Computer Operating System

Computer
Operating
System

Computer
Operating
System

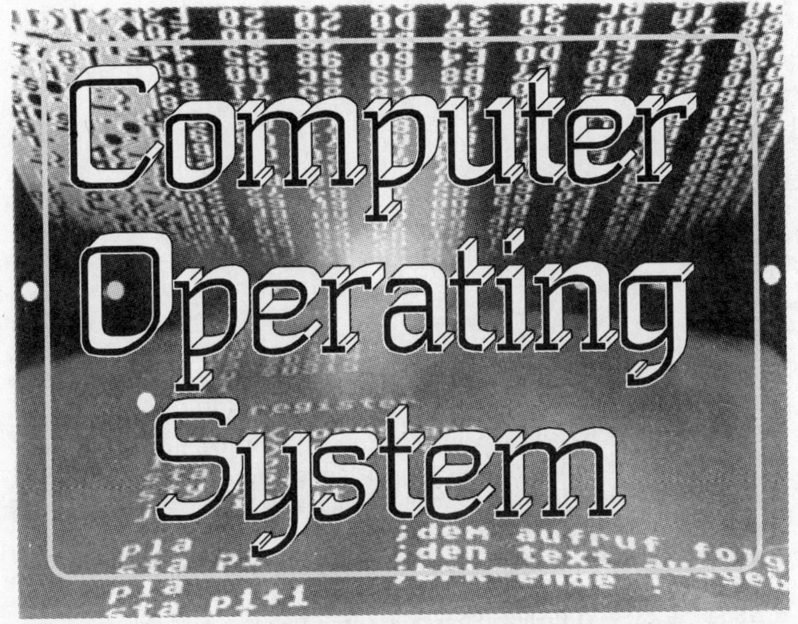

B Prasanalakshmi

King Saud University
Riyadh, Saudi Arabia

CBS Publishers & Distributors Pvt Ltd

New Delhi • Bangalore • Pune • Cochin • Chennai

ISBN : 978-81-239-1846-4

First Edition : 2010
Reprint : 2010

Published by Satish Kumar Jain and produced by V.K. Jain for
CBS Publishers & Distributors Pvt. Ltd.,
CBS Plaza, 4819/XI Prahlad Street, 24 Ansari Road, Daryaganj,
New Delhi - 110002, India. • Website: www.cbspd.com
e-mail: delhi@cbspd.com, cbspubs@vsnl.com, cbspubs@airtelmail.in
Ph.: 23289259, 23266861, 23266867 • Fax: 011-23243014

Branches:
- ***Bangalore:*** Seema House, 2975, 17th Cross, K.R. Road,
  Bansankari 2nd Stage, Bangalore - 560070 Ph.: 26771678/79
  Fax: 080-26771680 • e-mail: bangalore@cbspd.com
- ***Pune:*** Bhuruk Prestige, Sr. No. 52/12/2+1+3/2,
  Narhe, Haveli (Near Katraj-Dehu Road by Pass), Pune-411051
  Ph.: +91-20-32404169 • Fax: 020-24464059
  e-mail: pune@cbspd.com
- ***Cochin:*** 36/14, Kalluvilakam, Lissie Hospital Road,
  Cochin - 682018, Kerala • e-mail: cochin@cbspd.com
  Ph.: 0484-4059061-65 • Fax: 0484-4059065
- ***Chennai:*** 20, West Park Road, Shenoy Nagar, Chennai - 600030
  e-mail: chennai@cbspd.com Ph.: 044-26260666-26202620
  Fax: 044-45530020

Printed at :
Somya Printers, Delhi

to

---

my grandfathers
Sriram and Radhakrishnan

my parents
Raghu and Geetha

my husband
Bhala

and

my son
BN Kumar

Preface

Computer Operating System, a long-term dream of increasing the understandability of the concepts involved in operating system, has come true. A lenient language and presentation manner brings one well involved with the contents of this book. Assuming that the reader is somewhat introduced to the concepts of data structures, C programming and algorithms this book has been written. This would be quite useful to the graduate learners, beginners and even as a key reference to well trained people.

B Prasanalakshmi

e-mail: bplcse@yahoo.co.in

Acknowledgements

I would first of all like to thank Dr A Kannammal, CIT, Coimbatore and Dr T Senthil Kumar, Anna University, Trichirappalli who has been encouraging me with an idea and interest in bringing out this work. My lovable thanks to my family members who co-operated much with me to complete this book in a successful manner. Also I would like to acknowledge my collegues, students and my friend P Shanmugapriya who helped me much in correction and editing of the book. Also my sincere thanks to SCSVMV which provided me an environment in finishing this work. Finally I would like to bring out my heartfelt thanks to Mr YN Arjuna for giving me a scope in international level.

B Prasanalakshmi

Contents

2 HARDWARE AND SOFTWARE CONCEPTS

3 PROCESSES

7 MEMORY MANAGEMENT

8 VIRTUAL MEMORY MANAGEMENT

9 FILE SYSTEM INTERFACE AND IMPLEMENTATION

10 NETWORKING AND DISTRIBUTED SYSTEMS

1

Introduction

1.1 OPERATING SYSTEM—DEFINITION

An ***operating system*** is an important part of almost every computer system. A computer system is roughly divided into four components as:

(*i*) Hardware
(*ii*) Operating system
(*iii*) Application programs
(*iv*) Users

It performs no useful function by itself. It simply provides an environment within which other programs can do useful work. The operating system controls and co-ordinates the use of hardware among various application programs as shown in Fig. 1.1.

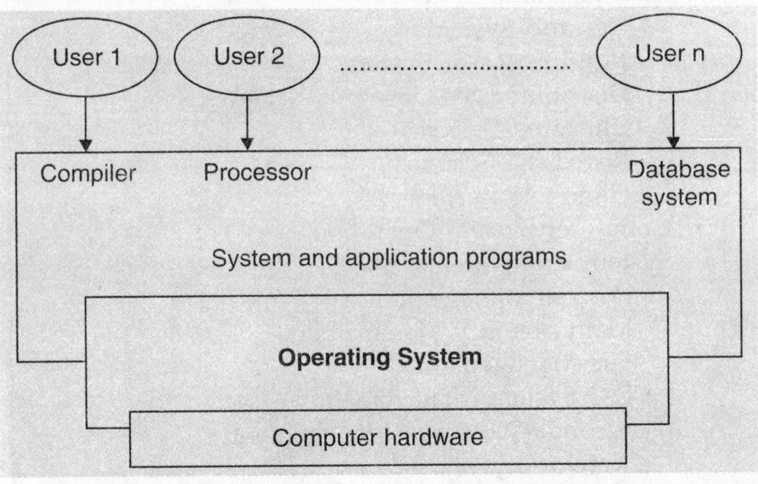

Fig. 1.1: Abstract view of components of computer system

Definition 1: An operating system is a program that manages the computer hardware. It also provides the basis for application programs and acts intermediate to the user of the computer and computer hardware. Personal computer operating system, mainframe operating system and handheld computer operating systems are some of the operating systems used today. Thus, some operating systems are designed to be convenient while others to be efficient and some are combinations of both.

The operating system can be explored from two viewpoints:

- User view
- System view

User view varies by the interface used. While considering a personal computer it facilitates *ease of use*, with some attention paid to performance and none paid to resource utilisation. When a terminal is connected to mainframe other users can access the same computer through other terminals. This *maximises resource utilisation,* i.e. CPU time, memory and I/O are used efficiently.

When considering workstations connected to network of other workstations and servers even though they have dedicated resources, some shared resources are also used. This is designed to *compromise between individual usability and resource utilisation*. Some computers today like embedded computers in home devices and automobiles have a little or no user view, with many hardware components but the operating system is designed to run without user interference.

System view shows the operating system as a program that is intimate with the hardware. Operating system here is a *resource allocator*. Even though a computer system has both hardware and software resources the operating system acts as a manager of these resources. While these resources meet complexity the operating system as a manager allocates resources to specific programs such that the system works efficiently.

Definition 2: Operating system is a *control program* that manages the execution of user programs to prevent errors and improper use of computer.

Fundamental goal of a computer system is to execute user programs for which the computer hardware is constructed. Since hardware alone cannot function, application programs were developed. These programs require certain common operations, which are controlled and allocated by the software called *operating system*.

Definition 3: Operating system is the one program running at all times on computer with all else being application program. Operating systems are called *kernel*.

An operating system can be defined by *what it does than by what it is*. While primary goal of some operating system is convenience for the user, for other operating system it is efficiency and convenience. Operating systems concentrate on the optimal use of computing resource. For example, Unix operating system started with keyboard and printer limiting the convenience of the users while later the port of the hardware changed making it user-friendly. Then many graphics user interface (GUI) were added to make it convenient for users. The operating system evolutes from the past and influenced the computer architecture, proposed changes took place in the hardware with the introduction of new hardware features.

1.2 OPERATING SYSTEM—OBJECTIVES

Modern operating systems generally have the following three major goals. Operating systems generally accomplish these goals by running processes in low privilege and providing service calls that invoke the operating system kernel in high-privilege state.

- ***To hide details of hardware by creating abstraction:*** An abstraction is software that hides lower level details and provides a set of higher-level functions. An operating system transforms the physical world of devices, instructions, memory, and time into virtual world that is the result of abstractions built by the operating system. There are several reasons for abstraction. First, the code needed to control peripheral devices is not standardized. Operating systems provide subroutines called device drivers that perform operations on behalf of programs for example, input/output operations. Second, the operating system introduces new functions as it abstracts the hardware. For instance, operating system introduces the file abstraction so that programs do not have to deal with disks. Third, the operating system transforms the computer hardware into multiple virtual computers, each belonging to a different program. Each program that is running is called a process. Each process views the hardware through the lens of abstraction. Fourth, the operating system can enforce security through abstraction.

- ***To allocate resources to processes (Manage resources):*** An operating system controls how processes (the active agents) may access resources (passive entities).
- ***Provide a pleasant and effective user interface:*** The user interacts with the operating systems through the user interface and usually interested in the 'look and feel' of the operating system. The most important components of the user interface are the command interpreter, the file system, on-line help, and application integration. The recent trend has been toward increasingly integrated graphical user interfaces that encompass the activities of multiple processes on networks of computers.

One can view Operating Systems from two points of view: *Resource manager and Extended machines*. From resource manager point of view, operating systems manage the different parts of the system efficiently and from extended machines point of view, operating systems provide a virtual machine to users that is more convenient to use. Structurally operating systems can be designed as a monolithic system, a hierarchy of layers, a virtual machine system, an external, or using the client-server model. The basic concepts of operating systems are processes, memory management, I/O management, the file systems and Security.

1.3 OPERATING SYSTEM—HISTORY

Historically operating systems have been tightly related to the computer architecture, it is a good idea to study the history of operating systems from the architecture of the computers on which they run.

Operating systems have evolved through a number of distinct phases or generations which correspond roughly to the decades.

The 1940's—First Generation

The earliest electronic digital computers had no operating systems. Machines of the time were so primitive that programs were often entered one bit at time on rows of mechanical switches (plug boards). Programming languages were unknown (not even assembly languages). Operating systems were unheard of.

The 1950's—Second Generation

By the early 1950's, the routine had improved somewhat with the introduction of Punch Cards. The General Motors Research Laboratories implemented the first operating systems in early 1950's for their IBM 701. The system of the 50's generally ran one job at a time. These were called single-stream batch processing systems because programs and data were submitted in groups or batches.

The 1960's—Third Generation

The systems of the 1960's were also batch-processing systems, but they were able to take better advantage of the computer's resources by running several jobs at once. So operating system designers developed the concept of multiprogramming in which several jobs are in main memory at once; a processor is switched from job to job as needed to keep several jobs advancing while keeping the peripheral devices in use.

For example, on the system with no multiprogramming, when the current job paused to wait for other I/O operation to complete, the CPU simply sat idle until the previous operation is finished. The solution for this problem that evolved was to partition memory into several pieces, with a different job in each partition. While one job was waiting for I/O to complete, another job could be using the CPU.

Another major feature in third-generation operating system was the technique called spooling (simultaneous peripheral operations on line). In spooling, a high-speed device like a disk interposed between a running program and a low-speed device involved with the program in input/output. Instead of writing directly to a printer, for example, outputs are written to the disk. Programs can run to completion faster, and other programs can be initiated sooner, when the printer becomes available, the outputs may be printed. Note that spooling technique is much like thread being spun to a spool so that it may be later unwound as needed.

Another feature present in this generation was time-sharing technique, a variant of multiprogramming technique, in which each user has an on-line (i.e. directly connected) terminal. Because the user is present and interacting with the computer, the computer system must respond quickly to user requests, otherwise user productivity could suffer. Time-sharing systems were developed to multiprogram a large number of simultaneous interactive users.

Fourth Generation

With the development of LSI (Large Scale Integration) circuits, chips, operating system entered in the personal computer and the workstation age. Microprocessor technology evolved to the point that it became possible to build desktop computers as powerful as the mainframes of the 1970s. Two operating systems have dominated the personal computer scene: MS-DOS, written by Microsoft, Inc. for the IBM PC and other machines using the Intel 8088 CPU and its successors, and UNIX, which is dominant on the large personal computers using the Motorola 6899 CPU family.

1.4 TYPES OF SYSTEMS

This section deals with types of systems as follows:

1. Mainframe systems
2. Desktop systems
3. Multiprocessor systems
4. Distributed systems
5. Clustered systems
6. Real-Time systems
7. Handheld systems.

1.4.1 Mainframe Systems

These were developed for many commercial and scientific applications. These further grew into:

(*a*) Batch systems
(*b*) Multiprogrammed systems
(*c*) Time-sharing systems

(a) Batch Systems

Early computers were physically large number of machines run from a console. Common input devices were card readers and tape drives. Common output devices were line printers, tape drives and card punches. Rather interacting directly with the computer the user prepared programs, data and control information then submitted to computer through punch cards. After some days the result appeared along with dump of memory and register contents.

In today's computers the OS* is made very simple just to transfer control automatically from one job to the next. OS is always residing in the memory as shown in Fig. 1.2.

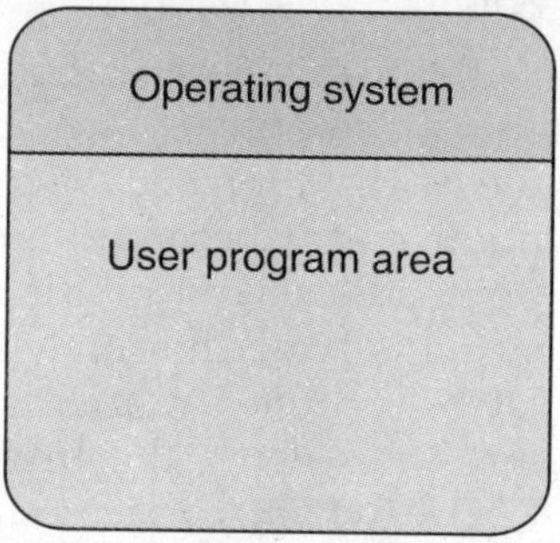

Operating system
User program area

Fig. 1.2: Memory layout for simple batch systems

To make processing speeder, programmers batched (scheduled) jobs of similar needs together and handed over them to operators. The operators after running each batch sent back the output of each batch to the appropriate programmer. In this process the CPU is often idle since mechanical input/output devices are very slower than electronic devices. On comparison a slow CPU executed thousands of instructions per second whereas a fast card reader may read 20 cards per second, which is one-third of magnitude.

(b) Multiprogrammed Systems

Job scheduling has the ability to multiprogram. Since a single user cannot keep the CPU always busy multiprogramming is used to increase CPU utilization.

The OS keeps several jobs in the memory simultaneously and hence keeps the several sets and subsets of jobs in job pool. Then the OS picks one of the jobs from the memory.

While there is necessity for a system to wait for an IO operation in a nonmultiprogramming system the CPU sits idle.

Whereas in a multiprogramming system a CPU simply switches to the next job as in Fig. 1.3. After completion of this job the CPU gets back to the pending job. Hence, the CPU is never idle in the multiprogrammed system. Multiple jobs

---

* OS herein after refers to Operating Systems

running concurrently include process scheduling, disk storage and memory management of all jobs.

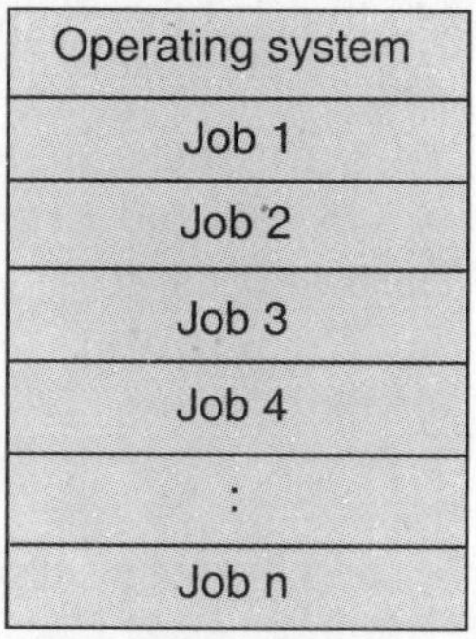

Operating system
Job 1
Job 2
Job 3
Job 4
:
Job n

Fig. 1.3: Memory layout for multi-programming system

(c) Time-Sharing Systems

Multiprogrammed batch systems provide an environment with high utilization of resources but the user cannot interact in it. Time-sharing or multitasking is an extension of multi-programming but users can interact with each program while running.

In interactive system the user communicates directly with the system using keyboard or mouse and waits for the result in a short response time, say one second.

In time-shared operating system even though many users share the computer simultaneously, the system appears to each user that it is dedicated to themselves. Time-shared OS uses CPU scheduling and multiprogramming to provide each user a small portion of time-shared computer. At least one separate program is loaded into memory, which is said to be 'process'.

Time-sharing OS are more complex than multiprogrammed OS. In both, several jobs are kept simultaneously in memory hence memory management is a must. To obtain reasonable response time jobs are swapped in and out of main memory. To achieve this a technique called 'Virtual Memory' is adopted to execute a job.

Main advantage of virtual memory is that:

(*a*) Programs can be larger than physical memory,
(*b*) Main memory has large and uniform array of storage,
(*c*) Logical memory (user view) is separated from physical memory.

1.4.2 Desktop Systems

PCs appeared in 1970's. During the first decade protection of OS from user programs were not considered. Hence, they were neither multi-user nor multitasking. Later to achieve goals of

OS instead of maximizing the CPU and peripheral utilization, user convenience and responsiveness were maximized.

OS for these systems were benefited from the development of OS for mainframes. Microcomputers were able to adopt themselves to the technology developed for larger OS. Microcomputers are of low hardware cost and high CPU utilization.

PCs needed no file protection on those days but since they are connected to LAN and the network they need file protection to avoid malicious access by other users. Programs become self-replicating via worms and viruses, which make file permissions and other means not enough for file protection.

1.4.3 Multiprocessor Systems

Most of the systems we use are single processor systems, which use only one main CPU. Today's importance is on multi-processor systems or parallel systems or tightly coupled systems. These systems have more than one processor all sharing computer bus, clock and sometimes memory and peripheral devices.

Three advantages of multiprocessor systems are:

(a) Increased Throughput

By increasing the number of processors we hope to get the work done in less time.

The speed up ratio with *N* processors is not *N* but less than *N*.

(b) Economy of Scale

It saves more money because they can share peripherals, storage and power supplies. Many processors can share data stored on one disk.

(c) Increased Reliability

If the functions are distributed properly among several processors then failure of one processor will not halt the system but only slows down. This ability to continue providing service proportional to the level of surviving (working) hardware is called *graceful degradation.* Systems designed for graceful degradation are called *fault tolerant.* Continued operation in the presence of failures requires a mechanism to allow the failure to be detected, diagnosed and if possible corrected. Two types of multiprocessing systems are used.

(*i*) ***Symmetric multiprocessing:*** If each processor runs an identical copy of the operating system and these copies communicate with one another as needed.

(*ii*) ***Asymmetric multiprocessing:*** If each processor is assigned a task and the master processor looks to it, this master-slave relationship brings asymmetric multiprocessing.

1.4.4 Distributed Systems

A network is a communication path between two or more systems. For this function distributed systems depend on network. Networks vary by protocols used, distance between nodes and transport media. Most operating systems support TCP/IP. To an operating system the network protocol needs interface device, device driver and software. Network is differentiated based on distance between nodes. Local area network exists within a room, floor or a building. Wide area network exists between buildings, cities and countries. Metropolitan area network to link buildings within city. Small area network to connect devices within feet of distance, e.g. Bluetooth. M dia varies as copper wires, fibre strands, satellites, microwave dishes and radios.

A. Client-Server Systems

Terminals connected to centralise systems are now parted as PCs. Hence, these centralised systems now act as *server systems* to satisfy requests generated by *client systems.*

Server systems are further classified as:

(*i*) ***Computer-server systems:*** Here clients send requests to server to perform action. Server executes it and returns result to clients.

(*ii*) ***File server systems:*** Here clients can themselves create, update, read and delete files.

B. Peer-to-Peer System

When PCs were introduced they were designed for personal use and were generally considered stand-alone computers.

Later when internet emerged many PCs were connected to computer network.

All modern PCs and workstations are capable of running a web browser for accessing hypertext document on web. Nowadays operating systems also include softwares like PPP, TCP/IP to enable internet access via LAN or telephone connection. These have collection of processors that do not share memory or clock. Since each processor has its own local memory, these processors communicate with each other through high-speed buses or telephone lines. Such systems are referred to as *loosely coupled systems* or *Distributed systems*.

1.4.5 Clustered Systems

Clustered systems are similar to parallel systems but differ in that two or more individual systems are coupled together. Clustered computers share storage and are closely linked via LAN network. Clustering enables to provide high availability. One node acts as monitoring machine, which monitors all other nodes while other are said to be monitored machines. When one of the monitor machines fails the monitoring machine takes up responsibility of the failed one. There are two models of clustering as:

(*i*) ***Asymmetric clustering:*** One machine is in hot stand by mode while the other is the running application. The hot stand by host does nothing but monitors the server. In the event of server failure it becomes the active server.

(*ii*) ***Symmetric clustering:*** Two or more hosts are running applications each monitoring one another. In distributed system most clusters do not allow shared access to data on disk. For this distributed file system must provide access control and locking into files to ensure no conflicting to occur. This type of service is known as *Distributed Lock Manager (DLM).*

1.4.6 Real-Time Systems

This is a special purpose operating system. This is used when rigid time requirements have been given for the operation of a processor or flow of data. Sensor devices, automobile engine fuel injection system, home appliance controller and weapon system are examples of real-time system. A real-time system has well-defined fixed time constraints. Processing must be done within defined constraints else the system fails. A real-time system functions correctly only if the result is returned within time constraint.

Real-time systems are of two types as:

(*i*) ***Hard real-time system:*** This guarantees critical tasks to be completed on time. Here the delays right from retrieval of stored data till the functioning of that request must be bound. Secondary storage of data is avoided instead short-term memory or ROM is used. ROM is non-volatile, which retains contents even on electric outage.

(*ii*) ***Soft real-time system:*** Here critical real time task gets priority over other tasks and retains this priority until completion. Kernel delays are to be bound. These have very limited utility than hard real-time systems. These systems need advanced operating system features that cannot be supported by hard real-time systems. Because of their expanded usage they are preferable in most operating systems.

1.4.7 Handheld Systems

Handheld systems include personal digital assistants (PDAs). Developers of handheld system applications face many changes due to the limited size of the devices, even small amount of memory storage and slow processors. Many handheld devices have between 512KB and 8MB of memory. Currently many handheld devices do not use virtual memory techniques instead work within limited physical memory.

Concerning the speed of processors used in the handheld devices, processors of handheld devices run at a fraction of speed of a processor in a PC. To speed up a processor it needs more power, which will be facilitated by large battery that is to be recharged more frequently. To reduce the size of the device the processors are slowed down. As a last issue the display screen is concerned. A home-based PC has 21 inches of display whereas handheld devices have a maximum of 3 inches square.

1.5 COMPUTER SYSTEM OPERATION

A general-purpose computer system consists of CPU and many device controllers connected through common bus providing access to shared memory.

Each device controller is in charge of specific type of device. CPU and device controllers can execute concurrently. Memory controller is used to synchronize access to memory hence, the orderly access to shared memory is ensured. For a computer to start running an initial program called *bootstrap* program which initialises each and every component from CPU registers to device controllers to memory contents is needed. The bootstrap program locates and loads into memory the operating system kernel. The operating system usually starts running from *init* the first process and waits for an event usually refereed to as an interrupt, which is caused by hardware or software. Hardware interrupt may be done by sending a signal to CPU through system bus. Software interrupt may be caused by special operation called *system call* or *monitor call*. Each interrupt has a service routine. Whenever an interrupt is raised CPU stops its functionality and transfers the control to the location of the service routine. CPU resumes by the completion of this service routine.

Concerning the computer architecture interrupts are important. As soon as the interrupt is encountered a generic routine is needed to examine the interrupt information. Interrupt routines can also be called indirectly through a table, which holds the pointer, values to interrupt routines. The pointer locations hold addresses of interrupt service routines for various devices. Unique device number indexes this array called interrupt vector.

If the interrupt routine needs to modify the processor state, by modifying register values it must explicitly save the current state and then restore that state before returning. Mostly operating system is *interrupt-driven*. If there are no processes to execute, no I/O devices to service and no users to whom to respond, an operating system will remain quiet, waiting for some process to happen. Events to be happened are signalled by occurrence of interrupt or *trap*. A trap is a software-generated interrupt caused either by an error or by a specific request from a user program that an operating system service be performed.

1.6 SYSTEM COMPONENTS

Even though, not all systems have the same structure many modern operating systems share the same goal of supporting the following types of system components.

1.6.1 Process Management

The operating system manages many kinds of activities ranging from user programs to system programs like printer spooler, name servers, file server, etc. Each of these activities is encapsulated in a process. A process includes the complete execution context (code, data, PC, registers, OS resources in use, etc.). It is important to note that a process is not a program. A process is only ONE instant of a program in execution. There are many processes running the same program. The five major activities of an operating system in regard to process management are:

- Creation and deletion of user and system processes.
- Suspension and resumption of processes.
- A mechanism for process synchronization.
- A mechanism for process communication.
- A mechanism for deadlock handling.

1.6.2 Main-Memory Management

Primary-memory or main-memory is a large array of words or bytes. Each word or byte has its own address. Main-memory provides storage that can be accessed directly by the CPU. That is to say for a program to be executed, it must in the main memory.

The major activities of an operating system in regard to memory-management are:

- Keep track of which part of memory are currently being used and by whom.
- Decide which process is loaded into memory when memory space becomes available.
- Allocate and deallocates memory space as needed.

1.6.3 File Management

A file is a collection of related information defined by its creator. Computer can store files on the disk (secondary storage), which provide long-term storage. Some examples of storage media are magnetic tape, magnetic disk and optical disk. Each of these media has its own properties like speed, capacity, data transfer rate and access methods. A file system is normally organized into directories to ease their use. These directories may contain files and other directions.

The five main major activities of an operating system in regard to file management are:

1. The creation and deletion of files.
2. The creation and deletion of directions.
3. The support of primitives for manipulating files and directions.
4. The mapping of files onto secondary storage.
5. The back up of files on stable storage media.

1.6.4 I/O System Management

I/O subsystem hides the peculiarities of specific hardware devices from the user. Only the device driver knows the peculiarities of the specific device to which it is assigned.

1.6.5 Secondary Storage Management

Generally speaking, systems have several levels of storage, including primary storage, secondary storage and cache storage. Instructions and data must be placed in primary storage or cache to be referenced by a running program. Because main memory is too small to accommodate all data and programs, and its data are lost when power is lost, the computer system must provide secondary storage to backup main memory. Secondary storage consists of tapes, disks and other media designed to hold information that will eventually be accessed in primary storage (primary, secondary, cache) is ordinarily divided into bytes or words consisting of a fixed number of bytes. Each location in storage has an address; the set of all addresses available to a program is called an address space.

The three major activities of an operating system in regard to secondary storage management are:

1. Managing the free space available on the secondary-storage device.
2. Allocation of storage space when new files have to be written.
3. Scheduling the requests for memory access.

1.6.6 Networking

A distributed system is a collection of processors that do not share memory, peripheral devices or a clock. The processors communicate with one another through communication lines called network. The communication-network design must consider routing and connection strategies, and the problems of contention and security.

1.6.7 Protection System

If a computer system has multiple users and allows the concurrent execution of multiple processes, the various processes must be protected from one another's activities. Protection refers to mechanism for controlling the access of programs, processes or users to the resources defined by a computer system.

1.6.8 Command-Interpreter System

A command interpreter is an interface of the operating system with the user. The user gives commands which are executed by operating system (usually by turning them into system calls). The main function of a command interpreter is to get and execute the next user specified command. Command-interpreter is usually not a part of the kernel, since multiple command interpreters (shell, in UNIX terminology) may be supported by an operating system, and they do not really need to run in kernel mode. There are two main advantages to separating the command interpreter from the kernel.

1. The way of look in command interpreter can be changed by changing the interface of command interpreter, but this cannot be done on a kernel.
2. If the command interpreter is a part of the kernel it is possible for a malicious process to gain access to certain part of the kernel that it showed not have to avoid this scenario it is advantageous to have the command interpreter separate from kernel.

1.7 GENERAL SYSTEM ARCHITECTURE

To improve the utilisation of computer system led to development of multiprogramming and time-sharing. Here the resources are shared leading to modification of computer architecture to allow operating system to maintain control over computer system. To establish this control dual mode of execution as user mode and monitor mode are developed. For more control privileged instructions are executed (only in monitor mode). These privileged instructions may be concerning I/O, memory management registers or timers. Since I/O instructions are privileged they are to be executed only by the operating system. By doing so the user programs are prevented from doing any I/O operations. To solve this problem the user requests the monitor to do I/O operation on the user's behalf. Such a request is called *system call* or *monitor call* or *operating system call*. Even if the processor varies the method to request action is the same.

Whenever the system call is executed, it is treated by the hardware as software interrupt. Control passes from interrupt vector to service routine and the mode bit is set to monitor type.

The monitor examines the interrupting instruction to determine the system call that occurred. Additional information needed for the request is passed in registers, on the stack or in memory. The monitor verifies these requests if they are legal and correct, executs the request and returns control to the instruction after the system call.

1.8 I/O STRUCTURE

A general-purpose computer system has a CPU and multiple device controllers connected through a bus. Each device controller is in charge of specific type of device. Device controller maintains some local buffer storage and set of optical purpose registers, and also for moving data between peripheral devices it controls. The size of local buffer rises from one controller to another.

1.8.1 I/O Interrupts

To start an I/O operation, CPU loads the corresponding registers within the device controllers, determines the action to take. Any communication between devices is accomplished by triggering an interrupt. Once when I/O is started two courses of action are possible, i.e. either at the I/O completion control is returned to user process which is called 'Synchronous I/O' else returns control to the user program without waiting for I/O to complete. This is said to be 'Asynchronous I/O'.

Waiting for an I/O completion may be done in one of the two ways:

(*i*) Special 'idle' instruction that idles the CPU until next interrupt.
(*ii*) Use of the tight 'wait' loop which continues until an interrupt occurs.

Whenever an I/O interrupt occurs the operating system knows which device is interrupting. This approach excludes the possibility of concurrent I/O operations to several devices and hence the possibility of overlapping is avoided.

As an alternative to the above discussed process the I/O can be started and then to continue other operating system or user program code. Here the operating system uses a table 'device status table' with an entry for each I/O device. The table as shown in Fig. 1.4 has entries indicating the device type, address and state (idle/busy/not functioning). Since there are possibilities for other processes to issue request to same device the operating system will maintain a wait queue for each I/O device with its corresponding waiting request.

Device name
Device status
Device driver file name or disk address
Entry point in main memory, if loaded (otherwise 0)
Device size

Fig. 1.4: Typical device status table

When service is needed I/O device interrupts which leads to the identification by the operating system and indexing to the I/O device table hence determining the status of device. The table entry is modified to reflect occurrence of interrupt. At completion the control is returned from I/O interrupt. If the process is in queue as recorded in the device status table, all waiting processes are served else returned back to the work done before encountering I/O interrupts. In a time-sharing system, the operating system switches to ready to running process. Main advantage of asynchronous I/O is increased system efficiency.

1.8.2 DMA Structure

When a line is to be read from the terminal, the first character typed is sent to the computer. When that character is retrieved the asynchronous, communication device interrupts the CPU. The address of this interrupts instructions is saved and the control is transferred to the interrupt service routine of that appropriate device, which saves the contents of any CPU registers needed to use and also checks for error conditions.

The interrupt routine must also adjust pointer and counter variables to be sure that the next input character is stored in the next location of buffer. The other parts are responsible for processing the data in buffer and transferring characters to the program requesting input.

Asynchronous I/O is usually assigned a low interrupt priority allowing more important interrupts to be processed.

A high-speed device will transmit information faster but would not leave much time for process execution. To solve this DMA (Direct Memory Access) is used in high-speed devices. There is no interference of CPU in DMA where data transfers directly between own buffer storage and memory.

After finding a free buffer from pool of buffers a portion of operating system called Device Driver sets the DMA controller registers to use correct source and destination address. While DMA controller performing data transfer CPU is free to perform other tasks. DMA controller interrupts the CPU when transfer has been completed.

1.9 PROTECTION AND SECURITY

1.9.1 Protection

Operating system shares resources, which allows program to run simultaneously hence system utilisation is improved. Multiprogramming works on several programs at the same time leading to maximum utilisation. There are also problems with this.

(*i*) In systems without sharing errors are caused only to processes that are on current working state.

(*ii*) In systems with sharing errors are caused to all processes on sharing.

Sometimes errors in one of the processes of multiprogramming system might modify the program or data of some other program or process, sometimes the resident monitor itself. A properly well-designed operating system must ensure to prevent such errors. Programming error detected by hardware are handled by operating system. If the user programs face a difficulty the hardware will trap the operating system, the trap transfers the control through interrupt vector to operating system like an interrupt. Whenever a program error occurs the operating system terminates the program abnormally after giving an appropriate error message that dumps the memory of the program. This memory dump is written to a file for enabling users to examine, correct and restart the program.

(a) Dual Mode Operation

The operating system should be protected for proper operation and also data be protected from malfunctioning. For this the operating system allows us to differentiate two modes of operation: user mode (1) and monitor mode (0). With this mode bit one can understand if the task is executed on behalf of operating system or on behalf of the user. Protection of operating system through dual mode operation is accomplished by the machine instructions. These privileged instructions are executed only in monitor mode. If attempted in user mode, the instruction is treated illegal and traps the operating system.

(b) I/O Protection

The user program may interrupt normal operation of the system by issuing illegal I/O instructions, by accessing memory location within operating system or by refusing to relinquish CPU. All I/O instructions are defined to be privileged instructions to prevent users from directly accessing the I/O instructions rather they could be accessed by the users only through operating system. Whenever an interrupt occurs the system executing in the user mode is switched to monitor mode by jumping to the address determined from interrupt vector. The user program could gain control of the system in monitor mode.

(c) Memory Protection

The interrupt vector should be protected from user program for correct operation. The interrupt service routine in operating system should not be modified else the user program overwrites the instruction in interrupt service routine. Memory protections should be made at least for interrupt vector and interrupt service routine. Generally the operating system should be protected from access by user's program and to protect itself from other user program. This protection is given by hardware. Protection is accomplished by the CPU hardware by comparing every address generated in user mode with registers. Any attempt by a program executing in user mode to access monitor memory or other users memory results in trap to the monitor (Fatal error). Base and limit registers are loaded only by the operating system which uses special privileged instruction (executed in monitor mode only). The monitor can change the register values but prevents user programs from changing the register contents.

1.9.2 Security

(i) Authentication

Many authorisation policies are based on the identity of the user associated with a process. Operating systems need some mechanism for authenticating a user interacting with the computer system. The most commonly used authentication technique is requiring the user to supply one or more pieces of information known only to the users. Knowledge of that information alone does not uniquely identify the individual. Either passwords or physical authentication may be used for authentication.

(ii) Prevention

The most desirable outcome of a security system is for it to prevent intruders from successfully penetrating the system's security. Preventive measures include the following:

- Limiting new passwords to those that pass a series of quality checks. Software exists that can check a password for length, diversity of characters, and the presence of words or permutations of words.
- Requiring passwords to be changed at periodic intervals.
- Encrypting data, either when it is transmitted or when it is stored. Programs like *ssh* allow communications to and from a remote site to be encrypted.
- Turning off unused or duplicate services. Reducing the number of system entry points reduces the probability of finding an entry point that can be exploited.
- Implementing an internal firewall. Some programs can be configured to deny network access, based on the remote location and/or the service to be accessed.

- Monitoring security advisories and updating software and configuration information as needed.

(iii) Detection

To reduce the negative effects detection should be promoted. Effective detection measures may also discourage intrusion attempts. Constant monitoring provides the best hope for fast discovery.

- Auditing systems record information about system events. Monitoring of system activities can detect unusual activities.
- Virus checkers search the contents of files and boot programs for the presence of known abnormalities.
- The existence of long-running process in a listing of currently executing processes may indicate suspicious activity.
- The current state of the system can be checked against a previous state. Some programs may record in its database a fingerprint of any file in the system and later be used to detect changes in the fingerprint for any file in the system.

(iv) Correction

After a system has been penetrated it is frequently necessary to take corrective action.

- Periodic backups should be performed so that a system can be rolled back to a previous state. Backups may be stored offline and even offsite to increase the probability is not compromised during the backup.
- If a backup does not exist or its integrity is unknown, a reload of the entire system may be necessary. An exact record of all currently installed software and updates simplifies the restoration effort.
- It may be necessary to change all resident security information. All users may be required to change their password.
- The vulnerability that allowed the system to be penetrated should be fixed. This may involve deactivating a service, installing a bug fix, or modifying the system configuration.

(v) Identification

To discourage intruders, it is desirable to identify the source of an attack. Identification is frequently the most difficult security task.

- Audit trails may provide useful identification information. However, depending on the nature of attack and the location of the log, the information contained in audit logs may have been tampered with by the intruder.
- Systems accessed through modems can keep track of the source of incoming calls using caller-id.
- Systems accessed through a network can record the address of the connecting computer. Attacks relayed through a series of computers must be traced to their origin.
- All services can be configured to require user authentication. For example, a mail server could refuse mail services to any unauthenticated client. If that server is used to relay an email virus, the authentication information may be useful in identifying its source.

2

Hardware and Software Concepts

2.1 INTRODUCTION

In this 21st century people use computers for many purposes as to access internet, browsing, display graphics, video, audio, games with all these aspects and more creativity. Large amounts of data are stored, manipulated or retrieved through much application. Similar to a human body a computer functions, it is even more than human.

A human is one with a body and a soul similarly a computer system is with a hardware and software. One cannot function without the other. A network (group) of computers can perform a bulk of calculations at a time in seconds. Linking the hardware and software brings all interactions in these computer systems. Not only this is sufficient for a system to function but also an operating system is needed to operate these. In short operating systems can be called of a *resource manager*. The resources, which this operating system manages, include processors, memory, secondary storage, I/O devices, processes, threads, files, databases and many. Nowadays hardware and software emerge into field with new innovations and techniques. So the operating system should also modify accordingly so as to fit the advancement only if the operating system is compatible to both the hardware and software, it can act as a perfect 'resource manager'.

2.2 EVOLUTION OF HARDWARE DEVICES

Always the operating systems remain the same but as time goes by hardware devices evolve and software to control them is emerging. A plug-in called the device driver is to be installed to the system in order for the operating system to adapt itself to the emerging hardware. Each and every time the hardware evolves, there is a technological development that has increased the computing speeds and capabilities to serve the demands of various resources which should also be advanced; hence the operating system gains much attention.

Generally there are two types of programming as system programming and application programming. System programs are codes written to perform hardware management and provide service to programs.

Application programs, which work in the environment of operating system, are development to request services and resources from the operating system to perform a task. Today many hardware components have been designed to interact with the operating system to facilitate its extensibility. For example, plug and play devices today do not need installation of software or device drivers rather can be used at time needed. A driver makes the operating system designer away from the details of hardware devices.

2.3 HARDWARE COMPONENTS

Hardware components are the workplace for the software. These physical devices may be processor, main memory, I/O devices and others.

2.3.1 Motherboard (Fig. 2.1)

Computers work properly by the interactions between hardware devices to satisfy the requirements of the system. Every component in the system at some point communicates through the motherboard either by directly plugging into it or by communicating through one of the motherboard ports. The main board provides a platform for all the other components and peripherals to talk with each other. This silicon layer containing microscopic electrical connections called *traces* provides connectivity on the board. These set of traces from a high-speed communication channel are known as *bus*.

'Motherboard Chipset' controls all the data that flow through the buses. This chipset directs data to the correct area of the motherboard.

Motherboard consists of a large Printed Circuit Board (PCB), which holds electronic components and also has physical connector (sockets, slots and header) into which other computer components may be inserted or attached.

In general a motherboard consists of the following at a minimum:

- Slots, where system's main memory is installed.
- Chipset, which forms an interface between CPU's front-side bus, main memory and peripheral buses.

- Non-volatile memory chips (flash ROM) containing system's firmware or bios.
- Clock generator to produce system clock signal.
- Expansion slots.
- Power connectors.

A current trend in motherboard design is integrating hardware components to PCB. Using add-on cards does this. On board devices reduce the overall system cost. There is also a disadvantage with this when all components are permanently attached and cannot be replaced easily.

The shape and layout of a motherboard is called the *Form factor*. Form factor is just one of the standards that apply to motherboards. Some of the other standards include:

- 'Socket' for the microprocessor determines what is the kind of CPU used.
- 'Chipset' is the motherboard's logic system that is made of two parts—the Northbridge and Southbridge. Then bridges connect the CPU to the other parts of the computer.
- 'Basic Input/Output System (BIOS)' chip controls the basic functions of computers and performs a self-test every time when computer is turned on.
- 'Real-time clock chip' is battery-operated chip that maintains the basic settings and system tie.

Some of the newer technological advances in motherboards are:

- RAID (Redundant Array of Independent Disk) controllers allow the computer to recognize multiple drives as a single drive.
- PCI express is a newer protocol that acts like a network than a bus. It eliminates the need for other ports including AGP port.

Some of the slots and ports found on a motherboard include:

- Peripheral components interconnect (PCI)-connections for video, sound and video capture cards.
- Accelerated graphics port (AGP)-dedicated port for video cards.
- Integrated drive electronics (IDE)-interface for hard drive.
- Universal serial bus or fire wire-external peripherals.
- Memory slots.

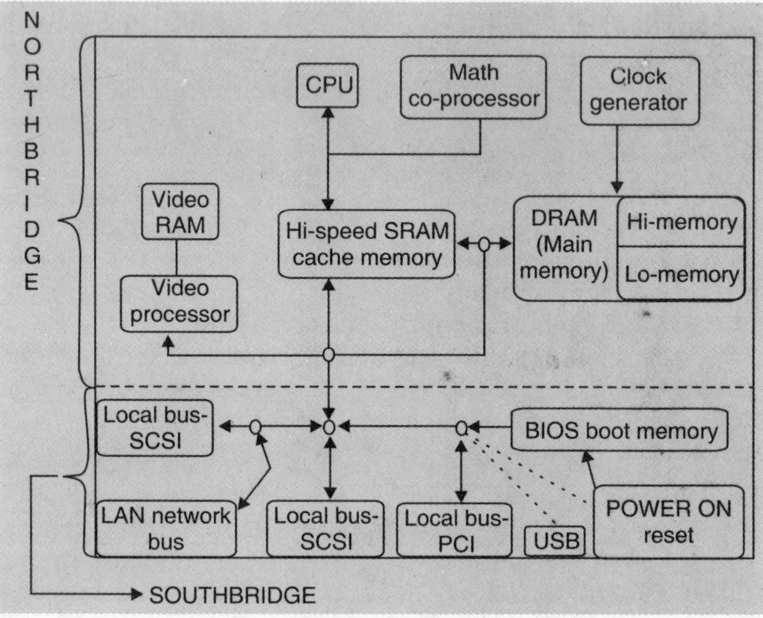

Fig. 2.1: Motherboard

2.3.2 Processor

Processor is a component that executes a stream of machine language instructions. This processor can be of many forms as central processing unit, graphics co-processor or a digital signal processor (DSP).

A processor can in general be referred to as CPU; regardless of the physical structure is execution of stored instructions called programs. For all Von Neumann CPU four kinds of operations are to be performed as: *fetch, decode, execute* and *write back.*

Fetch Operation

Retrieves an instruction from program memory. A program counter determines the location in program memory. This keeps track of the CPU's place in the current program. After fetching, the instruction must be retrieved from slow memory causing CPU to stall while waiting for the instruction to be returned. This instruction determines what the CPU must do.

Decode Operation

Here the instruction is broken up into parts, which gives importance to the other portions of CPU. A number called *opcode*, which is present in each instruction, determines the operation to be performed. Others in the instruction refers to the information required such as operands; register address to locate a value.

Execute Operation

During this step various portions of CPU are connected to complete the desired operation. For example, if an addition operation is requested and arithmetic logic unit will be connected to a set of inputs and a set of outputs, ALU contains a circuitry to perform simple arithmetic and logic operations. If the result produced is too long for the CPU to handle, an arithmetic overflow flag may be used.

Write Back Operation

This step writes back the results of execute step to some form of memory, later written to some internal CPU registers for quick access or utilization by subsequent instructions. Sometimes instructions may not produce the result directly rather may use jumps, flags and many.

Instruction set is the set of instructions a processor can execute. The size of each instruction called instruction length differs from one architecture to the other. Processor is also responsible for determining the amount of data that can be operated all at once.

Processor also increases the performance by supporting virtual memory and hardware interrupts. The processor is said to possess ALU (which was already discussed) registers, cache and bus.

Bus interfaces allow the processor to interact with memory and other devices. Since processors work at very high speed than that of main memory, cache is used to store copies of data in main memory—hence increasing the speed and efficiency.

These caches are in two levels as level *L*1, which is fastest and expensive and finds its location in processor whereas another level cache, level $L2$ is larger, slower and less expensive than $L1$ and finds its position in motherboard.

Registers are memories with high speed located in processor to hold immediate data, i.e. of immediate use in the processor. These are hardwired to processor circuitry. Registers are faster access than that of $L1$ cache. The number of bits the processor can operate all at once determines the size of the register. Registers that are reserved for use by applications are called general-purpose registers.

2.3.3 Clock

Clock rate is the fundamental rate in cycles per second (measured in hertz) at which the computer performs its most basic operation such as adding two numbers or transferring a value from one processor register to another. Generally, it is the frequency of the clock in any synchronous circuit. The term cycle refers to one complete oscillation of an electrical signal, which is provided by the system clock generator. This clock is used to determine the frequency at which buses transfer data. Different chips on motherboard have different clock rates but the term clock rate usually refers to the speed of CPU. This clock cycle toggles between logical zero and logical one state.

Generally '0' state withstands for a long time than '1' state due to thermal and electrical specification. For a CPU clock rates are determined at the end of manufacturing process thus fixing up price for a CPU.

Clock rate of a computer is useful in providing comparisons between computer chips in the same processor family. There are also many factors to be considered when comparing the speeds of entire computers like the clock rate of the computers front side bus (FSB), of the RAM, width of CPU's bus (in bits) and amount of $L1$, $L2$, $L3$ cache. Clock rates should not be used when comparing different computers or different processor families.

2.3.4 Memory Hierarchy

Most electronic devices transfer data using electrons passing through traces of PCB's. But there is a limit to the speed at which electrons can travel. Increase in length of wire increases the time to transfer. Speed of a processor controls how quickly a computer thinks. Speed of a chipset and buses controls the speed of communication with other parts of computer. Speed of RAM controls the speed of accessing instructions and data, thus giving a big impact on the system performance. Amount of memory available controls the amount of data available. RAM comprises the bulk of computer memory. Recently used memory is the dual data rate (DDR) memory. This means that the memory can transmit data twice per cycle instead of once which makes memory faster. Most motherboards have space for multiple memory chips and often connected to the Northbridge via a dual bus instead of a single bus. This further reduces the time taken by the processor to get information from the memory.

This hierarchical arrangement of storage in current computer architecture is called the memory hierarchy. It is designed to take advantage of memory locality in computer programs. Each level of the hierarchy has the properties of higher bandwidth, smaller size, lower latency then lower levels.

CPUs today are very fast hence the workload references of memory access and efficiency of the caching and memory transfers between different levels of hierarchy are the practical limitations on processing speed. As a result CPU spends much time waiting for memory I/O to complete.

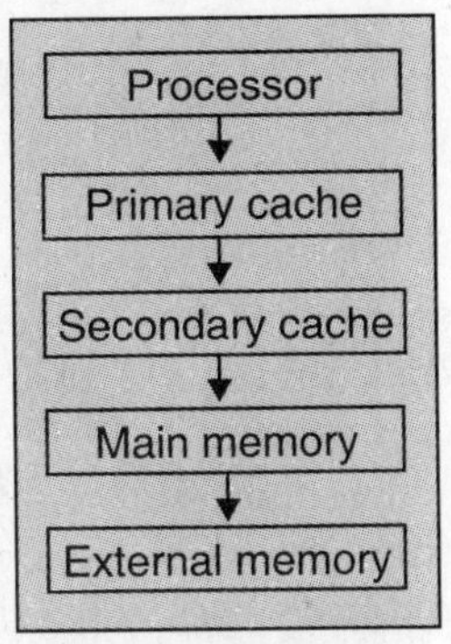

Fig. 2.2: Memory hierarchy

The memory hierarchy (Fig. 2.2) in most computers is:

- Processor register is the fastest possible access, which is usually 1 CPU cycle and only hundreds of bytes in size. Registers are the fastest and most expensive memory on a system. They operate at the same speed as processors.
- Cache memory is the speed of cache memory which is measured by its latency. Latency is nothing but the time required for data transfer in terms of nanosecond or processor cycles.

For instance $L1$ cache operates at a latency of 2 cycles and stores tens of KB of data. $L2$ cache operates at a latency of 10 cycles and stores hundreds of KB or MB of data. Today's existence $L3$ slower than $L2$ but faster than main memory. $L1$ and $L2$ are combined to get high-speed interconnections.

- Main memory (real or physical memory).

In general front side bus operates at a fraction of processor speeds. Since the data to pass through this front side bus main memory has additional latency. In today's architecture its latency is of tens or hundreds of processor cycles.

Main memory consists of volatile RAM (Random Access Memory) as the name implies can access data location in any (random) order. Some forms of RAM are:

1. Dynamic RAM (DRAM) which periodically refreshes the data or it will be lost.
2. Static RAM (SRAM) which is opposite to DRAM is usually faster and expensive. SRAM is commonly used in processor caches.

Memory modules are designed to reduce overall latency and increased bandwidth. Note that bandwidth is the amount of data transferred per unit of time.

- Secondary storage.

Secondary storage also called persistent storage or auxiliary storage stores large quantities of data and non-volatile hard disk drives are the mostly used secondary storage devices of computers.

Even though they store more than and cost less than RAM they are called only as secondary memory and not as main memory because of difference in access time. Secondary memory needs mechanical movements of heads for data access whereas main memory needs only electrical signals, which travels faster than mechanical movements. Hence its latency measures to milliseconds which is million times slower than that of CD, DVD, WORM disk, etc. Compact disk can store up to two layers per side and can store up to 5.6 GB of data per layer.

2.3.5 Bus

Bus is a collection of electrical connections that transport information between hardware devices. Two main components of a bus are data bus, which transports data and an address bus, which determines the recipient or sources of that data. A port is a bus that connects exactly two devices. I/O channel is bus shared by several devices. Then I/O channels are used to avoid collision of signals in a bus. Memory access by both I/O channels and processors are prioritised by a hardware called 'controller' and here I/O channels are given priority over processors. This is said to be 'cycle stealing'.

Bus speed are usually measured in MHz, an implementation which combines both chipset and RAM with two data transfers per cycle is said to be Double data rate (DDR). Another implementation, which allows 4 data transfers per second, is said to be 'Queue preparing'. Some examples of bus are PCI bus (peripheral component interface), AGP (accelerated graphics port), etc.

2.3.6 Direct Memory Access

For transfer of data between main memory and I/O device, PIO (programmed I/O) was used which transfers data in the range of byte or word. Until the transfer is complete some number of processor cycles are wasted. To avoid this wastage DMA is used. DMA devices and controllers are enabled thus enabling the processor to do its function. DMA is compatible to several bus architectures. The functions that actually take place in DMA are as follows:

1. A processor requests for an I/O to the disk through the I/O controller and then proceeds with its function.
2. Disk sends data to the I/O controller, which stores the received data in the memory address.
3. An interrupt regarding the job completion is sent to the processor.

2.3.7 Peripheral Devices

The devices connected internally or externally to a computer and used in the transfer of data are called peripheral devices. A personal computer or workstation processed information and strictly speaking, that is all the computer does. Data (unprocessed information) must get into the computer, and the processed information must get out. Entering and displaying information is carried out on a wide variety of accessory devices called peripherals, also known as input/output (I/O) devices. Some peripherals, such as keyboards, are only input devices; other peripherals, such as printers, are only output devices; and some are both. The monitor is the device on which images produced by the computer operator or generated by the program are displayed on a cathode-ray tube (CRT). Electron guns—one in a monochrome monitor, three in a color monitor—irradiate phosphors on the inside of the vacuum tube, causing them to glow. The flat-panel displays on most portable computers, known as liquid-crystal displays (LCDs), use two polarizing filters with liquid crystals between them to produce the image.

The computer keyboard, based on the typewriter keyboard, contains keys for entering letters, numbers, and punctuation marks, as well as keys to change the meaning of other keys. The function keys perform tasks that vary from program to program.

The mouse is a device that is rolled on the desktop to move the cursor on the screen. A ball on the bottom of the mouse translates the device's movements to sensors within the mouse and then through the connecting port to the computer. There are also mice that substitute optical devices for mechanical balls, and mice that use infrared rather than physical connections.

The trackball is essentially an upside-down mouse, with the ball that is used to move the cursor located on the top rather than on the bottom. The joystick is a pointing device used principally for games. The light pen performs the same functions as a mouse or trackball, but it is held up to the screen, where its sensors detect the presence of pixels and send a signal through a cable to the computer.

The graphics, or digitising tablet is a pad with electronics beneath the surface which is drawn upon with a pointed device called a stylus. The shapes drawn appear on the monitor's screen. The most common input or storage device in personal computers or workstations is a hard disk drive, a stack of magnetized platters on which information is stored by heads generating an electrical current to represent either 1 or 0 in the binary number system. The device is called hard, because the platters are inflexible, and is called a drive because it spins at

3600 revolutions or more a minute, within a sealed case. Diskettes, made of flexible film like that used in recording tape, are usually stored within a hard shell and are spun by their drives at about 360 revolutions per minute.

Data can also be stored and retrieved with light, the light of a laser beam reading a pattern of pits on an optical disk. The most familiar type of optical disk is the CD-ROM (compact disk-read only memory). Another kind of optical disk is the WORM (write once read many times).

As a consequence of their greater efficiency and speed, disk drives have quickly replaced tape drives as the primary means of data and program storage. Tape drives are still in use for backup storage, copying the contents of a hard disk as insurance against mechanical failure or human error.

The scanner converts an image of something outside the computer, such as text, a drawing, or a photograph, into a digital image that it sends into the computer for display or further processing. The image is viewed as a graphics image, not a text image, so it can be altered with a graphics program but cannot be edited with a word-processing program, unless the scanner is a part of a character-recognition system. To digitise photographs, a scanner may dither the image (put the dots a varying amount of space apart) or use the tagged image file format (TIFF), storing the image in 16 gray values. Some scanners can use standard video cameras to capture images for the computer. The printer puts text or other images produced with a computer onto paper or other surfaces. Printers are either impact or non-impact devices. Daisy wheel are so called from the shape of the elements bearing raised images of the characters. Their speed, perhaps 30 characters per second, is now considered unacceptably slow. Dot-matrix printers produce their images by striking a series of wire pins, typically, 9, 18, or 24, through the ribbon in the pattern necessary to form the letter, number, line or other character.

Ink-jet printers carry their ink in a well, where it is turned into a mist by heat or vibration and sprayed through tiny holes to form the pattern of the character on paper. Laser printers are similar to photocopying machines. The quality of laser-printer output is the highest generally available.

The modem connects one computer to another, ordinarily through the telephone lines, to exchange information.

2.4 HARDWARE SUPPORT FOR OPERATING SYSTEM

2.4.1 Processor

Also known as a *processor* or *microprocessor* the CPU was first developed by Intel and is acronym for **Central Processing Unit**. The computer CPU is responsible for handling all instructions and calculation it receives from other hardware components in the computer and software programs running on the computer. A special purpose processor that helps the CPU perform special operations such as math operations, encryption and computer graphics. A math **coprocessor**, which helps with floating point operations, allows the computer to perform more complicated mathematical instructions. Computer that has two separate processors that work together, *dual processors* are commonly used for intensive processing demands and improve the computer's overall processing efficiency. It is important to note that not all operating systems and software programs support dual processors. Often this is true with older operating systems such as Microsoft Windows 98; however, newer operating systems such as Microsoft Windows XP do support dual processors.

2.4.2 Timer and Clock

Also known as the internal clock or real-time clock (RTC), Acronym for Real-Time Clock, RTC is a battery-powered clock that is an IC located on the computer motherboard that allows the computer to keep time. The RTC keeps track of the second, minute, hour, day, month and year. A system clock or system timer is a continuous pulse that helps the computer clock keep the correct time. *Clock pulse* is also known as a CP, it is a vibration of a quartz crystal located inside the computer that helps in determining the speed of the computer's processor in MHz or GHz by counting each pulse. Clock speed is the speed that the microprocessor executes each instruction. It is also known as *clock rate*. The CPU requires a fixed number of clock ticks, or cycles, to execute each instruction. The faster the clock's rate, the faster the CPU, or the faster it can execute instructions. Clocks speeds are usually determined in MHz, 1 MHz representing 1 million cycles per second, or in GHz, 1 GHz representing 1 thousand million cycles per second.

Timer is a software program or hardware device that either keeps track of how much time has been spent doing something or counts down a specified duration of time. For example, a person may have a timer to keep track of how much time he or she spends on the internet, or a count down used to let the person know when to stop or start something.

2.4.3 Bootstrapping

Bootstrapping is also called Boot loader; a bootstrap loader is a program that resides in the computer's EPROM, ROM, or other non-volatile memory that is automatically executed by the processor when the computer is turned on. The bootstrap loader reads the hard disk drive's boot sector to continue the process of loading the computer's operating system. The boot loader has been replaced in computers that have an Extensible Firmware Interface (EFI). The boot loader is now a part of the EFI BIOS.

2.4.4 Plug and Play

Short for **Plug and Play**, **PnP** is an ability of a computer to detect and configure a new piece of hardware automatically, without the requirement of the user to physically configure the hardware device with jumpers or dipswitches. Plug and Play was introduced on IBM compatible computers with the release of Microsoft Windows 95, where Apple Macintosh computers have always supported the ability to automatically detect and install hardware.

For Plug and Play to operate properly on IBM compatible computers the user must have the following:

- BIOS supporting Plug and Play.
- Windows 95, 98, 2000 or other operating systems supporting PnP.
- Peripheral with PnP support.

Today, all new computers have PnP capabilities. Computers running Microsoft Windows XP no longer support non-PnP devices. Some users sarcastically refer to PNP as 'Plug and Play', indicating that they play for the device to work after plugging it in. This term was commonly used when PnP was first introduced because it was notorious for not working. This is a type of bipolar transistor.

2.5 CACHES AND BUFFERS

Cache is a high-speed access area that can be either a reserved section of main memory or a storage device. The two main types of cache are: memory cache and disk cache. Memory cache is a portion on memory of high-speed static RAM (SRAM) and is effective because most programs access the same data or instructions over and over. By keeping as much of this information as possible in SRAM, the computer avoids accessing the slower DRAM.

Like memory caching, disk caching is used to access commonly accessed data. However, instead of using high-speed SRAM, a disk cache uses conventional main memory. The most recently accessed data from the disk is stored in a memory buffer. When a program needs to access data from the disk, it first checks the disk cache to see if the data is there.

Most computers today come with *L*3 cache and/or *L*2 cache, while older computers included only *L*1 cache. Disk caching can dramatically improve the performance of applications because accessing a byte of data in RAM can be thousands of times faster than accessing a byte on a hard disk.

***L*1 cache is also known as primary cache**, or **internal cache**. When referring to computer processors, *L*1 cache is cache built onto the processor and is commonly the fastest cache in the computer.

Short for **Level 2 caching, *L*2** is also commonly referred to as **secondary cache** or **external cache.** Unlike Layer 1 cache, *L*2 cache is commonly located on the motherboard, although with most new processors it is being found on the processor. When *L*2 cache is found on the processor and if another cache is found on the motherboard, it is properly known as *L*3 cache.

*L*2 was first introduced with the Intel Pentium and Pentium Pro computers. In some cases this required that the user install or have installed optional *L*2 cache for *L*2 support.

*L*2 Cache on computers can range from 64 KB to 2 MB in size. However, early versions of the Intel Celeron had no *L*2 cache.

*L*3 Type of cache that is found on the motherboard instead of in the processor. Cache on the processor is known as *L*2 cache. ***L*3** or ***L*3 communication** is also a supplier of Intelligence, Surveillance and Reconnaissance systems and products, secure communication systems and products, microwave components, and space and navigation products.

When referring to memory, a **buffer** is a temporary storage in memory used to temporarily store information while other information is being processed. As in online one may see **buffering** with online streaming videos and music before they play. This buffering is done to help keep the media file from stopping when it does start to play by downloading a portion of the file first. Data Buffer is an alternate, generally temporary, location to store data while being moved from one location to another.

2.6 SOFTWARE OVERVIEW

2.6.1 Machine Language and Assembly Language

Programming Language Evolution

Early computers were programmed in *machine language* where the programmer writes instructions for direct execution on the hardware. Essentially this reduced to 'programming by number'. *Assembly languages* were introduced to reduce the errors associated with machine language programming. The main idea is to associate readable names with operations and data items. Some assembly languages offer more advanced features such as 'macro' operations that translate into more than one machine operation. Assembly language is usually not portable from one machine type to another. Hence the next step in programming language development was towards machine-independent languages also called *high-level programming languages*. Most of the history of programming languages is dominated by the development of different styles of high-level language.

Machine Language

In the early days of microcomputers, using switches on the front panel to enter the ones and zeros corresponding to the machine instructions that one wants to perform enters programs. This is called *machine language* programming. For instance if a number is to be added from memory location 20 to the number at memory location 21, and put the result at memory location 22. Here's what it looks like for the 6502 microprocessor:

```
1010 1101 0001 0100 0000 0000
0110 1101 0001 0101 0000 0000
1000 1101 0001 0110 0000 0000
```

Assembler

Programmers soon got tired of writing ones and zeros, and some very clever programmers decided to assign a *mnemonic* to each set of ones and zeros that corresponded to a machine instruction. One could then write their program using these easier-to-read mnemonics, and a program called an *assembler* would take those mnemonics and translate them into the ones and zeros. Here's the same program in assembler:

```
LDA    20
ADC    21
STA    22
```

That is better, but not by much. The mnemonics are a little bit unusual: LDA means 'load accumulator,' ADC means, 'add with carry,' and STA means 'store accumulator.' Two problems still remain. In assembler and machine language, you are responsible for figuring out where to put everything in memory. Also, the program is good only for one kind of platform, since different microprocessors have different combinations of ones and zeros to stand for 'add' or 'store.'

High Level Languages

In a high level language, you write in a notation that's familiar to you, and a program called a *compiler* takes that notation and translates it into the ones and zeros that the CPU understands. Here's a C++ statement to do the addition:

Result = First number + Second number;

All the problems are solved now. There is no worry about ones and zeros, or where things go in memory–the compiler figures all of that out for you. Since C++ compilers are available on almost every platform, you can write your program once and use it on many different types of computers.

The Linker

Back in the bad old days, everyone wrote all their own code. If you wanted to print something, you needed to write code to drive the printer mechanism. So did the next guy who wanted to print output. If you wanted to calculate square roots, you wrote the code for it.

This clearly was not a good use of people's time, so, again, some very clever programmers got together and wrote libraries of commonly used tasks like reading from the keyboard, writing to the screen or printer, and calculating heavy math stuff. They then wrote a program called a *linker* which combined the libraries with your code. This, again, made everyone's life easier.

2.6.2 Interpreter and Compiler

An **Interpreter** is a *program* that implements or simulates a *virtual machine* using the base set of instructions of a *programming language* as its *machine language*. It is a *program* that implements a library containing the implementation of the basic instruction set of a *programming language* in *machine language*. It reads the statements of a program, analyses them and then executes them on the virtual machine by calling the corresponding instructions of the library.

A **Compiler** is a *program* that translates code of a *programming language* in *machine code*, also called *object code*. The object code can be executed directly on the machine where it was compiled.

So using a *compiler* separates *translation* and *execution* of a program. In contrast of an *interpreted* program the *source code* is translated only once.

The *object code* is *machine-dependent* meaning that the compiled program can only be executed on a machine for which it has been compiled, whereas an *interpreted* program is not *machine-dependent* because the *machine-dependent* part is in the interpreter itself.

The first phase of preparing a program for the computer to execute is the entry of the program instructions at an appropriate language level, and this will usually be done with a text editor as already described. The language used to describe the procedure to be followed is almost always quite different from the machine language level. Thus some form of translation from one language level to a lower level is required. In the early days of electronic computers, this was done by hand assembling the machine instructions to execute each high level instruction. One of the first routine tasks to be automated was the process of such a translation, resulting in either an *interpreted* or a *compiled* execution environment for the program.

The distinction between the terms *interpret* and *compile* arises when we consider that most useful tasks in scientific computing involve highly repetitive instruction sequences, usually called *loops* of one form or another. For a program which involves significant looping, the process of translating from the high level language to the machine level for each iteration can consume a large fraction of the computer time, while for a program that does not have to execute many repetitive instructions, the cost of interpreting is relatively low.

2.6.3 High Level Language

Very early in the development of computer's attempts were made to make programming easier by reducing the amount of knowledge of the internal workings of the computer that was needed to write programs. If programs could be presented in a language that was more familiar to the person solving the problem, then fewer mistakes would be made. High-level programming languages allow the specification of a problem solution in terms closer to those used by human beings. These languages were designed to make programming far easier, less error-prone and to remove the programmer from having to know the details of the internal structure of a particular computer. These high-level languages were much closer to human language. One of the first of these languages was Fortran II which was introduced in about 1958. In Fortran II our program above would be written as:

$$C = A + B$$

which is obviously much more readable, quicker to write and less error-prone. As with assembly languages the computer does not understand these high-level languages directly and hence they have to be processed by passing them through a program called a *compiler* which translates them into internal machine language before they can be executed.

Another advantage arrives from the use of high-level languages if the languages are standardised by some international body. Then each manufacturer produces a *compiler* to compile programs that conform to the standard into their own internal machine language. Then it should be easy to take a program, which conforms to the standard, and implement it on many different computers merely by re-compiling it on the appropriate computer. This great advantage of portability of programs has been achieved for several high-level languages and it is now possible to move programs from one computer to another without too much difficulty. Unfortunately many compiler writers add new features of their own which means that if a programmer uses these features then their program becomes non-portable. It is well worth becoming familiar with the standard and writing programs, which obey it, so that your programs are more likely to be portable.

As with assembly language human time is saved at the expense of the compilation time required to translate the program to internal machine language. The compilation time used in the computer is trivial compared with the human time saved, typically seconds as compared with weeks.

COBOL	Business application
FORTRAN	Engineering and scientific applications
PASCAL	General use and as a teaching tool
C and C++	General purpose
PROLOG	Artificial intelligence
JAVA	General purpose

2.6.4 Structured Programming

Structured programming is a logical construct that allows for the efficient operation of a program. With this in mind, many programmers understand structured programming as being one of the disciplines that make up the overall process of procedural programming. One of the advantages to the implementation of a structured model of programming is the ability to either eliminate or at least reduce the necessity of employing the GOTO statement.

The essential composition of any type of structured programming tends to include three basic elements. *Concatenation* is the element that has to do with the logical sequence of the statements that make up the basics for the order to be executed. Each step in the sequence must logically progress to the following step without invoking any undesirable activities.

Selection is the second element included in a process of structural programming. Essentially, this step allows for the selection of any one of a number of statements to execute, based on the current status of the program. Generally, the selection statements will contain keywords that help to identify the order as a logical executable, such as 'if,' 'then', 'endif' or 'switch'.

A third component in structural programming is *repetition*. Within this element, a selected statement remains active until the program reaches a point where there is a need for some other action to take place. A repetition normally will include keywords such as 'repeat', 'for', or 'do...until'. Essentially, the repetition instructs the program how long to continue the function before requesting further instructions.

The exact nature of structured programming will vary, depending on the purpose and function of the program. Most forms of structured programming will begin with a single point of entry, but may allow for more than one point of exit. Some types of structured programming, sometimes called modular programming, will allow for the creation of subsets or modules within the overall structure of the program that interact with one another, based on the type of order that is executed.

Structured programming is one of the several different ways in which a programming language can be constructed. It was originally introduced as a means of getting away from the 'spaghetti' code that was used in the early days and to provide some means by which programmers could more easily follow code written by other programmers. Structured programming is a procedure-oriented method of designing and coding a program.

A structured programming language does not allow just things to happen in any order within the code. There are a limited number of constructs that can be used within the code to define the execution flow. A structured program is one that only uses the constructs that are listed within this document. Most so-called structured (or procedural) programming languages also permit constructs to be used that are not listed in this document. These additional constructs are to be avoided if a true structured program is to be produced.

A structured program may be written out using pseudo code prior to being translated into whatever programming language that the program is to be written in. This pseudo code forms part of the program specification and is readable by anyone who understands structured programming regardless of whether or not they know the specific language in which the program has been written.

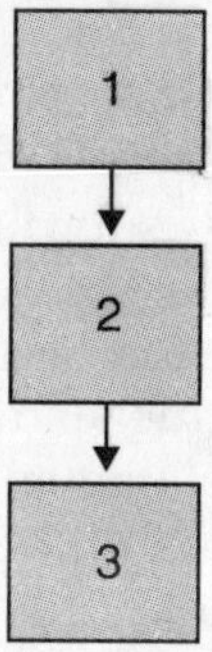

Sequence

Structured programming provides a number of constructs that are used to define the sequence in which the program statements are to be executed.

1 → 2 → 3

Consecutive

Statements within a structured program are normally executed in the same sequence as they are listed within source code. If a code fragment consists of three statements following one another, statement one will execute first, statement two second and statement three last. To change from this straight consecutive execution sequence requires the use of one of the other structured programming constructs which are described below.

Pseudo Code

```
Statement-1
  Statement-2
  Statement-3
```

Example

```
Input a
  b = 5 + 2 * a
  Print b
```

Block

Statements may be blocked together. A block of statements may be substituted wherever a single statement is allowed.

The symbol or keyword used to indicate the start and end of each block differs depending on the programming language used.

Pseudo Code

```
  {
  Statement-1
  Statement-2
  Statement-3
  }
```

Subroutine

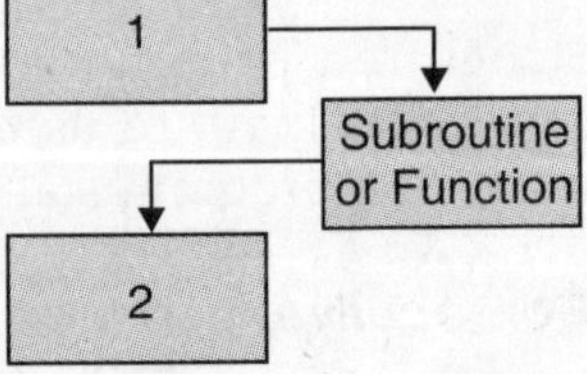

A subroutine is a code segment that has been separated from the preceding and following code. A subroutine usually consists of a series of statements that perform a particular task. The task performed is usually identified by the name given to the subroutine.

1

Subroutine or Function

2

Once a subroutine has been defined it can then be called from one or more places within the program. This allows a program to perform the same task a number of times without having to repeat the same code. A single call statement replaces (stands in for) all of the statements contained within the subroutine. Parameters can be passed to a subroutine which will supply the data required to perform the task and perhaps to return values for use by the subsequent processing.

A subroutine can be compiled either with the calling program or separately .

Pseudo Code

```
Call subroutine-1 (var 1, var 2)
   Subroutine-1 (var 1, var 2)
   {
   Statement-1
   Statement-2
   }
```

Example

```
Call output (a, b)
   Output (a, b)
   {
   Print a
   Print b
   }
```

Function

A function is similar to a subroutine except that a function always returns a value to the calling program. A function is usually called implicitly by embedding the function call into another statement in place of the returned value rather than having a separate call statement.

A function works in the same way as a subroutine except in the way that it is called. A function can be compiled internally or externally. Some programming languages also provide functions built into the language itself.

Pseudo Code

```
Var 2 = function-1 (var 1)
   Function-1 (var1)
   {
   Statement-1
   Statement-2
   Return var-2
   }
```

Example

```
b = cube (a)
   Cube (a)
   {
   b = a * a * a
   Return b
   }
```

Branching

There are two types of branching statements. The if statement is used for conditional execution of a single statement or to select which of two statements is to be executed. The case statement allows for selection of one statement out of three or more that should be executed.

If

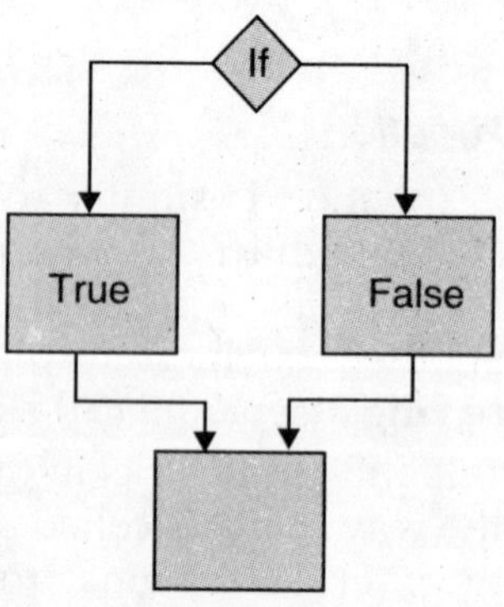

Statements can be executed conditionally by using an if statement. The if statement specifies a condition which gets tested when the if statement is executed. If the condition is true then the following statement is executed otherwise processing skips that statement.

Optionally a second statement can be attached to the if statement that will be executed if the condition is false.

Pseudo Code

If condition
True-statement
Else
False-statement

Example

If $x > y$
Print 'x is bigger than y'
Else
Print 'x is not bigger than y'

Case

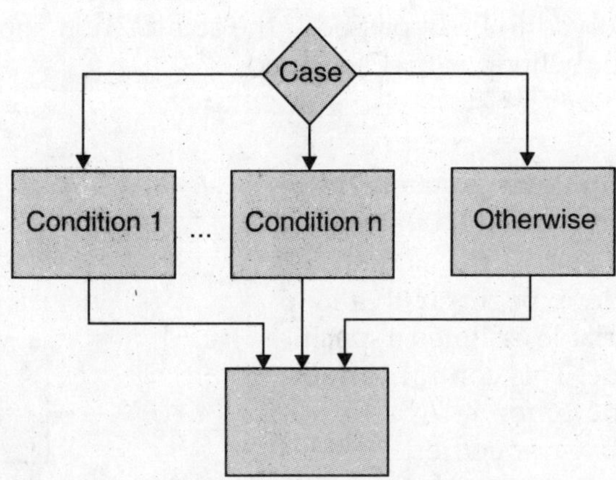

A case or select statement allows for one of a number of statements to be executed depending on the value of a field. There is usually also an additional statement which is executed if none of the specified values is matched.

Pseudo Code

Case field name
Value 1: statement-1
Value 2: statement-2
Value 3: statement-3
Otherwise: Other statement

Example

Case size

1: print 'small'

2: print 'medium'

3: print 'large'

Otherwise: Print 'unknown'

Loops

Loops allow for the same statement to be executed a number of times in succession. There are three different loop constructs that can be used depending on whether the number of repetitions is known and also (where the number of repetitions is not known and is dependent on a condition) whether the loop is allowed to be bypassed if the termination condition is met before the loop is first executed.

For

A for loop allows a statement to be executed a specified number of times.

The for loop begins with a loop control variable assigned a specific initial value. This control variable in then incremented (or decremented) by a specified amount each time around the loop until a specified terminating value is reached at which time the statement following the loop is then executed.

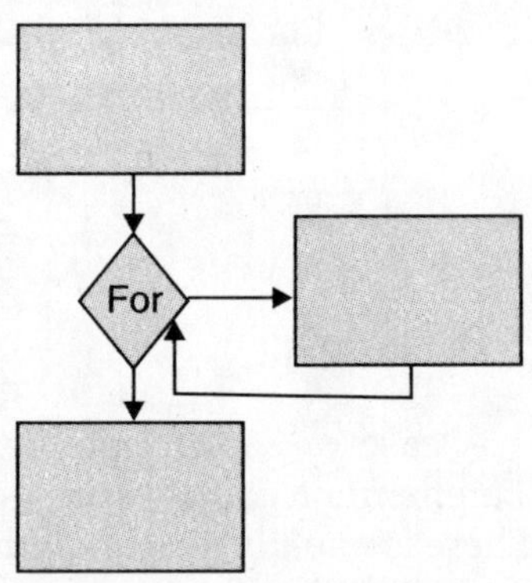

Pseudo Code

For (initial-value, final-value, increment)

Statement-1

Example

For ($a = 3, a > 12, a = a + 2$).

Print *a*

This example will output 3 5 7 9 11.

While

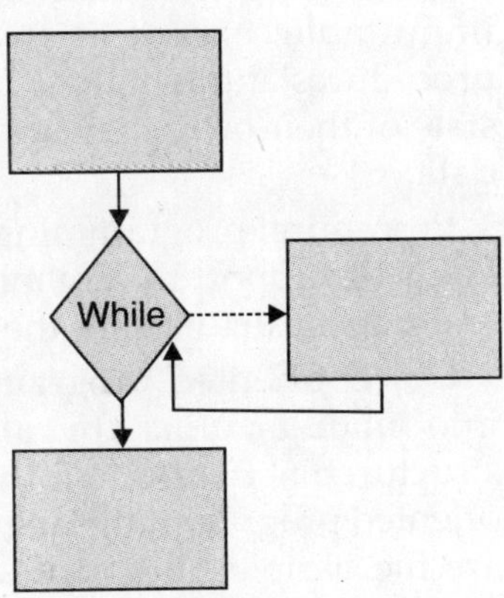

A while loop allows a statement to be executed until a given condition is met. If the condition is met prior to executing the loop then the loop will not be executed. As soon as the condition is met, execution continues with the statement following the loop.

Pseudo Code

```
While not condition
   Statement-1
```

Example

```
While not end-of-file
   {
   Read record
   Write record
   }
```

Until

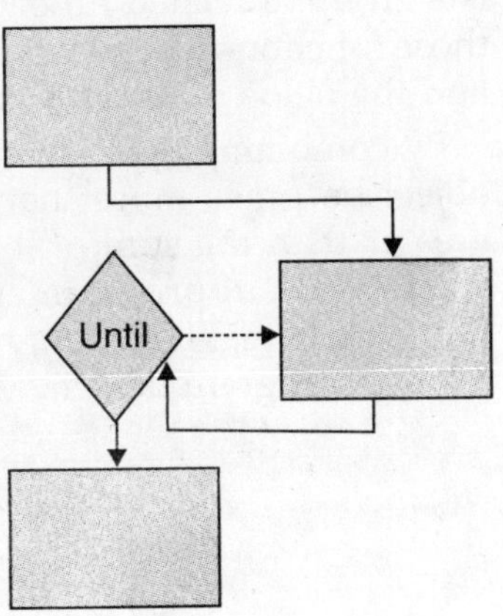

An until loop also allows a statement to be executed until a given condition is met but the condition will not be tested until after the loop has been executed once. Once the condition is met the statement following the loop will be executed.

Pseudo Code

```
Do
   Statement-1
   Until condition
```

2.6.5 Object-Oriented Programming

Programming languages have traditionally divided the world into two parts—data and operations on data. Data is static and immutable, except as the operations may change it. The procedures and functions that operate on data have no lasting state of their own; they are useful only in their ability to affect data.

Procedural programming language like C, may offer various kinds of support for organizing data and functions. Functions and data structures are the basic elements of design.

Object-oriented programming group operations and data into modular units are called *objects* and are combined into structured networks to form a complete program. In an object-oriented programming language, objects and object interactions are the basic elements of design. Every object has both state (data) and behaviour (operations on data).

Abstractions reveal causes and effects, expose patterns and frameworks, and separate what's important from what's not. They are at the root of understanding. To invent programs, same kinds of abstractions are to be discovered and expressed in the program design.

The insight of object-oriented programming is to combine state and behaviour—data and operations on data—in a high-level unit, an *object*, and to give it language support. An object is a group of related functions and a data structure that serves those functions. The functions are known as the object's *methods*, and the fields of its data structure are its *instance variables*.

By combining both state and behaviour in a single unit, an object becomes more than either alone; the whole really is greater than the sum of its parts. An object is a kind of self-sufficient 'subprogram' with jurisdiction over a specific functional area. It can play a full-fledged modular role within a larger program design.

3

Processes

3.1 PROCESS—DEFINITION

A process is a sequential program in execution. The components of a process are:

- The object program to be executed (usually a text editor).
- The *data* used for executing the program.
- *Resources* required by the program.
- The *status* of the process's execution.

3.2 MANAGING PROCESSES

Multiprogramming systems explicitly allow multiple processes to exist at any given time, where only one is using the CPU at any given moment, while the remaining processes are performing some I/O operations or may be waiting. The process manager is one of the four major parts of the operating system which implements the process abstraction. This is done by creating a model for the way the process uses CPU. When multiple processes are about to share the hardware all at the same time the complexity of the operating system starts. As a result the process manager implements CPU sharing which is referred to as *scheduling*, process *synchronization* mechanisms, and a *deadlock* strategy. The process manager also implements part of the operating system's protection and security. *Process Descriptor* or *Process Control Block* is a data structure in operating system that manages the process which is currently executed. Process can be dealt in as an entity and also as a program under execution.

Each process has its own address space which consists of text region, data region and stack region. Text region stores the code that the processor executes. Data region stores variables and allocates memory to be used by the process during execution. Stack region stores instructions and local variables for procedure call.

3.3 STATES OF A PROCESS

During the lifespan of a process, its execution status may be in one of four states:

- *Executing:* The process is currently running and has control of a CPU.

- ***Waiting:*** The process is currently able to run, but must wait until a CPU becomes available.
- ***Blocked:*** The process is currently waiting on I/O, either for input to arrive or output to be sent.
- ***Suspended:*** The process is currently able to run, but for some reason the OS has not placed the process on the ready queue.
- ***Ready:*** The process is in memory, will execute in given CPU time.

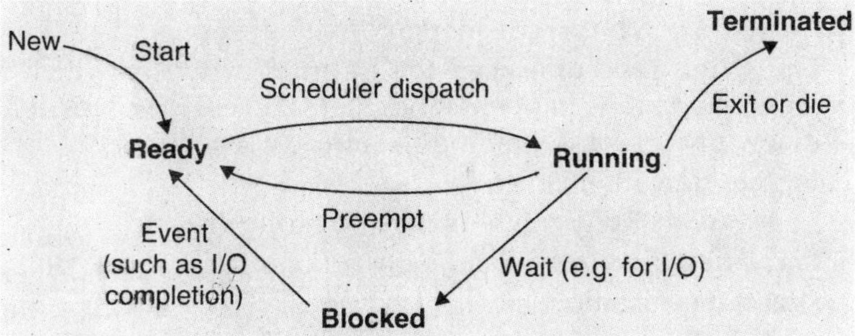

Fig. 3.1: Process state transition

3.4 PROCESS STATE TRANSITIONS (FIG. 3.1)

Possible six transitions among the above-discussed five states as in Fig. 3.1 are:

From state	*Event*	*To state*
New	Accepted	Ready
Ready	Scheduled//Dispatch	Running
Running	Need I/O	Waiting
Running	Scheduler time out	Ready
Running	Completion/Error/Killed	Terminated
Waiting	I/O completed or wake up event	Ready

Transition 1 occurs when a process recognizes that it cannot continue. If running process initiates an I/O operation before its allotted time expires, the running process voluntarily refreshes the CPU.

This state transition is represented as below.

Block (process-name): *Running* → *Block*.

Transition 2 occurs when the scheduler decides that the running process has run long enough for a sufficient amount of time and it is time to let another process have CPU time.

This state transition is represented as below.

Time-Run-Out (process-name): *Running* → *Ready.*

Transition 3 occurs when all other processes have completed their work at their scheduled time share and it is the turn for the first process to run again. This state transition is represented as below.

Dispatch (process-name): *Ready* → *Running.*

Transition 4 occurs when the external event for which a process was waiting happens .The external event may be arrival of a new process or delimiting the already scheduled process. This state transition is:

Wakeup (process-name): *Blocked* → *Ready.*

Transition 5 occurs when a new process is created.

This state transition is:

Admitted (process-name): *New* → *Ready.*

Transition 6 occurs when the process has finished execution.

This state transition is:

Exit (process-name): *Running* → *Terminated.*

3.5 PROCESS CONTROL BLOCK

A data package called *Process Control Block* (PCB) holds the track information of switching of process. For each process, its PCB is used to track the process's execution status which includes the following,

- An ID number that identifies the process.
- Pointers to the locations in the program and its data where processing last occurred.
- Register contents.
- States of various flags and switches.
- Pointers to the upper and lower bounds of the memory required for the process.
- A list of files opened by the process.
- The priority of the process.
- The status of all I/O devices needed by the process.

Each process has a status associated with it. Many processes consume zero CPU time until they get some sort of input. While it is waiting, it is said to be '**suspended**'. When the status of the process changes, from pending to active, or from suspended to running, the information in the process control block must be used.

Swapping of processes as per need or constraint happens without direct user interference and each process gets enough CPU cycles to accomplish its task in a reasonable amount of time. Trouble can begin if the user tries to have too many processes functioning at the same time. The operating system itself requires some CPU cycles to perform the saving and swapping of all the registers, queues and stacks of the application processes. If enough processes are started, and if the operating system hasn't been carefully designed, the system can begin to use the vast majority of its available CPU cycles to swap between processes rather than running the processes. This instance is called **thrashing**, and it usually requires some sort of direct user intervention to stop processes and bring order back to the system.

3.6 SYMMETRIC AND ASYMMETRIC PROCESS

In a system with two or more CPUs, the operating system must divide the workload among the CPUs, trying to balance the demands of the required processes with the available cycles on the different CPUs. This comes under two main categories as *Symmetric* and *Asymmetric* operating system (Figs 3.2 and 3.3).

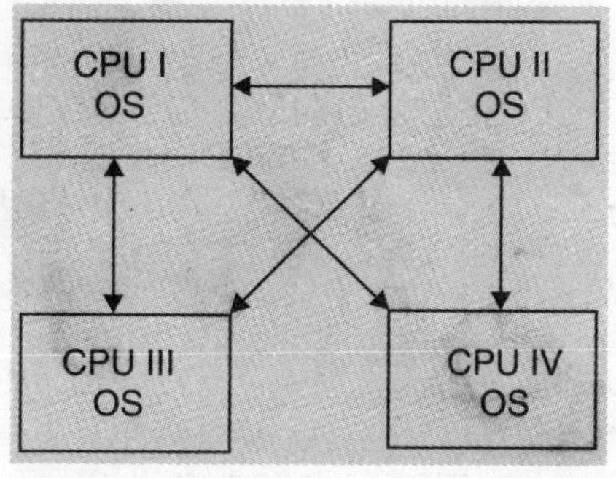

Fig. 3.2: Symmetric operating system

Asymmetric operating systems use one CPU for their own needs and divide application processes among the remaining CPUs. If the operating system is the only software with execution needs, the CPU is not the only resource to be scheduled. Memory management is the next crucial step in making sure that all processes run smoothly.

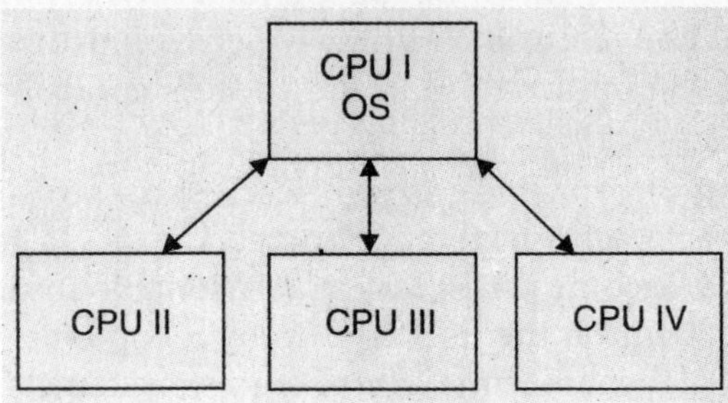

Fig. 3.3: Asymmetric operating system

3.7 OPERATIONS ON PROCESS

A process should be created or deleted dynamically which involves the following stages.

3.7.1 Process Creation

In general-purpose systems, some steps should be adapted to create processes as need raises during operation. There are four basic and important events that led to processes creation.

- System initialisation.
- Execution of a process.
- Creating system calls by a running process.
- A user request to create a new process.
- Initialisation of a batch job.

Foreground processes interact with users directly. Background processes that stay sleeping in background suddenly get life to handle internal or sudden activity. Background processes are called daemons. This call to handle new process creates an exact clone of the calling process. A process may create a new process by some create process command such as *fork*. In such a case the creating process is called parent process and the created one is called the child process. Only one parent is needed to create a child process. This creation of process (processes) yields a hierarchical structure of processes. Each child has only one parent but each parent may have many children. After the fork, the two processes, the parent and the child, have the same memory image, the same environment strings and the same open files. After a process is created, both the parent and child have their own distinct address space. If either process changes a word in its address space, the change is not visible to the other process.

3.7.2 Process Termination

A process terminates when it finishes executing its last statement of request. Its resources are returned to the system, it is purged from any system lists or tables, and its process control block (PCB) is refreshed and its memory space is returned to a free memory pool. The new process terminates the existing process, usually due to following reasons:

- *Normal exist:* Most processes terminate because they have done their job. This call exists in UNIX.
- *Error exist:* When process discovers a fatal error. For example, a user tries to compile a program that does not exist.
- *Fatal error:* An error caused by process due to a bug in program for example, executing an illegal instruction, referring non-existing memory or dividing by zero.
- *Killed by another process:* A process executes a system call telling the Operating Systems to terminate some other process. In UNIX, this call is kill.

3.8 INTERPROCESS COMMUNICATION

One of the benefits of multitasking is that several processes can be made to cooperate in order to achieve their ends. To do this, they must do one of the following.

1. *Communicate:* Interprocess communication (IPC) involves sending information from one process to another. This can be achieved using a 'mailbox' system, a socket which behaves like a virtual communication, network (loopback), or through the use of 'pipes'. Pipes are a system construction, which enables one process to open another process as if it were a file for writing or reading.

2. ***Share data:*** A segment of memory must be available to both processes. Most memory is locked to a single process.
3. ***Waiting:*** Some processes wait for other processes to give a signal before continuing. This is an issue of synchronization.

A major problem with interprocess communication is synchronizing the cooperating processes that takes part in IPC. For example, suppose two processes modify the same file. If both processes tried to write simultaneously the result would be a nonsensical mixture. Processes synchronization should be done so that even concurrent processes must also stay in line to access shared data *serially*. Synchronization is a tricky problem in multiprocessor systems, but it can be achieved with the help of *critical sections* and *semaphores/locks*.

3.9 PROCESS HIERARCHY: CHILDREN AND PARENT PROCESSES

When a user creates a process using the command interpreter, the new process becomes the *child* of the command interpreter. Similarly the command interpreter process becomes the parent for the child. Processes, therefore, form a hierarchy.

The processes are linked by a tree structure. If a parent is signaled or killed, usually all its children receive the same signal or are destroyed with the parent. It is possible to detach children from their parents—but in many cases it is useful for processes to be linked in this way.

When a child is created it may do one of the following:

- Duplicate the parent process.
- Load a completely new program.

Similarly the parent may do one of two things:

- Continue executing alongside its children.
- Wait for some or all of its children to finish before proceeding.

3.10 PROCESS SYNCHRONIZATION

There are two important primitives for any communication as *send* and *receive*. Communication between process also takes place by placing calls to those primitives. This message passing can be either blocking (Synchronous) or non-blocking (Asynchronous).

Synchronous

- *Send:* Sending process is blocked till the receiving process receives the message.
- *Receive:* The receiver blocks until the message is available.

Asynchronous

- *Send:* Sending process sends the message and continues its work.
- *Receive:* The receiver gets a valid message or a null message.

The primitives must be from different category. If both are from same category then a tie sustains between the sender and receiver.

3.10.1 Cooperating Processes

An *Independent* process is not affected by other running processes. *Cooperating processes* may affect each other, in some controlled way. Cooperating processes are used for:

- Computational speed up.
- Modularity or convenience.
- Information sharing.

In a computer system processes do not cooperate. For the processes to cooperate, they must have a way to communicate with each other. Two common methods are:

- Shared variables—some segment of memory accessible to both processes
- Message passing—a process sends an explicit message that is received by another process.

Here the shared-memory communication is considered.

3.10.2 Producer-Consumer Problem

The classic example for studying cooperating processes is the Producer-Consumer problem.

One or more producers may produce processes as 'producing' data. This data is stored in a buffer to be 'consumed' by one or more consumer processes as in Fig. 3.4.

The buffer may be:

- ***Unbounded:*** We assume that the producer can continue producing items and storing them in the buffer at all times.

Fig. 3.4: Producer-consumer problem

However, the consumer must wait for an item to be inserted into the buffer before it can take one out for consumption.

- ***Bounded:*** The producer must also check to make sure there is space available in the buffer.

Bounded Buffer and Buffer Size n

For simplicity, we will assume the objects being produced and consumed are *int* values.

This solution leaves one buffer entry empty at all times:

- Shared data

```
int buffer (n);
int in = 0;
int out = 0;
```

- Producer process

```
while (1) {
...
produce item;
...
while [[(in + 1)% n] = = out); /*busy wait*/
buffer (in) = item;
in = (in + 1)% n;
}
```

- Consumer process

```
while (1) {
while (in = = out); /*busy wait*/
item = buffer (out);
out = (out + 1) % n;
...
consume item;
...
}
```

These processes can be interleaved in any order—the system could preempt the producer at any time and run the consumer. Things to be careful about are shared references to variables.

Note that only one of the processes can *modify* the variables in and out. Both use the values, but only the producer modifies in and only the consumer modifies out. The entire buffer space allocated may be used but there are chances of overriding the entire buffer space. To keep track of the buffer usage a counter variable may be added as below to keep track of the number of items in the buffer.

- Shared data

```
int buffer (n);
int in = 0;
int out = 0;
int counter = 0;
```

- Producer process

```
while (1) {
...
produce item;
...
while (counter = = n); /*busy wait*/
buffer (in) = item;
in = (in + 1) % n;
counter = counter + 1;
}
```

- Consumer process

```
while (1) {
while (counter = = 0); /*busy wait*/
item = buffer (out);
out = (out + 1) % n;
counter = counter – 1;
...
consume item;
...
}
```

Consider the two statements that modify counter:

Producer	Consumer
P_1 R_0 = counter;	C_1 R_1 = counter;
P_2 $R_0 = R_0 + 1$;	C_2 $R_1 = R_1 - 1$;
P_3 counter = R_0;	C_3 counter = R_1;

Consider one possible ordering: P_1 P_2 C_1 P_3 C_2 C_3, where counter = 17 before starting. Here the scenario of '*Race condition*' occurs. Some of the most difficult bugs to find in software, often in operating systems, arise from race conditions. This is tedious to be recovered when executing in real-time processes.

Consider two processes modifying a linked list, one inserting and one removing. A context switch at the wrong time can lead to a corrupted structure:

```
struct node {
...
struct node *next;
}
struct node *head, *tail;
void insert(val) {
struct node *newnode;
newnode = getnode();
newnode-> next = NULL;
if (head == NULL){
head = tail = newnode;
} else { // ⇐ THE WRONG PLACE
tail-> next = newnode;
tail = newnode;
}
}
void remove () {
// ... code to remove value ...
head = head-> next;
if (head = = NULL) tail = NULL;
return (value);
}
```

If the process-executing insert is interrupted at 'the wrong place' and then another process calls remove until the list is empty, when the insert process resumes, it will be operating on invalid assumptions and the list will be corrupted. In the bounded buffer, we need to make sure that when one process starts modifying counter, that it finishes before the other can try to modify it. This requires *synchronization* of the processes.

If there were mutliple producers or consumers, we would have the same issue with the modification of in and out, so we cannot rely on the 'empty slot' approach in the more general case. We need to make those statements that increment and decrement counter *atomic*. We say that the modification of counter is a *critical section*.

3.10.3 Critical Section

The critical-section problem:

- n processes, all competing to use some shared data.
- each process has a code segment (the critical section) in which shared data is accessed

```
While (1) {
< CS entry >
Critical section
< CS exit >
Non-critical section
}
```

- Need to ensure that when one process is executing in its critical section, no other process is allowed to do so

Example: Intersection/traffic light analogy

Example: One-lane bridges during construction

Any solution to the critical section problem must satisfy three conditions:

1. ***Mutual exclusion:*** If process P_i is executing in its critical section, no other processes can be executing in their critical sections. 'One at a time.'
2. ***Progress***: If no process is executing in its critical section and there exist some processes that wish to enter their critical section, the selection of the processes that will enter the

critical section next cannot be postponed indefinitely. 'No unnecessary waiting.'

3. ***Bounded waiting:*** A bound must exist on the number of times that other processes are allowed to enter their critical sections after a process has made a request to enter its critical section and before that request is granted (We must assume that each process executes at non-zero speed, but makes no assumptions about relative speeds of processes).

One possible way to deal with this is to make sure the problematic context switch doesn't happen. If we disable interrupts so a context switch isn't possible while we're executing the critical section, we will prevent the interference.

However, this is a bit extreme, since it doesn't just restrict another process that will be modifying the same shared variable from being switched in, it prevents ANY other process from being switched in. This approach would also not work in a multiprocessor environment when the interference could be from two processes running truly concurrently.

3.10.4 Algorithmic Approaches for 2 Processes

We first attempt to solve the above for two processes, P_0 and P_1. They share some variables to synchronize. We fill in < CS entry > and < CS exit > from above with code that should satisfy the three conditions.

Critical Section Algorithm 1

- Shared data

  Int turn = 0;

- Process P_i (define j = 1 – i, the other process)

```
While (1) {
While (turn! = i); /*busy wait*/
/*critical section*/
Turn = j;
/*non-critical section*/
}
```

Note the semicolon at the end of the while statement's condition at the line labeled 'busy wait' above. This means that

P_i just keeps comparing turn to i over and over until it succeeds. This is sometimes called a *spin lock*. For now, this is our only method of making one process wait for something to happen.

Critical Section Algorithm 2

We'll avoid this alternation problem by having a process wait only when the other has "indicated interest" in the critical section.

- Shared data
```
boolean flag (2);
flag (0) = false;
flag (1) = false;
```
- Process P_i
```
while (1) {
flag (i) = true;
while [flag (j)];
/*critical section*/
flag (i) = false;
/*non-critical section*/}
```
Flag (i) set to true means that P_i is requesting access to the critical section.

This one also satisfies mutual exclusion, but not progress.

Both can set their flags, then both start waiting for the other to set flag (j) back to false. If we swap the order of the flag (i) = true; and while [flag (j)]; statements, we no longer satisfy mutual exclusion.

Critical Section Algorithm 3

We combine the two previous approaches:

- Shared data
```
int turn = 0;
boolean flag (2);
flag (0) = false;
flag (1) = false;
```
- Process P_i
```
while (1) {
```

```
flag (i) = true;
turn = j;
while [flag (j) and and turn = = j];
/*critical section*/
flag (i) = false;
/*non-critical section*/
}
```

So, we first indicate interest. Then we set turn = *j*; effectively saying 'no, you first' to the other process. Even if both processes are interested and both get to the while loop at the 'same' time, only one can proceed. Whoever set turn first gets to go first. This one satisfies all three of our conditions. This is known as *Peterson's Algorithm.*

3.10.5 Algorithmic Approach for n Processes: Bakery Algorithm

The idea is that each process, when it wants to enter the critical section, takes a number. Whoever has the smallest number gets to go in. This is more complex than the bakery ticket-spitters because two processes may grab the same number (to guarantee that they would not require mutual exclusion—exactly the thing we are trying to implement), and because there is no attendant to callout the next number—the processes all must come to agreement on who should proceed next into the critical section. We break ties by allowing the process with the lower process identifier (PID) to proceed. For *Pi*, we call it i. This assumes PIDs from 0 to $n - 1$ for n processes, but this can be generalized.

Although two processes that try to pick a number at about the same time may get the same number, we do guarantee that once a process with number k is in, all processes-choosing numbers will get a number $> k$.

Notation used below: an ordered pair (number, pid) fully identifies a process's number. We define a *lexicographic order* of these:

- $(a, b) < (c, d)$ is $a < c$ or if $a = c$ and $b < d$

The algorithm:

- Shared data, initialized to 0's and false

```
boolean choosing (n);
int number (n);
```

- Process P_i

```
while (1) {
choosing (i) = true;
number (i) = max [number (0), number (i), ..., number
(n – 1)] + 1;
choosing (i) = false;
for (j = 0; j < n; j ++) {
while [choosing (j)];
while [[number (j)! = 0] and and
[[number (j), j] < [number (i), i]]];
}
/*critical section*/
number (i) = 0;
/*non-critical section*/
}
```

Before choosing a number, a process indicates that it is doing so. Then it looks at everyone else's number and picks a number one larger. Then it says it's done choosing. Then look at every other process. First, wait for that process not to be choosing. Then make sure we are allowed to go before that process.

To leave the CS, just reset the number back to 0.

So great, we have a solution. But...problems:

1. That's a lot of code. Lots of while loops and for loops. Could be expensive if we're going to do this a lot.
2. If this is a highly popular critical section, the numbers might never reset, and we could overflow our integers. Unlikely, but think what could happen if we did.
3. It's kind of inconvenient and in some circumstances, unreasonable, to have these arrays of n values. There may not always be n processes, as some may come and go.

Synchronization Hardware

Hardware support can make some of this a little easier. Problems can arise when a process is pre-empted within a single high-level language line. But pre-emption in the middle of a machine instruction is not possible.

If a single machine instruction that checks the value of a variable and sets it **atomically**, it is called a **Test-and-Set** or Test and Set Lock instruction, and does this, atomically:

```
Boolean Test and Set (boolean *target) {
Boolean orig_val = *target;
*target = TRUE;
return orig_val;
}
```

So it sets the variable passed in to true, and tells us if it was true or false *before* we called it. So if two processes do this operation, both will set the value of target to true, but only one will get a return value of false.

Really, this would be an instruction that takes two operands: TAS *R*, *X*.

Where R is a CPU register and X is a memory location. After the instruction completes (atomically), the value that was in memory at *X* is copied into R, and the value of *X* is set to 1. *R* contains a 0 if *X* previously contained a 0. If two processes do this operation concurrently, only one will actually get the 0.

The Intel *x*86 BTS instruction sets a single bit in memory and sets the carry bit of the status word to the previous value. Think about how one might implement an atomic test and set on, for example, a micro programmed architecture.

Any of these can be used to implement a 'test and set' function as described above. Armed with this atomic test-and-set, we can make a simple mutual exclusion solution for any number of processes, with just a single shared variable:

- Shared data

```
boolean lock = false;
```

- Process P_i

```
while (1) {
while [Test and Set (and lock)]; /*busy wait*/
/*critical section*/
lock = false;
/*non-critical section*/
}
```

This satisfies mutual exclusion and progress, but not bounded waiting (a process can leave the CS and come back around and grab the lock again before others who may be waiting ever get a chance to look).

A solution that does satisfy bounded waiting is still fairly complicated:

- Shared data

  boolean lock = false;

  boolean waiting (*n*); /*all initialized to false*/

- Process P_i and its local data

```
int j;
boolean key;
while (1) {
waiting (i) = true;
key=true;
while [waiting (i) and key)
key = Test and Set (and lock);
waiting (i) = false;
/*critical section*/
j = (i + 1) % n;
while [(j! = i) and !waiting (j)]
j = (j + 1)% n;
if (j = = i) lock = false;
else waiting (j) = false;
/*non-critical section*/
}
```

Another hardware instruction that might be available is the atomic *swap* operation:

```
Void swap (boolean *a, boolean *b) {
boolean temp = *a;
*a = *b;
*b = temp;
}
```

Different architectures have variations on this one, including the *x*86 XCHG instruction.

An algorithm to use this, minus the bounded wait again, is straight forward:

- Shared data

  boolean lock = false;

- Process P_i

```
boolean key = true;
while (1) {
while (key = = true) swap (and key, and lock); /* busy wait
*/
/*critical section*/
lock = false;
/*non-critical section*/
}
```

It's pretty similar to what we saw before with Test and Set( ).

3.10.6 Semaphores

All that busy waiting in all of our algorithms for mutual exclusion is pretty annoying. It's just wasted time on the CPU. If we have just one CPU, it doesn't make sense for that process to take up its whole quantum spinning away waiting for a shared variable to change that can't change until the current process relinquishes the CPU!

This inspired the development of the *semaphore*. The name comes from old-style railroad traffic control signals, where mechanical arms swing down to block a train from a section of track that another train is currently using. When the track was free, the arm would swing up, and the waiting train could now proceed. A semaphore *S* is basically an integer variable, with two atomic operations:

```
Wait (S):
while (S < = 0); /*wait*/
S—;
Signal (S):
S++;
```

Wait and signal are also often called down and up (from the railroad semaphore analogy) and occasionally are called *P* and *V* (because Dijkstra, who invented them, was Dutch, and these are the first letters of the Dutch words *proberen* (to test) and *verhogen* (to increment)).

Important!!! Processes using a semaphore in its most pure form are not allowed to set or examine its value. They can use the semaphore *only* through the wait and signal operations.

Note, however, that we don't want to do a busy-wait. A process that has to wait should be put to sleep, and should wake up only when a corresponding signal occurs, as that is the only time the process has any chance to proceed. Semaphores are built using hardware support, or using software techniques such as the ones we discussed for critical section management. Since the best approach is just to take the process out of the ready queue, some operating systems provide semaphores through system calls. We will examine their implementation in this context soon.

Given semaphores, we can create a much simpler solution to the critical section problem for *n*

Processes:

- Shared data
  Semaphore mutex = 1;
- Process P_i
  While (1) {
  Wait (mutex);
  /* critical section */
  Signal (mutex);
  /* non-critical section */
  }

The semaphore provides the mutual exclusion for sure, and should satify progress, but depending on the implementation of semaphores, may or may not provide bounded waiting. A semaphore implementation might look like this:

Struct semaphore {
int value;
proclist *L*;
};

- *block* operation suspends the calling process, removes it from consideration by the scheduler.

- *Wakeup (P)* resumes execution of suspended process *P*, puts it back into consideration.
- Wait (*S*):

```
S.value – –;
if (S.value < 0) {
add this process to S.L;
block;
}
```

- Signal (*S*):

```
S.value ++;
if (S.value <= 0) {
remove a process P from S.L;
wakeup (P);
}
```

There is a fairly standard implementation of semaphores on many Unix systems: POSIX semaphores

- Create a shared variable of type sem t
- Initialize it with sem init (3)
- Wait operation is sem wait (3)
- Signal operation is sem post (3)
- Deallocate with sem destroy (3)

Note that what we have been looking at are *counting semaphores*. This means that the semaphore's value is 0 and there are two signal operations, its value will be 2. This means that the next two wait operations will not block. This means that semaphores can be used in more general situations than simple mutual exclusion. Perhaps we have a section that we want at most 3 processes in at the same time. We can start with a semaphore initialized to 3. Semaphores can also be used as a more general-purpose synchronization tool. Suppose statement *B* in process P_j can be executed only after statement *A* in P_i. We use a semaphore called flag, initialised to 0:

P_i	P_j
...	...
A;	Wait (flag);
Signal (flag);	*B*;
...	...

Here, P_j will be forced to wait only if it arrives at the wait call before P_i has executed the signal. Of course, we can introduce *deadlocks* (two or more processes waiting indefinitely for an event that can only be caused by one of the waiting processes).

Consider semaphores Q and R, initialized to 1, and two processes that need to wait on both. A careless programmer could write:

P_0	P_1
Wait (Q);	Wait (R);
Wait (R);	Wait (Q);
...	...
Signal (R);	Signal (Q);
Signal (Q);	Signal (R);
...	...

Things might be fine, but they might not be. There's also the possibility that a process might just forget a signal and leave one or more other processes (may be even itself) waiting indefinitely. We will look into the implementation of semaphores and mutexes later, but for now we will look more at how to use them as a synchronization tool.

Executable code for implementation of multiple producer—multiple consumer problem using semaphores:

```
#include<stdio.h>
#include<semaphore.h>
#include<pthread.h>
#include<math.h>
#define NBUFF10
#define MAXTHREADS 25
int nitems, nproducers, nconsumers;
struct{
int buff[NBUFF];
int nput;
int nputval;
int ngetval;
int nget;
```

```
sem_t mutex, nempty, ntored;
} shared;
void*produce(void*);
void*consume(void*);
int main(int argc,char**argv)
{
int i,nl,n2;
int count(MAXTHREADS),ccount(MAXTHEADS);
pthread_ttid_produce(MAXTHEADS),tid_consume (MAXTHREADS);
shared.nput=0;
shared.nputval=0;
if(argc=4)
{
printf(Usage:filename<nitems> <nproducers>");
return0;
}
nitems=atoi[argv(1)];
nl=atoi[argv(2)];
if(nl>MAXRHREADS)
nprodcers=MAXTHREADS;
else
nproducers=nl;
if(n2>MAXTHREADS)
nconsumers=MATHREADS;
else
nconsumers=n2;
printf("\n\nMultiplleproducer-multiple consumer problem using semphore\n");
printf("..........................\n\n");
sem_init(and shared.mutex,0,1);
sem_init(and shared.nempty,0,NBUFF);
sEM_INIT(and SHARED.NSTORED,0,0);
pthread_setconcurrency(nproducers+nconsumers);
```

```
for(i=0;i<nproducdefs;i++)
{
pcount(i)=0;
pthread_create[and tid_produce[i],
NULL,produce, and pcount(i)];
}
for(i=0;i<nconsumers;i++)
{
ccount(i)=0;
pthread_creat[and tid_consume(i),
NULL,consume,and ccount(i)];
}
for(i=0;i<nproducers;i++)
pthread_join[tid_produce(i),NULL];
for(i=0;i<nconsumers;i++)
pthread_join[tid_consume(i),NULL];
sem_destroy(and shared.mutex);
sem_destroy(and shared.nempty);
sem_destroy(and shared.nstored);
}
void*produce(void*arg)
{
for(;;)
{
sem_wait(and shared.nempty);
sem_wait(and shared.mutex);
if(shared.nput>=nitems
sem_post(and shared.nempty);
sem_post(and shared.mutex);
return (NULL);
}
shared.buff(shared.nput%NBUFF)
=shared.nputval;
printf("\t producer%d.....",*)arg));
printf(buff(%d\n\n",shared.nput,
shared.nput,shared.buff
(shared.nput%NBUFF)];
```

```
shared,nput++;
shared.nputval++;
sem_post(and shared.mutex);
sem_post(and shared.nstored);
*(int*)arg+=1;
sleep(5);
}
}
void*consume(void*arg)
{
int i;
for(;;)
{
sem_wait(and shared.nstored);
sem_wait(and shared.mutex);
if(shared.nget>=nitems)
{
sem_post(and shared.nstored);
sem_post(and shared.mutex);
return (NULL);
}
I=shared.nget%NBUFF;
printf("\t Consumer...%d",*((int*)arg));
printf["buff(%d)=%d\n\n\n",i,
shared.buff(i)];
shared.nget++;
shared.ngetval++;
sem_poot(and shared.mutex);
sem_post(and shared.nempty);
*((int*)arg)+=1;
sleep(3);
}
returnNULL;
}
```

Executable code for implementation of multiple producer—one consumer problem using semaphores:

```
#include<stdio.h>
#include<semaphore.h>
#include<pthread.h>
#include<math.h>
#define NBUFF 10
#define MAXTHREADS25
int nitems,nproducers;
struct{
int buff[NBUFF];
int nout;
int nputval;
sem_tmurex,nempty,nstored;
} shared;
void*produce(void*);
void*consume(void*);
int i,n;
int count[MAXTHREADS];
pthread_t tid_produce[MAXTHREADS],
tid_consume;
shared.nput=0;
shared.nputval=0;
if(argc!=3)
{
int i,n;
int count[MAXTHREADS];
pTHREAD_T TID_PRODUCE[MAXTHREADS],
tid_consume;
shared.nput=0;
shared.nputval=0;
if(argc!=3)
{
printf("Usage:filename<nitems>
<nproducers>");
```

```
return 0;
}
nitems=atoi[argv(1)];n=atoi[argv(2)];
if(n>MAXTHREADS)
nproducers=MAXTHREADS;
else
nproducers=n;
printf("\n\nMultiplle producer - one consumer
oroblem using semphore\n");
printf(.........................\n\n");
sem_init(and shared.mutex,o,1);
sem_init(and shared.nempry,o,NBUFF);
sem_init(and shared.nstored,o,o);
pthread_setconcurrency(nproducers+1);
for(i=0;i<nproducers;i++)
{
count(i)=0;
pthread_create[and tid_produce(i),
NULL,produce,and count(i)];
}
pthreadcreate(tid_consume,NULL,
consume,NULL);
for(i=0;i<nproducers;i++)
pthread_join(tid_produce[i],NULL);
pthread_join(tid_consume,NULL);
sem_destroy(and shared.mutex);
sem_destroy(and shared.nempty);
sem_destroy(and shared.nstored);
}
void produce(void*arg)
{
for(;;)
{
dem_wait(and shared.nempty);
sem_wait(and shared.mutex);
if(shared.nput>=nitems)
}
```

```
sem_post(and shared.nempty);
sem_post(and shared.mutex);
return (NULL);
}
shared.buff[shared.nput%NBUFF]
=shared.nputval;
printf("t producer %d........",arg);
printf("buff%d]=%d\n\n",shared.nput,
shared,buff[shared.nput%NBUFF];
shared.nput++;
shared.nputval++;
sem_post(and shared.mutex);
sem_post(and shared.nstored);
*(in*)arg+=1;
sleep(3);
}
}
void*consume(void*arg)
{
int i;
for(i=0;i<nitems;i++)
{
sem_wait(and shared.nstored);
sem_wait(and shared.mutex);
printf(\t consumer..........");
printf"buff[(%d)=%d\n\n\n",i,shared.buff
(i%NBUFF)];
sem_post(and shared.mutex);
sem_post(and shared.nimpty);
sleep(3);
}
return NULL;
}
```

3.10.7 Classical Problems of Synchronization

Dining Philosophers

- One way to tell a computer scientist from other people is to ask about the dining philosophers.
- Five philosophers with alternate thinking and eating.
- Need 2 forks to do so (eating spaghetti), one from each side
- Keep both forks until done eating, then replace both.

Since fork is the name of a C function, we'll use a different (and possibly more appropriate) analogy of chopsticks. The philosophers need two chopsticks to eat rice.

- Shared data:

```
semaphore chopstick (5);
chopstick (0..4) = 1;
```

- Philosopher i:

```
while (1) {
wait [chopstick (i)];
wait {chopstick [(i + 1)% 5]};
/*eat*/
signal [chopstick (i)];
signal {chopstick [(i + 1)% 5]};
/*think*/
}
```

This solution may deadlock.

One way to reduce the chances of deadlock might be to think first, since each might think for a different amount of time.

Another possibility

Each philosopher:

1. Picks up their left chopstick.
2. Checks to see if the right chopstick is in use.
3. If so, the philosopher puts down their left chopstick, and starts over at 1.
4. Otherwise, the philosopher eats.

Consider this all could pick up their left chopstick, look right, put down the left, and repeat indefinitely.

How to solve this? Must either

1. Introduce an asymmetry, or
2. Limit the number of concurrently hungry philosophers to $n - 1$.

Here's one that includes an asymmetry, by having odd numbered philosophers pick up to the right first. The code for philosopher i and problem size n.

```
void philosopher ( ) {
think;
if [odd (i)] {
wait {chopstick [(i + 1) % n]};
wait [chopstick (i)];
}
else {
wait [chopstick (i)];
wait {chopstick [(i + 1) % n]);
}
eat;
if [odd (i)] {
signal {chopstick [(i + 1) % n]};
signal [chopstick (i)];
}
else {
signal [chopstick (i)];
signal (chopstick[(i +1) % n]);
}
}
```

Readers-Writers

We have a database and a number of processes that need access to it. We would like to maximize concurrency.

- There are multiple 'reader processes' and multiple 'writer processes'.
- Readers see what's there, but don't change anything. Like a person on a travel website seeing what flights have seats available.

- Writers change the database. The act of making the actual reservation.
- It's bad to have a writer in with any other writers or readers—may sell the same seat to a number of people (airline, sporting event, etc.). Remember counter ++ and counter – –.
- Multiple readers are safe, and in fact we want to allow as much concurrent access to readers as we can. Since we don't want to keep potential customers waiting.

A possible solution:

- Shared data:

```
semaphore wrt, mutex;
int readcount; wrt = 1; mutex = 1; readcount = 0;
```

- Writer process:

```
while (1) { wait (wrt);
/*perform writing*/ signal(wrt);
}
```

- Reader process:

```
while (1) {
wait (mutex); readcount ++; if (readcount = = 1) wait (wrt);
signal (mutex);
/*perform reading*/
wait (mutex); readcount –; if (readcount = = 0) signal (wrt);
signal (mutex);
}
```

Note that the semaphore mutex protects readcount and is shared among readers only. Semaphore wrt indicates whether it is safe for a writer, or the first reader, to enter. Danger: A reader may wait (wrt) while inside mutual exclusion of mutex. This is a reader-preference solution.

Sleeping Barber

Problem: A certain barber shop has a single barber, a barber's chair, and n chairs in a waiting area. The barber spends his life in the shop. If there are no customers in the shop, the barber sleeps in the chair until a customer enters and wakes him. When customers are in the shop, the barber is giving one a haircut, and will call for the next customer when he finishes with each. Customers arrive periodically. If the shop is empty and the barber is asleep in the barber's chair, he wakes the barber and gets a haircut. If the barber is busy, but there are chairs available in the waiting room, he sleeps in one of those chairs until called. Finally, if there are no available chairs in the waiting room, the customer leaves and comes back another time.

A possible solution:

- Shared Data

  constant CHAIRS = maximum number of chairs (including barber chair).

  semaphore mutex = 1, next_cust = 0, barber_ready = 0;

  int cust_count = 0;

- Customer process

  while (1) { /* live your non barber-shop life until you decide you need a haircut */

  wait (mutex); if (cust_count > = CHAIRS) { signal (mutex);

  exit; /* leave the shop if full, try tomorrow */

  }

  cust_count++; /* increment customer count */

  signal (mutex); signal (next_cust); /* wake the barber if he's sleeping */

  wait (barber_ready); /* wait in the waiting room */

  /* get haircut here */ wait (mutex); cust_count –; /* leave the shop, freeing a chair */

  signal (mutex);

  }

- Barber process

  while (1) {

  wait (next_cust); /* sleep until a customer shows up */

  signal (barber_ready); /* tell the next customer you are ready */

  /*give the haircut here*/

  }

4

Threads

4.1 THREADS—INTRODUCTION

Even if it is true that a thread must execute in process, the process and its associated threads are different concepts. Processes are used to group resources together and threads are the entities scheduled for execution on the CPU. *A thread is a single sequence stream within a process*. Because threads have some of the properties of processes, they are sometimes called *lightweight processes*. These LWPs are independently scheduled parts of a single program. A task is multithreaded if it is composed of several independent subprocesses, which work on common data, and if each of those subprocesses could run parallel. If a program uses threads there is only one program, one executable file, one task in the normal sense. Threads simply enable the program to be split into logically separate pieces, and have the pieces run independent of each other, until they need to communicate. In a process, threads allow multiple executions of streams. In many respect, threads are popular way to improve application through parallelism. The CPU switches rapidly back and forth among the threads giving illusion that the threads are running in parallel. Like a traditional process, i.e. process with one thread, a thread can be in any of several states (Running, Blocked, Ready or Terminated). Each thread has its own stack. Since thread will generally call different procedures and thus a different execution history. The basic unit of CPU utilization is a thread. A thread has or consists of a program counter (PC), a register set, and a stack space. Threads are not independent of one another like processes, as a result threads share with other threads their code section, data section, OS resources also known as task, such as open files and signals.

4.2 PROCESS *Vs* THREADS

The point is that threads are cheaper than normal processes, and that they can be scheduled for execution in a user-dependent way, with less overhead. Threads are cheaper than a whole process because they do not have a full set of resources each. Whereas the process control block for a heavyweight process is large and costly to context switch, the PCBs for threads are much smaller, since each thread has only a stack and some registers to manage. It has no open file lists or resource lists, no accounting structures to update. All of these resources are shared by all threads within the process. Threads can be assigned priorities—a higher priority thread will get put to the front of the queue.

To summarize some of the similarities and differences:

Similarities

- Like processes, threads share CPU and only one thread is active (running) at a time.
- Like processes, threads within a process execute sequentially.
- Like processes, thread can create children.
- Like process, if one thread is blocked, another thread can run.

Differences

- Unlike processes, threads are not independent of one another.
- Unlike processes, all threads can access every address in the task.
- Processes might or might not assist one another because processes may originate from different users, threads are designed to assist one another.

4.3 WHY THREADS?

Following are some reasons why threads are used in designing operating systems.

1. A process with multiple threads makes a great server for example printer server.
2. Because threads can share common data, they do not need to use interprocess communication.
3. Because of the very nature, threads can take advantage of multiprocessors.

Threads are cheap in the sense that:

1. They only need a stack and storage for registers therefore, threads are cheap to create.
2. Threads use very little resources of an operating system in which they are working. That is, threads do not need new address space, global data, program code or operating system resources.
3. Context switching are fast when working with threads. The reason is that we only have to save and/or restore PC, SP and registers.

But this cheapness comes with the biggest drawback of null protection between threads.

Using threads it is possible to organize the execution of a program in such a way that something is always being done, whenever the scheduler gives the heavyweight process CPU time, because even if the scheduler does not know what the program does the programmer knows it.

Advantages of Threads

- Threads allow a programmer to switch between lightweight processes when it is best for the program.

- A process, which uses threads, does not get more CPU time than an ordinary process—but the CPU time it gets is used to do work on the threads. It is possible to write a more efficient program by making use of threads.
- Inside a heavyweight process, threads are scheduled on a FCFS basis, unless the program decides to force certain threads to wait for other threads. If there is only one CPU, then only one thread can be running at a time.
- Threads context switch without any need to involve the kernel—a user level library performs the switching, so time is saved because the kernel doesn't need to know about the threads.

4.4 LEVELS OF THREADS

In modern operating systems, there are two levels at which threads operate: system or kernel threads and user level threads. If the kernel itself is multithreaded, the scheduler assigns CPU time on a thread basis rather than on a process basis. A kernel level thread behaves like a virtual CPU, or a power point to which user-processes can connect in order to get computing power. The kernel has, as many system level threads as it has CPUs and each of these must be shared between all of the user-threads on the system. In other words, the maximum number of user level threads, which can be active at any one time, is equal to the number of system level threads, which in turn is equal to the number of CPUs on the system.

Since threads work 'inside' a single task, the normal process scheduler cannot normally tell which thread to run and which not to run, that is up to the program. When the kernel schedules a process for execution, it must then find out from that process which is the next thread it must execute. If the program is lucky enough to have more than one processor available, then several threads can be scheduled at the same time.

Some important implementations of threads are:

- The Mach System/OSF1 (user and system level)
- Solaris 1 (user level)
- Solaris 2 (user and system level)
- OS/2 (system level only)

- NT threads (user and system level)
- IRIX threads
- POSIX standardized user threads interface

User-Level Threads

User-level threads implement in user-level libraries, rather than via systems calls, so thread switching does not need to call operating system and to cause interrupt to the kernel. In fact, the kernel knows nothing about user-level threads and manages them as if they were single-threaded processes.

Advantages

The most obvious advantage of this technique is that a user-level threads package can be implemented on an Operating System that does not support threads. Some other advantages are:

- User-level thread does not require modification to operating systems.
- ***Simple representation:*** Each thread is represented simply by a PC, registers, stack and a small control block, all stored in the user process address space.
- ***Simple management:*** This simply means that creating a thread, switching between threads and synchronization between threads can all be done without intervention of the kernel.
- ***Fast and efficient:*** Thread switching is not much more expensive than a procedure call.

Disadvantages

- There is a lack of coordination between threads and operating system kernel. Therefore, process as a whole gets one time slice irrespective of whether process has one thread or 1000 threads within. It is up to each thread to relinquish control to other threads.
- User-level threads require non-blocking systems call, i.e. a multithreaded kernel. Otherwise, entire process will be blocked in the kernel, even if there are runnable threads left in the processes. For example, if one thread causes a page fault, the process blocks.

Kernel-Level Threads

In this method, the kernel knows about and manages the threads. No runtime system is needed in this case. Instead of thread table in each process, the kernel has a thread table that keeps track of all threads in the system. In addition, the kernel also maintains the traditional process table to keep track of processes. Operating Systems kernel provides system call to create and manage threads. The implementation of general structure of kernel-level thread is:

Advantages

- Because kernel has full knowledge of all threads, scheduler may decide to give more time to a process having large number of threads than process having small number of threads.
- Kernel-level threads are especially good for applications that frequently block.

Disadvantages

- The kernel-level threads are slow and inefficient. For instance, thread operations are hundreds of times slower than that of user-level threads.
- Since kernel must manage and schedule threads as well as processes. It requires a full thread control block (TCB) for each thread to maintain information about threads. As a result there is significant overhead and increased in kernel complexity.

4.5 THREADS AND MULTIPROCESSES

Advantages of threads over multiprocessors:

- *Context switching:* Threads are very inexpensive to create and destroy, and they are inexpensive to represent. For example, they require space to store, the PC, the SP, and the general-purpose registers, but they do not require space to share memory information, information about open files of I/O devices in use, etc. With so little context, it is much faster to switch between threads. In other words, it is relatively easier for a context switch using threads.

- *Sharing:* Threads allow the sharing of a lot resources that cannot be shared in process, for example, sharing code section, data section, Operating System resources like open file, etc.

Disadvantages of Threads over Multiprocesses

- *Blocking:* The major disadvantage is that if the kernel is single-threaded, a system call of one thread will block the whole process and CPU may be idle during the blocking period.
- *Security:* Since there is an extensive sharing among threads there is a potential problem of security. It is quite possible that one thread overwrites the stack of another thread (or damaged shared data) although it is very unlikely since threads are meant to cooperate on a single task.

Threads are of obvious importance in connection with parallel processing. There are two approaches to scheduling on a multiprocessor machine:

- *Asymmetric:* One CPU does the work of the system, the other CPUs service user requests.
- *Symmetric:* All processors can be used by the system and users alike. No CPU is special.

The asymmetric variant is potentially more wasteful, since it is rare that the system requires a whole CPU just to itself. This approach is more common on very large machines with many processors, where the job the system has to do is quite difficult and warrants a CPU to itself.

4.6 MULTITHREADING MODELS

There are multithreading models for the systems, which support both user and kernel threads. Some of the common multithreading models are:

(*i*) 1 : 1 model
(*ii*) *n* : 1 model
(*iii*) *n* : *n* model

1 : 1 Model

As name implies, one user thread is associated with one kernel thread. This model allows many thread to run in parallel on

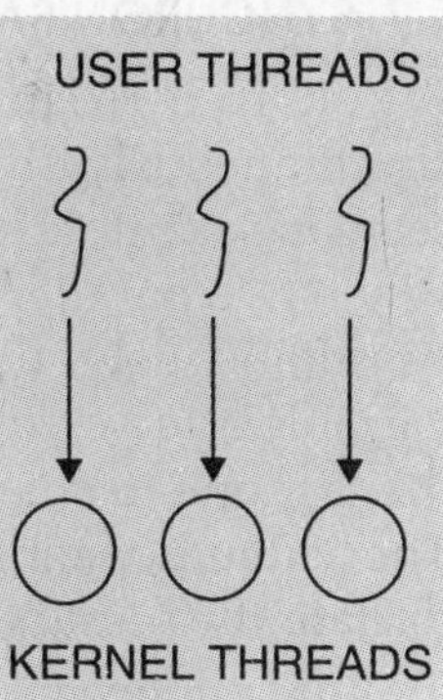

multiprocessors. Also if the system makes blocking calls on one thread the others exists to run. Creating a kernel thread is a burden to the performance of the applications. The drawback with this model is that, creation of user thread must be immediately accompanied by the creation of kernel thread leading to performance slow down. This model is used in Windows NT, Windows 2000 and OS/2.

n : 1 Model

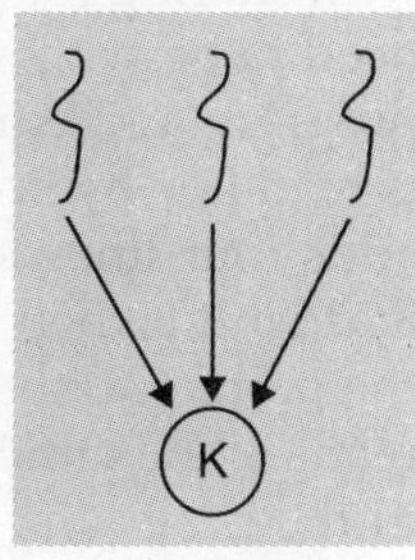

Here many user threads are associated with only one kernel thread. It has good efficiency since the management is done in user space. But unlike 1 : 1 model, only one thread can access the kernel at a time and hence multiple threads cannot run in parallel on multi-processors. Also if a system block is called the entire process will be blocked. OS which do not support kernel thread use this model. **Green threads** are threads libraries of *n* : 1 model used in Solaris 2.

n : *n* Model

This model multiplexes the user level threads to equal no. of kernel threads. Number of kernel threads depends on the machine or application. Drawback with 1 : 1 model is that even if concurrency exists, here too many thread creation for an application cannot be created by the developer and with *n* : 1 even if desired no. of threads are created by the developer, concurrency does not exists. Since kernel can schedule only one thread at a time, overcoming these drawbacks, *n* : *n* model allows developer to create as many desired number of threads (concurrency not affected).

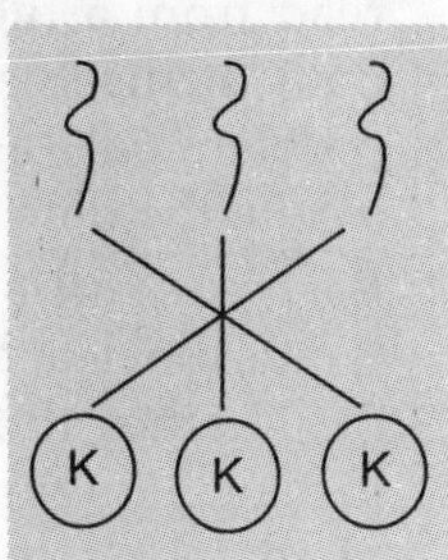

4.7 SYNCHRONISATION OF PROCESS AND THREADS

When two or more processes work on the same data simultaneously strange things can happen. We have already seen one example in the threaded file reader in previous section. When two parallel threads attempt to update the same variable simultaneously, the result is unpredictable. The value of the variable afterwards depends on which of the two threads was the last one to change the value. This is called a *race condition*. The value depends on which of the threads wins the race to update the variable.

What we need in a multitasking system is a way of making such situations predictable. This is called *serialization*. Problems with sharing for processes are that it is not only threads which need to be synchronized. Suppose one user is running a script program and editing the program simultaneously. The script is read line by line. During the execution of the script, the user adds four lines to the beginning of the file and saves the file. Suddenly, when the next line of the executing script gets read, the pointer to the next line points to the wrong location and it reads in the same line it already read four lines ago! Everything in the program is suddenly shifted by four lines, without the process executing the script knowing about it.

This example (which can actually happen in the UNIX shell) may or may not turn out to be serious—clearly, in general, it can be quite catastrophic. It is a problem of *synchronization* on the part of the user and the file system.

We must consider programs which share data.

1. *When do we need to prevent programs from accessing data simultaneously*? If there are 100 processes which we want to read from a file, this will cause no problems because the data themselves are not changed by a read operation. A problem only arises if more than one of the parties want to *modify* the data.
2. *Is it even sensible for two programs to modify data simultaneously*? It must be clear about whether such collisions can be avoided, or whether they are a necessary part of a program. For instance, if two independent processes want to add entries to a database, this is a reasonable thing to do. If two unrelated

processes want to write a log of their activities to the same file, it is probably not sensible: A better solution would be to use two separate files.

3. *How should we handle a collision between processes?* There is no universal answer to this question—in some cases it might be logically incorrect for two processes to change data at the same time if two processes try to change one numerical value then one of them has to win. On the other hand, if two processes try to add something to a list, that makes sense, but we have to be sure that they do not write their data on top of each other. The writing must happen serially, not in parallel.

Serialization

The key idea in process synchronization is *serialization*. This means that we have to go to some pains to *undo* the work we have put into making an operating system perform several tasks in parallel. As we mentioned, in the case of print queues, parallelism is not always appropriate.

Synchronization is a large and difficult topic, so we shall only undertake to describe the problem and some of the principles involved here.

There are essentially two strategies to serializing processes in a multitasking environment.

- The scheduler can be disabled for a short period of time, to prevent control being given to another process during a critical action like modifying shared data. This method is very inefficient on multiprocessor machines, since all other processors have to be halted every time one wishes to execute a critical section.

- A protocol can be introduced which all programs sharing data must obey. The protocol ensures that processes have to queue up to gain access to shared data. Processes which ignore the protocol ignore it at their own peril (and the peril of the remainder of the system!). This method works on multiprocessor machines also, though it is more difficult to visualize.

The responsibility of serializing important operations falls on programmers. The OS cannot impose any restrictions on silly behaviour—it can only provide tools and mechanisms to assist the solution of the problem.

Mutexes: Mutual Exclusion

Another way of talking about serialization is to use the concept of mutual exclusion. We are interested in allowing only one process or thread access to shared data at any given time. To serialize access to these shared data, we have to exclude all processes except for one. Suppose two processes A and B are trying to access shared data, then: if A is modifying the data, B must be excluded from doing so; if B is modifying the data, A must be excluded from doing so. This is called *mutual exclusion*.

Mutual exclusion can be achieved by a system of *locks*. A mutual exclusion lock is colloquially called a *mutex*. You can see an example of mutex locking in the multithreaded file reader in the previous section. The idea is for each thread or process to try to obtain locked-access to shared data:

```
get_Mutex(m);
//Update shared data
release_Mutex (m);
```

The mutex variable is shared by all parties, e.g. a global variable. This protocol is meant to ensure that only one process at a time can get past the function Get_Mutex. All other processes or threads are made to wait at the function Get_Mutex until that one process calls Release_Mutex to release the lock. A method for implementing this is discussed below. Mutexes are a central part of multithreaded programming.

User Synchronization: File Locks

A simple example of a protocol solution, to the locking problem at the user level, is the so-called *file-lock* in UNIX. When write-access is required to a file, a lock is obtained by creating a *lock-file* with a special name. If another user or process has already obtained a lock, then the file is already in use, and we are denied permission to edit the file. If the file is free, a 'lock' is placed on the file by creating the file lock. This indicates that the file now belongs to the new user. When the user has finished, the file lock is deleted, allowing others to use the file.

In most cases a lock is simply a text file. If we wanted to edit a file blurb, the lock might be called blurb lock and contain the user identifier of the user currently editing the file. If other users then try to access the file, they find that the lock file exists and are denied access. When the user is finished with the file, the lock is removed.

The same method of locks can also be used to prevent two instances of a program from starting up simultaneously. This is often used in mail programs such as the ELM mailer in UNIX, since it would be unwise to try to read and delete incoming mail with two instances of the mail program at the same time.

We can implement a lock very easily. Here is an example from UNIX in which the lock file contains the *process identifier*. This is useful because if something goes wrong and the editor crashes, the lock will not be removed. It is then possible to see that the process the lock referred to no longer exists and the lock can be safely removed.

```
//*************************************************************
//
// Example of a program which uses a file lock to ensure.
// That no one starts more than one copy of it.
//
//*************************************************************
#include <iostream.h>
#include <fstream.h>
//*************************************************************
// Include file
//*************************************************************
extern 'C' int getpid ( );
extern 'C' void unlink (char *);
int locked ( );
void remove lock( );
const int true = 1;
const int false = 0;
const int exitstatus = 1;
```

```
//********************************************************************
// Main program
//********************************************************************
main ( )
{
if [locked ( )]
{
cout << 'This program is already running!\n';
return exitstatus;
}
// Program here
remove lock ( );
}
//********************************************************************
// Toolkit: locks
//********************************************************************
locked ( )
{ if stream lock file;
int pid;
lock file.open ('/tmp/lockfile', ios::in);
if (lock file)
{
return true;
}
lock file.open ('/tmp/lockfile', ios::out);
if (! lock file)
{
cerr << 'Cannot secure a lock!\n';
return true;
}
pid = getpid ( );
lock file.out << pid;
lock file.close ( );
return false;
}
//********************************************************************
```

```
void remove lock ( )
{
unlink ('/tmp/lockfile');
}
```

Exclusive and Non-exclusive Locks

To control both read and write access to files, we can use a system of exclusive and non-exclusive locks.

If a user wishes to read a file, a non-exclusive lock is used. Other users can also get non-exclusive locks to read the file simultaneously, but when a non-exclusive lock is placed on a file, no user may write to it.

To write to a file, we must get an exclusive lock. When an exclusive lock is obtained, no other users can read or write to the file.

Critical Sections: The Mutex Solution

A critical section is a part of a program in which it is necessary to have *exclusive access* to shared data. Only one process or thread may be in a critical section at any one time.

In the past it was possible to implement this by generalizing the idea of interrupt masks. By switching off interrupts (or more appropriately, by switching off the scheduler) a process can guarantee itself uninterrupted access to shared data. This method has drawbacks: (*i*) masking interrupts can be dangerous—there is always the possibility that important interrupts will be missed, (*ii*) it is not general enough in a multiprocessor environment, since interrupts will continue to be serviced by other processors—so all processors would have to be switched off; (*iii*) it is too harsh. We only need to prevent two programs from being in their critical sections simultaneously if they share the same data. Programs A and B might share different data to programs C and *D*, so why should they wait for C and *D*?

The modern way of implementing a critical section is to use mutexes as we have described above. In 1981 G.L. Peterson discovered a simple algorithm for achieving mutual exclusion between two processes with PID equal to 0 or 1. The code goes like this:

```
int turn;
int interested (2);
void Get_Mutex (int pid)
{ int other;
other = 1 – pid;
interested (pid) = true;
turn = pid;
while [turn = = pid && interested (other)] / /loop until no one
{ / / else is interested
}
}
void Release_Mutex (int pid)
{
interested (pid) = false;
}
```

Where more processes are involved, some modifications are necessary to this algorithm. The key to serialization here is that, if a second process tries to obtain the mutex, when another already has it, it will get caught in a loop, which does not terminate until the other process has released the mutex. This solution is said to involve *busy waiting*, i.e. the program actively executes an empty loop, wasting CPU cycles, rather than moving the process out of the scheduling queue. This is also called a *spin lock*, since the system 'spins' on the loop while waiting.

Flags and Semaphores

Flags are similar in concept to locks. The idea is that two cooperating processes can synchronize their execution by sending very simple messages to each other. A typical behaviour is that one process decides to stop and *wait* until another process *signals* that it has arrived at a certain place.

For example, suppose we want to ensure that procedure 1 ( ) in process 1 gets executed before procedure 2 ( ) in process 2.

```
// Process 1                    // Process 2
Procedure 1 ( );                Wait (my signal);
Signal (my signal);             Procedure 2 ( );
...                             ...
```

These operations are a special case of *interprocess communication*. A semaphore is a flag which can have a more general value than just true or false. A semaphore is an integer counting variable and is used to solve problems where there is competition between processes. The idea is that one part of a program tends to increment the semaphore while another part tends to decrement the semaphore. The value of the flag variable dictates whether a program will wait or continue, or whether something special will occur. There are many uses for semaphores and we shall not go into them here. A simple example is reading and writing via buffers, where we count how many items are in the buffer. When the buffer becomes full, the process which is filling it must be made to wait until space in the buffer is made available.

Monitors

Some languages (like Modula) have special language class-environments for dealing with mutual exclusion. Such an environment is called a monitor.

- A monitor is a language-device which removes some of the pain from synchronization. Only one process can be 'inside' a monitor at a time—users don't need to code this themselves, they only have to create a monitor.
- A procedure or function defined under the umbrella of a monitor can only access those shared memory locations declared within that monitor and vice-versa.
- Wait and signal operations can be defined to wait for specific condition variables. A process can thus wait until another process sends a signal or semaphore which changes the condition variable.

4.8 MORE THREAD ISSUES

(a) Application that Benefits from Threads

A proxy server satisfying the requests for a number of computers on a LAN would be benefited by a multi-threaded process. In general, any program that has to do more than one task at a time could benefit from multitasking. For example, a program that reads input, process it, and outputs could have three threads, one for each task.

(b) Application that cannot Benefit from Threads

Any sequential process that cannot be divided into parallel task will not benefit from thread, as they would block until the previous one completes. For example, a program that displays the time of the day would not benefit from multiple threads.

(c) Resources Used in Thread Creation and Process Creation

When a new thread is created it shares its code section, data section and operating system resources like open files with other threads. But it is allocated with its own stack, register set and a program counter. The creation of a new process differs from that of a thread mainly in the fact that all the shared resources of a thread are needed explicitly for each process. Though two processes may be running at the same piece of code they need to have their own copy of the code in the main memory to be able to run. Two processes also do not share other resources with each other. This makes the creation of a new process very costly compared to that of a new thread.

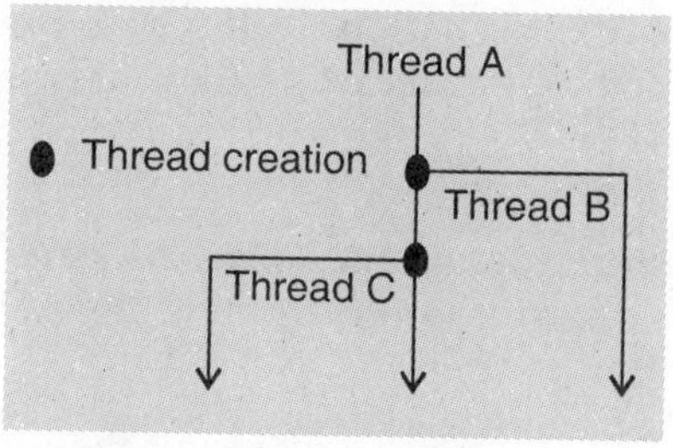

(d) Context Switch

To give each process on a multiprogrammed machine a fair share of the CPU, a hardware clock generates interrupts periodically. This allows the operating system to schedule all processes in main memory (using scheduling algorithm) to run on the CPU at equal intervals. Each time a clock interrupt occurs, the interrupt handler checks how much time the current running process has used. If it has used up its entire time slice, then the CPU scheduling algorithm (in kernel) picks a different process to run. Each switch of the CPU from one process to another is called a context switch.

Major Steps of Context Switching

- The values of the CPU registers are saved in the process table of the process that was running just before the clock interrupt occurred.
- The registers are loaded from the process picked by the CPU scheduler to run next.

In a multiprogrammed Uniprocessor computing system, context switches occur frequently enough that all processes appear to be running concurrently. If a process has more than one threads, the Operating System can use the context switching technique to schedule the threads so they appear to execute in parallel. This is the case if threads are implemented at the kernel level. Threads can also be implemented entirely at the user level in run-time libraries. Since in this case no thread scheduling is provided by the Operating System, it is the responsibility of the programmer to yield the CPU frequently enough in each thread so all threads in the process can make progress.

Action of Kernel to Context Switch among Processes

Context switches among processes are expensive. Before a process can be switched its process control block (PCB) must be saved by the operating system. The PCB consists of the following information:

- The process state.
- The program counter, PC.
- The values of the different registers.
- The CPU scheduling information for the process.
- Memory management information regarding the process.
- Possible accounting information for this process.
- I/O status information of the process.

When the PCB of the currently executing process is saved the operating system loads the PCB of the next process that has to be run on CPU. This is a heavy task and it takes a lot of time.

Action of Kernel to Context Switch among Threads

The threads share a lot of resources with other peer threads belonging to the same process. So a context switch among threads for the same process is easy. It involves switch of register set, the program counter and the stack. It is relatively easy for the kernel to accomplish this task.

Thread Cancellation

Terminating a thread before completion is said to be thread cancellation. Thread to be cancelled is said to be target thread. Cancellation occurs in two ways.

1. ***Asynchronous cancellation:*** One thread terminating immediately the target thread.
2. ***Deferred cancellation:*** Target thread should check itself if it should terminate, if a situation raises, it should terminate. This cancellation is analysed in safer side. The point at which cancellation may be done is said to be cancellation points.

(e) Thread Pools

The working of a thread pool is to create many threads for a process and store within itself. The created thread waits in the pool and is awaked by the server when it receives request. After its job gets to end, it resides back at the pool waiting for other request to serve. If at instance, the pool contains no available threads, the server waits until one becomes free.

Some benefits from thread pools are:

- It is usually faster to service a request with an existing thread than waiting to create a thread.
- Thread pool limits the number of threads that exist at any point. This importance is established for systems which do not support larger number of concurrent threads.

Number of threads in pool exclusively depends on:

- Number of CPUs in the system.
- Amount of physical memory.
- Expected number of client requests to be executed concurrently.

4.9 EXAMPLES OF THREADS

Example 1: POSIX Pthreads

The POSIX standardization organization has developed a standard set of function calls for use of user-level threads. This library is called the *pthread* interface.

Let's look at an example program which counts the number of lines in a list of files. This program will serve as an example for the remainder of this chapter. We shall first present the program without threads, and then rewrite it, starting a new thread for each file. The threaded version of the program has the possibility of reading several of the files in parallel and is in principle more efficient, whereas the non-threaded version must read the files sequentially.

The non-threaded version of the program looks like this:

```
// Count the number of lines in a number of files, non-
threaded version.//
#include <iostream.h>
#include <fstream.h>
const int buf size = 100;
void parse file (char *);
int LINE COUNT = 0;
/*************************************************************/
main ( )
{
cout << 'Single threaded parent...\n';
parse file('proc 1');
parse file('proc 2');
parse file('proc 3');
parse file('proc 4');
cout << 'Number of lines = % d\n', LINE COUNT;
}
/*************************************************************/
void parse file (char * file name)
{ fstream file;
char buffer (buf size);
```

```
cout << 'Trying to open' << filename << end l;
file.open (file name, ios::in);
if (! file)
{
cerr << 'Couldn't open file\n';
return;
}
while [!file.eof ( )]
{
file.getline (buffer, buf size);
cout << file name << ':' <<buffer << end l;
LINE COUNT ++;
}
file.close ( );
}
```

This program calls the function parse file ( ) several times to open and count the number of lines in a series of files. The number of lines is held in a global variable called LINE COUNT. A global variable is, by definition, shared data. This will cause a problem when we try to parallelize the program using threads. Here is the threaded version:

```
// This program uses POSIX threads (pthreads)
//
#include <iostream.h>
#include <fstream.h>
#include <pthread.h>
#include <sched.h>
const int bufsize = 100;
const int maxfiles = 4;
void * parse file (char *);//Must be void*, defined in pthread.h !
int LINECOUNT = 0;
pthread_mutex_tMUTEX=PTHREAD_MUTEX_INITIALIZER;
main ( )
```

```
{ pthread_t tid (maxfiles);;
int i, ret;
// Create a thread for each file
ret = pthread_create {& [tid (0)], NULL, Parse file,'proc 1'};
ret = pthread_create {& [tid (1)], NULL, Parse file,'proc 2'};
ret = pthread_create {& [tid (2)], NULL, Parse file,'proc 3'};
ret = pthread_create {& [tid (3)], NULL, Parse file,'proc 4'};
cout << 'Parent thread waiting...\n';
// If we don't wait for the threads, they will be killed before
 they can start...
for (i = 0; i < maxfiles; i ++)
{
ret = pthread_join [tid (i), (void **) NULL];
}
cout << 'Parent thread continuing\n';
cout << 'Number of lines ='<< LINECOUNT << end l;
}
void *parse file (char *file name)
{ fstream file;
char buffer (buf size);
int ret;
cout << 'Trying to open' << file name << end l;
file.open (file name, ios::in);
if (! file)
{
cerr << 'Couldn't open file\n';
return NULL;
}
while [!file.eof ( )]
{
file.getline (buffer, buf size);
cout << file name << ':' <<buffer << end l;
//Critical section
ret = pthread_mutex_lock (& MUTEX);
```

```
LINECOUNT ++;
ret = pthread_mutex_unlock (& MUTEX);
//Try uncommenting this ....
//Yield the process, to allow next thread to be run
//sched_yield ( );
}
file.close ( );
}
```

In this version of the program, a separate thread is spawned for each file. First, we call the function pthread_create ( ) for each file we encounter. A new thread is spawned with a pointer to the function the thread should execute (in this case the same function for all threads), called parse file ( ), which reads lines from the respective files and increments the global variable LINE COUNT. Several things are important here.

The main program is itself a thread. It is essential that we tell the main program to wait for the additional threads to *join* the main program before exiting, otherwise the main program will exit and kill all of the child threads immediately. Thread join-semantics are like wait-semantics for normal processes.

Each of the threads updates the same global variable. Suppose now that two threads are running on different CPUs. It is possible that both threads would try to alter the value of the variable LINE COUNT simultaneously. This is called a *race condition* and can lead to unpredictable results. For this reason we use a *mutex* to lock the variable while it is being updated. We shall discuss this more in the next section.

A final point to note is the commented outlines in the parse file ( ) function. The call sched_yield( ) tells a running thread to give itself up to the scheduler, so that the next thread to be scheduled can run instead. This function can be used to switch between several threads. By calling this function after each line is read from the files, we can spread the the CPU time evenly between each thread. Actually, it is difficult to predict precisely which threads will be scheduled and when, because the threads in our program here are only a small number, compared to the total number of threads waiting to be scheduled by the system. The interaction with disk I/O can also have a complicated effect on the scheduling. On a single CPU system, threads are usually scheduled FCFS in a queue. If we yield after every instruction, it has the effect of simulating round-robin scheduling.

Example 2: LWPs in Solaris 1

Early solaris systems had user-level threads only, which were called lightweight processes. Since the kernel was single-threaded, only one user-level thread could run at any given time.

To create a threaded process in solaris 1, one simply has to execute a LWP system call. The 'lightweight processes library' then converts the normal process into a process descriptor plus a thread. Here is the simplest example

```
/* Creating a lightweight process in SunOS 4.1.3   */
#include <lwp/lwp.h>
#include <lwp/stackdep.h>
#define MINSTACKSZ 1024
#define STACKSIZE 1000 + MINSTACKSZ
#define MAXPRIORITY 10
stkalign_t stack (STACKSIZE);
/* Zone 0   */
main ( )
{ thread_t tid;
int task( );
pod_setmaxpri (MAXPRIORITY);
/* This becomes a lwp here */
lwp_create [& tid, task, MAXPRIORITY, 0, STKTOP
  (stack), 0];
print f ('Done!–Now other threads can run...\n');
}
/*Zone 1                              */
task ( )
{
print f ('Task: next thread after main ( ) !\n');
}
```

Here is an example program containing several threads which wait for each other.

```
/* Creating a lightweight process in sunos 4.1.3 (Solaris 1)
*/
/* Yielding to other processes */
#include <lwp/lwp.h>
#include <lwp/stackdep.h>
#define MINSTACKSZ 1024
#define STACKCACHE 1000
#define STACKSIZE STACKCACHE + MINSTACKSZ
#define MAXPRIORITY 10
#define MINPRIORITY 1
/**************************************************************/
stkalign_t stack (STACKSIZE);
/* Zone 0 */
main ( )
{ thread_t tid_main;
thread_t tid_prog 1;
thread_t tid_prog 2;
int prog 1 ( ), prog 2 ( );
lwp_self(& tid_main);   /* Get main's tid */
lwp_setstkcache(STACKCACHE,3);
/* Make a cache for each prog */
lwp_create [& tid_prog 1, prog 1, MINPRIORITY,
 0, lwp_newstk ( ), 0];
lwp_create [& tid_prog 2, prog 2, MINPRIORITY,
 0, lwp_newstk ( ), 0];
print f ('One');
lwp_yield (THREADNULL);
print f ('Four');
lwp_yield (tid_prog 2);
print f ('Six');
exit (0);
}
/* Zone 1, 2.. */
```

```
prog 1 ( )
{
print f ('Two');
if [lwp_yield (THREADNULL) < 0]
{
lwp_perror ('Bad yield');
return;
}
print f ('Seven\n');
}
/*************************************************************** /
prog 2 ( )
{
print f ('Three');
lwp_yield (THREADNULL);
print f ('Five');
}
```

Executable code for implementation of Dekker's algorithm (Mutual Exclusion):

```
#include<stdio.h>
#include<math.h>
#include<unistd.h>
#include<pthread.h>
int turn=0;
int need(2)=(0,0);
int shard=0;
void dwait(int me)
{
int other;
other=1-me;
need(me)=1;
while[need(other)]
{
if(turn==otner)
{
```

```
need(me)=0;
while(turn==other)
}
need(me)=1;
{
}
void dsignal(intme)
{
need(me)=1;
turn=1-me;
}
void*p1()
{
while(1)
{
dwait[need(0)];
shared++;
printf('p1 is in its crictial section\n');
dsignal[need(0)];
printf('%d',shared);
sleep(2);
}
{
void*p2()
{
while(1)
{
dwait[need(1)];
shared–;
printf(p2is its critical section\n');
printf(%d',shared);
dsignal[need(1)];
sleep(2);
```

```
}
}
int main()
{
pthread_t tid_process1,tid_process 2;
pthread_setconcurrency (2);
pthread_create(&tid_process1,
NUULL,p1,NULL);
pthread_create(&tid_process2,
NUULL,p2,NULL);
pthread_join(tid_process1,NULL);
pthread_join(tid_process2,NULL);
exit(0);
}
```

5

Deadlock

5.1 INTRODUCTION

Operating system is also defined as a resource allocator. There are many resources that can be allocated to only one process at a time. Some of the operating systems with this feature are mutexes, semaphores or file locks.

Sometimes a process has to reserve more than one resources. For example, a process which copies files from one tape to another generally requires two tape drives. A process which deals with databases may need to lock multiple records in a database.

In general, resources allocated to a process are not preemptable; this means that once a resource has been allocated to a process, there is no simple mechanism by which the system can take the resource back from the process unless the process voluntarily gives it up or the system administrator kills the process. This can lead to a situation called *deadlock*. A set of processes or threads is deadlocked when each process or thread is waiting for a resource to be freed which is controlled by another process. Here is an example of a situation where deadlock can occur.

```
Mutex M1, M2;
/* Thread 1 */
while (1) {
non-critical section ( )
Mutex_lock (& M1);
Mutex_lock (& M2);
critical section ( );
Mutex_unlock (& M2);
Mutex_unlock(& M1);
}
/* Thread 2 */
while (1) {
non-critical section ( )
Mutex_lock (& M2);
Mutex_lock (& M1);
critical section ( );
Mutex_unlock (& M1);
Mutex_unlock (& M2);
}
```

Suppose thread 1 is running and locks $M1$, but before it can lock $M2$, it is interrupted. Thread 2 starts running; it locks $M2$, when it tries to obtain and lock $M1$, it is blocked because $M1$ is already locked (by thread 1). Eventually thread 1 starts running again, and it tries to obtain and lock $M2$, but it is blocked because $M2$ is already locked by thread 2. Both threads are blocked; each is waiting for an event which will never occur.

Traffic gridlock is an everyday example of a deadlock situation.

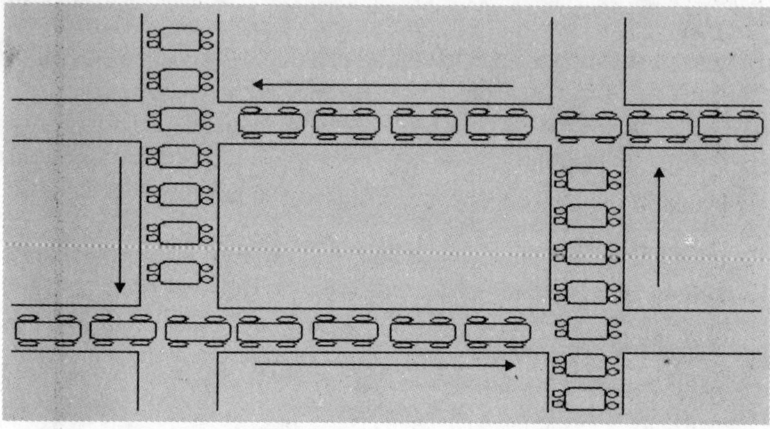

The dining philosophers problem discussed in an earlier section is a classic example of deadlock. Each philosopher picks up his or her left fork and waits for the right fork to become available, but it never does.

Deadlock can be modeled with a directed graph. In a deadlock graph, vertices represent either processes (circles) or resources (squares). A process which has acquired a resource is show (shown) with an arrow (edge) from the resource to the process. A process which has requested a resource which has not yet been assigned to it, is modeled with an arrow from the process to the resource. If these create a cycle, there is deadlock.

The deadlock situation in the above code can be modeled like this.

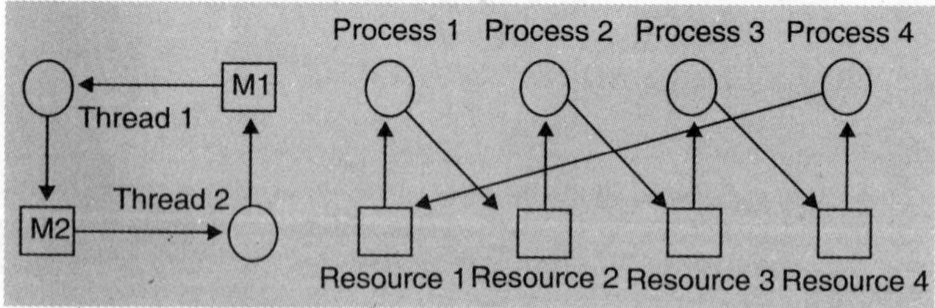

This graph shows an extremely simple deadlock situation, but it is also possible for a more complex situation to create deadlock. Here is an example of deadlock with four processes and four resources. There are a number of ways that deadlock can occur in an operating situation. We have seen some examples, here are two more.

- Two processes need to lock two files, the first process locks one file the second process locks the other, and each waits for the other to free up the locked file.
- Two processes want to write a file to a print spool area at the same time and both start writing. However, the print spool area is of fixed size, and it fills up before either process finishes writing its file, so both wait for more space to become available.

5.2 CAUSES OF DEADLOCK

Deadlock occurs when a number of processes are waiting for an event which can only be caused by another of the waiting processes.

These are the essential requirements for a deadlock:

1. ***Circular waiting:*** There must be a set of processes $P_{1..}$ P_n where P_1 is waiting for a resource or signal from P_2, P_2 is waiting for P_3... and P_n is waiting for P_1.
2. ***Mutual exclusion:*** It is not possible to share the resources or signals which are being waited for. If the resource can be shared, there is no reason to wait.
3. ***No preemption:*** The processes cannot be forced to give up the resources they are holding.
4. ***Hold and wait:*** Process request resources incrementaly and hold on to what they have got.

Difference from avoidance is that here, the system itself is build in such a way that there are no deadlocks. Deadlock prevention requires a system overhead.

5.3 STRATEGIES OF HANDLING DEADLOCKS

1. ***Prevention:*** We can try to design a protocol which ensures that deadlock never occurs.
2. ***Detection and recovery:*** We can allow the system to enter a deadlock state and then recover.
3. ***Ostrich method:*** We can pretend that deadlocks will never occur and live happily in our ignorance. This is the method

used by most operating systems. User programs are expected to behave properly. The system does not interfere. This is understandable: it is very hard to make general rules for every situation which might arise.

Make sure at least one of the 4 deadlock conditions is never satisfied.

This may however be even more conservative than deadlock avoidance strategy.

Attacking Mutex Condition

- Never grant exclusive access but this may not be possible for several resources.

Attacking Preemption

- Note something you want to do.

Attacking Hold and Wait Condition

- Make a process hold at the most 1 resource at a time.
- Make all the requests at the beginning. All or nothing policy. If you feel, retry, e.g. 2-phase locking.

Attacking Circular Wait

- Order all the resources.
- Make sure that the requests are issued in the correct order so that there are no cycles present in the resource graph. Resources numbered 1 ... *n*. Resources can be requested only in increasing order, i.e. you cannot request a resource whose number is less than any you may be holding.

5.4 DEADLOCK PREVENTION

The simplest possibility for avoidance of deadlock is to introduce an extra layer of software for requesting resources in addition to a certain amount of accounting. Each time a new request is made, the system analyses the allocation of resources before granting or refusing the resource. The same applies for wait conditions.

The problem with this approach is that, if a process is not permitted to wait for another process the system would have to reject or terminate programs which could enter deadlock, returning an error condition. Another method is that, one might demand that all programs declare what resources they will need in advance. Similarly all wait conditions should be declared. The system could then analyse and re-analyse each time a new process arrives the resource allocation and pinpoint possible problems.

The detection of deadlock conditions is also a system overhead. At regular intervals the system is required to examine the state of all processes and determine the interrelations between them. Since this is quite a performance burden, it is not surprising that most systems ignore deadlocks and expect users to write careful programs.

5.5 DEADLOCK AVOIDANCE

To recover from a deadlock, the system must either terminate one of the participants, and go on terminating them until the deadlock is cured, or repossess the resources, which are causing the deadlock from some processes until the deadlock is cured. The latter method is somewhat dangerous since it can lead to incorrect program execution. Processes usually wait for a good reason, and any interruption of that reasoning could lead to incorrect execution. Termination is a safer alternative.

Avoid actions that may lead to a deadlock. Think of it as a state machine moving from 1 state to another as each instruction is executed.

Safe State

Safe state is one where:

- It is not a deadlocked state.
- There is some sequence by which all requests can be satisfied.

To avoid deadlocks, we try to make only those transitions that will take you from one safe state to another. We avoid transitions to unsafe state (a state that is not deadlocked, and is not safe)

e.g.

Total # of instances of resource = 12

(Max, Allocated, Still needs)

$P0$ (10, 5, 5) $P1$ (4, 2, 2) $P2$ (9, 2, 7) Free = 3 – Safe.

The sequence is a reducible sequence—the first state is safe.

What if $P2$ requests 1 more and is allocated 1 more instance?
—results in unsafe state.

So do not allow $P2$'s request to be satisfied.

Banker's Algorithm for Deadlock Avoidance

When a request is made, check to see if after the request is satisfied, there is a (at least one!) sequence of moves that can satisfy all the requests, i.e. the new state is safe. If so, satisfy the request, else make the request wait.

How do you Find if a State is Safe?

n process and m resources

```
Max (n * m)
Allocated (n * m)
Still_needs (n * m)
Available (m)
Temp (m)
Done (n)
While ( ) {
Temp (j) = Available (j) for all j
Find an i such that
(a) Done (i) = False
(b) Still_needs (i, j) < = Temp (j)
If so {
Temp (j) + = Allocated (i, j) for all j
Done (i) = TRUE }
}
Else if done (i) = TRUE for all i then state is safe
Else state is unsafe
}
```

Ignore Deadlock

This can also be referred to as the *Ostrich algorithm*. Just hope that deadlock doesn't happen. In general, this is a reasonable strategy. Deadlock is unlikely to occur very often; a system can run for years without deadlock occurring.

If the operating system has a deadlock prevention or detection system in place, this will have a negative impact on performance (slow the system down) because whenever a process or thread requests a resource, the system will have to check whether granting this request could cause a potential deadlock situation.

If deadlock does occur, it may be necessary to bring the system down, or at least manually kill a number of processes, but even that is not an extreme solution in most situations.

Executable code for Banker's algorithm:

```
#include<stdio.h>
#include<conio.h>
#define true 1
#define false 0
int np=5,nr=3;
intavail()=(0,0,0);
int max(5)(3)=[(0,1.0),(4,0,2),(3,0,3),
(3,1,1),(0,0,4)];
int need(10)(5);
intallot(5)(3)=[(0,1,0),(2,0,0),(3,0,3),
(2,1,1),(0,0,2)];
void main()
{
int i,j,res,req(10),finish(10);
int process(10),p=0;
char c='A';
clrscr();
printf("\t\tBankers algorithm\n");
printf("\t\t........\n\n");
printf("process Allocation\t Max\n");
printf("............\n\t");
for(i=0;<nr;i++)
printf("%c ",c++);
c='A';
```

```
for(i=0;i<nr;i++)
printf(%c ",c++);
printf('________\n');
for(i=0<np;i++)
{
printf('p%d\t',i);
for(j=0;k<nr;j++)
printf['%d',allot(i)(j)];
for(j=0;j<nr;j++)
printf[' %d',max(i)(j)];
printf('\n');
}
printf('\n\t Availabln');
printf('\t.......\n');
for(i=0i<dr;i++)
printf['\t%d',avail(i)];
printf('\n\n');
for(i=0 i<np;i++)
{
for(j=0;j<nr;j++)
{
if[max(i)(j)==0]
need(i)(j)=0;
else
need(i)(j)=max(i)(j)-allot(i)(j);
}
finish(i)=false;
}
find:
for(i=0;i<np;i++)
{
if[!finish(i)]
{
printf('pricess=p%d',i);
printf('\trequest available\n\t');
```

```
for(j=0;j<nr;j++)
{
req(j)=need(i)(j);
printf[‘%d’,req(j);
}
printf(‘\t’);
for(j=0;j<nr;j++)
{
printf(‘%d’,avail[j];
}
printf(‘\n’);
res=safety(req,i);
if(res==true)
{
finish(i)=true;
printf(‘%d has finished’,i);
process(p==)=i;
}
printf(‘%d hasnot finshed’,i);
getch();
}
}
if(p<np)
goto find;
for(i=0;i<np;i++)
{
if[finish(i)==false]
{
printf(‘not in safe state’);
return;
}
}
printf(‘safe sequence is <’);
for(i=0;i<np;i++)
```

```
Print f(‘p%d’,process(i);
print f(‘>\n\n’);
}
int k,j,reqvalid=true;
for(j=0;j<nr;j++)
if[req(j)<avail(j)]
{
reqvalid=false;
break;
}
if(reqvalid==true)
{
for(j=0;j<nr;j++
{
avail(j)+=allot(i)(j)+req(j);
need(i)(j)=0;
allot(i)(j)=0;
}
return true;
}
else
return false;
}
```

5.6 DEADLOCK DETECTION AND RECOVERY

As we saw above, if there is only one instance of each resource, it is possible to detect deadlock by constructing a resource allocation/request graph and checking for cycles. Graph theorists have developed a number of algorithms to detect cycles in a graph. It uses only one data structure *L* a list of nodes.

A Cycle Detection Algorithm

For each node N in the graph

1. Initialize *L* to the empty list and designate all edges as unmarked.

2. Add the current node to *L* and check to see if it appears twice. If it does, there is a cycle in the graph.
3. From the given node, check to see if there are any unmarked outgoing edges. If yes, go to the next step, if no, skip the next step.
4. Pick an unmarked edge, mark it, then follow it to the new current node and go to step 3.
5. We have reached a dead end. Go back to the previous node and make that the current node. If the current node is the starting node and there are no unmarked edges, there are no cycles in the graph. Otherwise, go to step 3.

Let's work through an example with five processes and five resources. Here is the resource request/allocation graph.

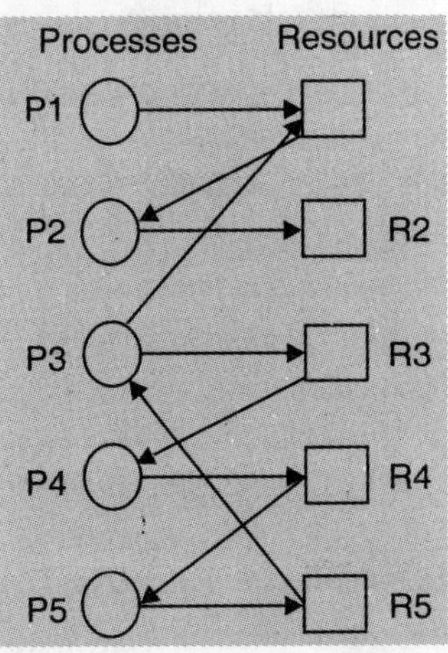

The algorithm needs to search each node; let's start at node *P*1. We add *P*1 to *L* and follow the only edge to *R*1, marking that edge. *R*1 is now the current node so we add that to *L*, checking to confirm that it is not already in *L*. We then follow the unmarked edge to *P*2, marking the edge, and making *P*2 the current node. We add *P*2 to *L*, checking to make sure that it is not already in *L*, and follow the edge to *R*2. This makes *R*2 the current node, so we add it to *L*, checking to make sure that it is not already there. We are now at a dead end so we back up, making *P*2 the current node again. There are no more unmarked edges from *P*2 so we back up yet again, making *R*1 the current node. There are no more unmarked edges from *R*1 so we back up yet again, making *P*1 the current node. Since there are no more unmarked edges from *P*1 and since this was our starting point, we are through with this node.

We move to the next unvisited node *P*3, and initialize *L* to empty. We first follow the unmarked edge to *R*1, putting *R*1 on *L*. Continuing, we make *P*2 the current node and then *R*2. Since we are at a dead end, we repeatedly back up until *P*3 becomes the current node again.

L now contains *P*3, *R*1, *P*2, and *R*2. *P*3 is the current node, and it has another unmarked edge to *R*3. We make *R*3 the current node, add it to *L*, follow its edge to *P*4. We repeat this process, visiting *R*4, then *P*5, then *R*5, then *P*3. When we visit *P*3 again we note that it is already on *L*, so we have detected a cycle, meaning that there is a deadlock situation.

Once deadlock has been detected, it is not clear what the system should do to correct the situation. There are three strategies.

- ***Preemption:*** We can take an already allocated resource away from a process and give it to another process. This can present problems. Suppose the resource is a printer and a print job is half completed. It is often difficult to restart such a job without completely starting over.
- ***Rollback:*** In situations where deadlock is a real possibility, the system can periodically make a record of the state of each process and when deadlock occurs, roll everything back to the last checkpoint, and restart, but allocating resources differently so that deadlock does not occur. This means that all work done after the checkpoint is lost and will have to be redone.
- ***Kill one or more processes:*** This is the simplest and crudest, but it works.

5.7 ADDRESSING DEADLOCK IN REAL-TIME SYSTEMS

There is a variant of deadlock called *livelock*. This is a situation in which two or more processes continuously change their state in response to changes in the other process(es) without doing any useful work. This is similar to deadlock in that no progress is made but differs in that neither process is blocked or waiting for anything.

A human example of livelock would be two people who meet face-to-face in a corridor and each moves aside to let the other pass, but they end up swaying from side to side without making any progress because they always move the same way at the same time.

Deadlock is a terrific theoretical problem for graduate students, but none of the solutions discussed above can be implemented in a real world, general purpose operating system. It would be difficult to require a user program to make requests for resources in a certain way or in a certain order. As a result, most operating systems use the ostrich algorithm.

Some specialized systems have deadlock avoidance/ prevention mechanisms. For example, many database operations involve locking several records, and this can result in deadlock, so database software often has a deadlock prevention algorithm.

The Unix file locking system lockf has a deadlock detection mechanism built into it. Whenever a process attempts to lock a file or a record of a file, the operating system checks to see if that process has locked other files or records, and if it has, it uses a graph algorithm similar to the one discussed above to see if granting that request will cause deadlock, and if it does, the request for the lock will fail, and the lockf system call will return and errno will be set to EDEADLK.

5.8 DEADLOCK—OTHER DISCUSSIONS

Signals

Recall that an interrupt is an asynchronous event which can happen at any time. When an interrupt occurs, the processor stops executing instructions in the current running process and executes an interrupt handler function in the kernel. Unix systems have a software interrupt mechanism called signals.

An example of a signal that you are probably familiar with is an interrupt signal which is sent by the user to a running process when the user enters Control-C. The default action of this signal is to kill the process.

A signal is represented as an integer. These integers are assigned symbolic names in the header file signal.h. The interrupt signal has the value 2 but you should use the symbolic name SIGINT.

Every signal has a default action. The default action for SIGINT is to abort the program. A program can modify the default action for most signals or they can choose to ignore a signal.

The system call which does this has the following function prototype.

Void {*signal [int sig, void (*disp) (int)]} (int);

This says that the function signal takes two arguments, the first, sig is a signal, and the second is function name. This function takes one argument, an integer and returns a pointer. The call to signal changes the signal handling function for its first argument from the default to the function of its second argument.

Here is a simple example.

```
#include <signal.h>
#include <stdio.h>
void *SigCatcher (int n)
{
printf ('Ha Ha, you can't kill me\n');
signal {SIGINT, [void (*)] SigCatcher};
return (void*) NULL;
}
int main ( )
{
int i;
signal {SIGINT, [void (*)] SigCatcher};
for (i = 0; i < 10; i ++) {
sleep (1);
print f ('Just woke up, i is %d\n', i);
}
return 0;
}
```

The main function calls signal to change the default action to the function SigCatcher then enters a loop where it alternately sleeps for one second, then displays a message on stdout. Normally, the user could kill this program by hitting

Control-C while it was running, but because the default signal action has changed, when the user hits Control-C while this program is running, instead of the program dying, it displays the message Ha Ha, you can't kill me. Notice that the signal handler function calls signal. On some Unix systems, once a signal handler has been called, the system resets the handler to the default unless it is reset again.

Killing Zombies

Recall that if a child dies before its parent calls wait, the child becomes a zombie. In some applications, a web server for example, the parent forks off lots of children but doesn't care whether the child is dead or alive. For example, a web server might fork a new process to handle each connection, and each child dies when the client breaks the connection. Such an application is at risk of producing many zombies, and zombies can clog up the process table. When a child dies, it sends a SIGCHLD signal to its parent. The parent process can prevent zombies from being created by creating a signal handler routine for SIGCHLD which calls wait whenever it receives a SIGCHLD signal. There is no danger that this will cause the parent to block because it would only call wait when it knows that a child has just died.

There are several versions of wait on a Unix system. The system call waitpid has this prototype

```
# include <sys/types.h>
# include <sys/wait.h>
Pid_t waitpid(pid_t pid, int *stat_loc, int options).
```

This will function like wait in that it waits for a child to terminate, but this function allows the process to wait for a particular child by setting its first argument to the pid that we want to wait for. However, that is not our interest here. If the first argument is set to zero, it will wait for any child to terminate, just like wait. However, the third argument can be set to WNOHANG. This will cause the function to return immediately if there are no dead children. It is customary to use this function rather than wait in the signal handler.

Here is some sample code

```
#include <sys/types.h>
#include <stdio.h>
#include <signal.h>
#include <wait.h>
#include <unistd.h>
void *zombiekiller (int n)
{
int status;
waitpid (0, and status, WNOHANG);
signal (SIGCHLD, zombiekiller);
return (void*) NULL;
}
int main()
{
signal (SIGCHLD, zombiekiller);
....
}
```

Pipes

A second form of redirection is a pipe. A pipe is a connection between two processes in which one process writes data to the pipe and the other reads from the pipe. Thus, it allows one process to pass data to another process. The Unix system call to create a pipe is int pipe [int fd (2)]. This function takes an array of two ints (file descriptors) as an argument. It creates a pipe with fd (0) at one end and fd (1) at the other. Reading from the pipe and writing to the pipe are done with the read and write calls that you have seen and used before. Although both ends are opened for both reading and writing, by convention a process writes to fd (1) and reads from fd (0). Pipes only make sense if the process calls fork after creating the pipe. Each process should close the end of the pipe that it is not using. Here is a simple example in which a child sends a message to its parent through a pipe.

```
#include <unistd.h>
#include <stdio.h>
int main ( )
{ pid_t pid;
int retval;
int fd (2);
int n;
retval = pipe (fd);
if (retval < 0) {
print f ('Pipe failed\n'); /*pipe is unlikely to fail*/
exit (0);
}
pid = fork( );
if (pid = = 0) { /*child*/
close [fd (0)];
n = write [fd (1), 'Hello from the child', 20);
exit (0);
}
else if (pid > 0) {/*parent*/
char buffer (64);
close [fd (1)];
n = read [fd (0), buffer, 64];
buffer (n) = '\0';
print f ('I got your message: %s\n',buffer);
} return 0;
}
```

There is no need for the parent to wait for the child to finish because reading from a pipe will block until there is something in the pipe to read. If the parent runs first, it will try to execute the read statement, and will immediately block because there is nothing in the pipe. After the child writes a message to the pipe, the parent will wake up. Pipes have a fixed size (often 4096 bytes) and if a process tries to write to a pipe which is full, the write will block until a process reads some data from the pipe. Here is a program which combines dup2 and pipe to redirect the output of the ls process to the input of the more process as would be the case if the user typed ls | more at the Unix command line.

```
#include <stdio.h>
#include <unistd.h>
void error(char *msg)
{
perror(msg);
exit(1);
}
int main()
{
int p (2), retval;
retval = pipe (p);
if (retval < 0) error ('pipe');
retval = fork ( );
if (retval < 0) error ('forking');
if (retval = = 0) {/*child*/
dup2 [p (1), 1]; /*redirect stdout to pipe*/
close [p (0)]; /*don't permit this process to read from pipe*/
execl ('/bin/ls', 'ls', '-l', NULL);
error ('Exec of ls');
}
/*if we get here, we are the parent*/
dup2 [p (0), 0]; /*redirect stdin to pipe*/
close [p (1)]; /*don't permit this process to write to pipe*/
execl ('/bin/more', 'more', NULL); error ('Exec of more');
return 0;}
\
```

Summary of detection, prevention and avoidance approaches for operating systems

Principle	*Resource allocation policy*	*Different schemes*	*Major advantages*	*Major dis-advantages*
DETECTION	Very liberal; requested resources are granted where possible.	Invoke periodically to test for deadlock.	Never delays process initiation. Facilitates on-line handling.	Inherent preem-ption losses.
PREVENTION	Conservative; under commits resources.	Requesting all resources at once. Preemption. Resource ordering.	'Works well for processes that perform a single burst of activity. 'No preemption necessary.' 'Works well for processes that perform a single burst of activity.' 'No preemption necessary.' Feasible to enforce via compile-time checks. 'Needs no run-time computation since problem is solved in system design.'	Ine_cient. 'Delays process initiation.' 'Pree-mpts more often than necessary.' ' Subject to cyclic restart. Preempts without much use.' 'Disallows incremental resource requests.'
AVOIDANCE	Selects midway between that of detection and prevention.	Manipulate to_nd at least one safe path.	No preemption necessary.	'Future resource requirem-ents must be known.' 'Processes can be blocked for long periods.'

6

Processor Scheduling

6.1 PROCESSOR SCHEDULING

In a multiprogramming system, multiple processes are maintained in main memory to maximize CPU utilisation. In a Uniprocessor system only one process may run at a time, any other process must wait until the CPU is free and can be rescheduled. Each process alternates between using a processor and waiting for I/O to be performed or for some other event occur. The processor(s) are kept busy by executing one process while the others wait. The key to multiprogramming is scheduling. In fact, four types of scheduling are typically involved.

Scheduling is a fundamental function of operating system. Most of the resources are scheduled before their use. CPU is one of such primary resources. Hence, its scheduling is important to operating system design.

6.2 TYPES OF SCHEDULING (TABLE 6.1)

The aim of processor scheduling is to assign processes to be executed by the processor in a way that meets system objectives such as response time, throughput and processor efficiency. In many systems, this scheduling activity is broken down into separate functions: long, medium and short-term scheduling. The names suggest the relative frequency with which these functions are performed.

Table 6.1: Types of scheduling

Long-term scheduling	The decision to add to a pool of processes to be executed.
Medium-term scheduling	The decision to add the number of processes that are partially or fully in main memory.
Short-term scheduling	The decision as to which available process will be executed by the processor.
I/O scheduling	The decision as to which process's pending I/O request shall be handled by an available I/O device.

Figure 6.1 shows the scheduling functions to a process state transition diagram. Long-term scheduling is performed when a new process is created. The creation of a new process results from the decision to add a new process to a set of currently active process. Medium-term scheduling is part of the swapping function and results from a decision to add a process to those that are at least partially in main memory and therefore, available for execution. Short-term scheduling is the actual decision of which ready process to execute next.

Figure 6.2 shows the queuing system for scheduling. Scheduling affects the performance of the system because it determines which processes will wait and which will progress.

Fundamentally, scheduling is matter of managing queues to minimize queuing delay and to optimize performance in a queuing environment.

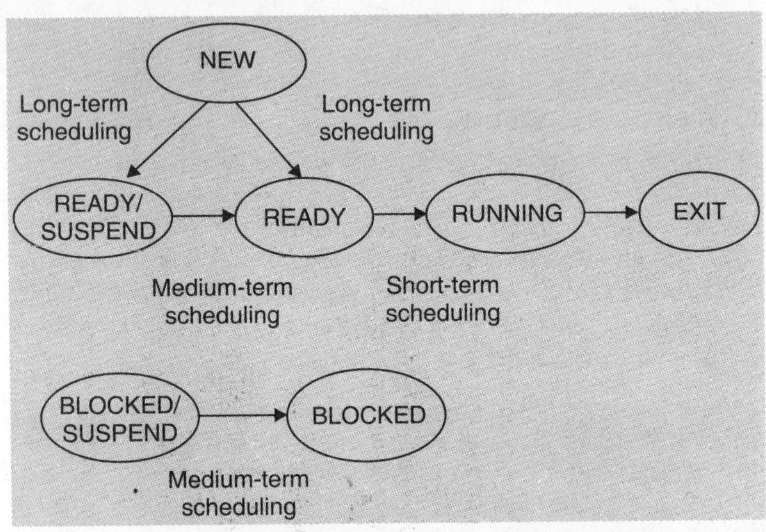

Fig. 6.1: Scheduling and process state transitions

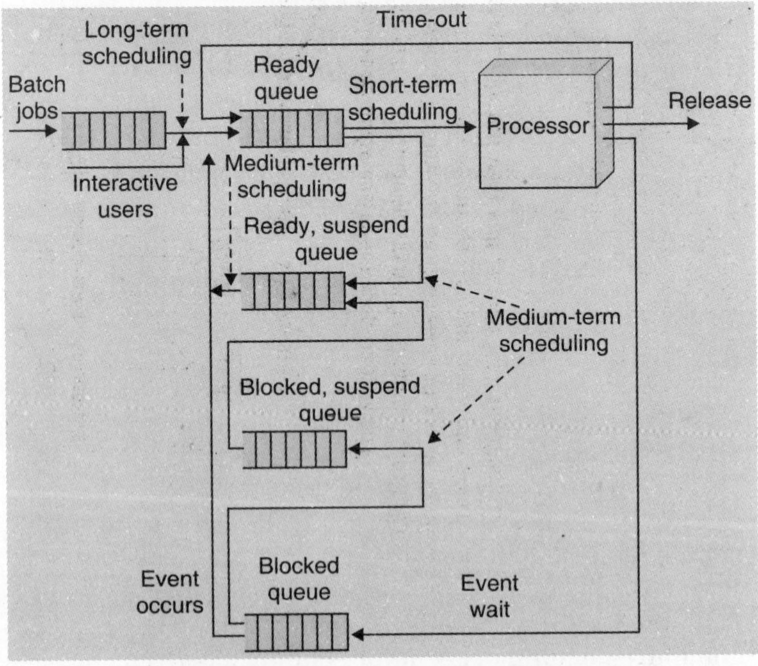

Fig. 6.2: Queuing system for scheduling

6.2.1 Long-Term Scheduling

Long-term scheduling determines which programs are admitted to the system for processing. Thus, it controls the degree of multiprogramming. Once admitted a job or user program becomes a process and is added to the queue for the short-term scheduler. In some systems, a newly created process begins in a swapped condition, in which case it is added to a queue for the medium-term scheduler.

In a batch system or batch processor of the general purpose operating system, newly submitted jobs are routed to disk and held in batch queue. The long-term scheduler creates processes from the queue when it can. Two decisions are to be taken. First the scheduler must decide that the operating system can take on one or more additional processes. Second the scheduler must decide which job/ jobs to accept and turn into processes.

The decision about when to create a new process is generally driven by the degree of multiprogramming. The more processes that are created the smaller is the percentage of time that each process can be executed. Thus, the long-term scheduler may limit the degree of multiprogramming to provide satisfactory services to the current set of processes. Each time a job terminates, the scheduler may make the decision to add one or more new jobs. Additionally, if the fraction of time that the processor is ideal exceeds a certain threshold, the long-term scheduler may be invoked.

The decision as to which job to admit next can be on a first come, first served (FCFS) basis, or it can be a tool to manage system performance. The criteria used may in lived priority, expected execution time and I/O requirements. For example, if the information is available, the scheduler may attempt to keep a mix of processor-bound and I/O- bound processes. Also in an attempt to balance I/O use, the decision may be made depending on which I/O resources are to be requested.

For interactive programs in a time-sharing systems a process request is generated when a user attempts to connect to the system. Time-sharing users are not simply queued up and kept waiting until the system can accept them. Rather the operating system accepts all authorized comers until the system is saturated by using some predefined measure of saturation. At this point, a connection request is met with a message indicating that the system is full and the user should try again later.

6.2.2 Medium-Term Scheduling

Medium term scheduling is essentially concerned with memory management, hence it's very often designed as a part of the memory management subsystem of an OS. Its efficient interaction with the short-term scheduler is essential for system performances, especially in virtual memory systems. This is the reason why in paged system the pager process is usually run at a very high (dispatching) priority level.

6.2.3 Short-Term Scheduling

Short-term scheduling concerns with the allocation of CPU time to processes in order to meet some pre-defined system performance objectives. The definition of these objectives (scheduling policy) is an overall system design issue, and determines the 'character' of the operating system from the user's (i.e. the buyer's) point of view, giving rise to the traditional distinctions among 'multi-purpose, time shared', 'batch production', 'real-time' systems, and so on.

From a user's point of view, the performance criteria can be stated as follows:

- ***Response time:*** The interval of time from the moment a service is requested until the response begins to be received. In time-shared, interactive systems this is a better measure of responsiveness from a user's point of view than turnaround time, since processes may begin to produce output early in their execution.
- ***Turnaround time:*** The interval between the submission of a process and the completion of its execution, including the actual running time, plus the time spent sleeping before being dispatched or while waiting to access various resources. This is the appropriate responsiveness measure for batch production, as well as for time-shared systems that maintain multiple batch queues, sharing CPU time among them.
- ***Meeting deadlines:*** The ability of the OS to meet pre-defined deadlines for job completion. It makes sense only when the

minimal execution time of an application can be accurately predicted.

- ***Predictability:*** The ability of the system to ensure that a given task is executed within a certain time interval, and/or to ensure that a certain constant response time is granted within a strict tolerance, no matter what the machine load is.

When the overall system performance is considered, additional scheduling criteria must be taken into account:

- ***Throughput:*** The rate of completion of processes (processes completed per unit time). This is a "raw" measure of how much work is performed, since it depends on the execution length of processes, but it's obviously affected by the scheduling policy.
- ***User processor utilisation:*** Time (percentage of unit time) during which the CPU is running user processes. This is a measure of how well the system can serve the payload and keep at minimum time spent in housekeeping chores.
- ***Overall processor utilisation:*** Time percentage during which the CPU is busy. It is a significant criterion for expensive hardware, that must be kept busy as much as possible in order to justify its cost, e.g. supercomputers for numerical calculus applications.
- ***Resource utilisation balance:*** It extends the idea of processor utilisation to take into account all system resources. A good scheduler should try to keep all the hardware resources in use at any time.

When the interaction between user's needs and overall system performance is considered, additional criteria to be accounted for arise:

- ***Fairness:*** No process should be left to starve waiting for CPU time; CPU time should be shared fairly: all processes that are equivalent, according to a pre-defined, scheduling policy related definition, should be treated equally by the scheduler.
- ***Enforcing priorities:*** Within the limits of a fair scheduling policy, preference should be given to high priority processes, when priorities are defined.

The design of the short-term scheduler is one of the critical areas in the overall system design, because of the immediate effects on system performance from the user's point of view.

It is usually one of the trickiest as well: since most processor architectures support their own task switching facilities, the implementation of the process switch mechanism is generally machine-dependent. The result is that the actual process switch software is usually written in the assembly language of a particular machine, whether the operating system is meant to be portable across different machines or not.

Independently of the adopted scheduling policy, three basic issues in short-term scheduler design can be individuated:

- The process switch must be done efficiently, otherwise the users will suffer from poor system responsiveness. This is a platitude, yet it has an immediate translation in terms of performance specification: the time spent to switch one process out and the next one in must be in the order of a few microseconds. Since most of the time taken to carry out the process switch is sacrificed in saving and restoring the context of processes, it is important that the amount of information to be saved and restored be reduced to the absolute minimum. An effective way to achieve fast process (and context) switches is to remap the (virtual) addresses of the new running process's PCB into an address that the kernel knows about. This requires simply the remapping of one address, as opposed to copying the whole PCB data into some storage area.
- Since many data structures are shared among processes (e.g. device tables, timing information, relative priorities, etc.), there must be a consistent method for allowing data access between them. The only obvious answer is to store these data structures in memory.
- Since the system manages multiple processes, each of which assumes the only process running on the time-shared machine, the system must choose a scheme in which processes have a fair share of time, where the "fairness" is conditioned by the overall system policy. This is discussed in the following sections.

6.3 SCHEDULING OBJECTIVES

If we assume we only have one processor and there are two or more processes in a ready state, how do we decide which process to schedule next? Or more precisely, which *scheduling algorithm* does the *scheduler* use in deciding which process should be moved to a running state?

In trying to schedule processes, the scheduler tries to meet a number of objectives.

1. ***Fairness:*** Ensure each process gets a fair share of the CPU.
2. ***Efficiency:*** Ensure the CPU is busy 100% of the time. In practice, a measure of between 40% (for a lightly loaded system) to 90% (for a heavily loaded system) is acceptable.
3. ***Response times:*** Ensure interactive users get good response times.
4. ***Turnaround:*** Ensure batch jobs are processed in acceptable time.
5. ***Throughput:*** Ensure a maximum number of jobs are processed.

The scheduler cannot meet all of these objectives to an optimum level. For example, in trying to give interactive users good response times, the batch jobs may have to suffer.

Many large companies, that use mainframes, address these types of problems by taking many of the scheduling decisions themselves. For example, a company the lecturer used to work for, did not allow batch work during the day. Instead they gave the TP (Transaction Processing) system all the available resources so that the response times for the users was as fast as possible.

The batch work was run overnight when the interactive workload was much less, typically only operations staff and technical support personnel.

However, these types of problems are likely to increase as the world becomes 'smaller'. If a company operates a mainframe that is accessible from all over the world then the concept of night and day no longer hold and there may be a requirement for TP access 24 hours a day and the batch work somehow has to be fitted in around this workload.

6.4 ALTERNATIVE SCHEDULING METHODS

Short-term scheduling methods can be classified according to the 'selection criterion' they use to decide *which* process, among the ready ones, should be executed next, and to the 'decision mode' used to determine *when* the process switch is to take place.

Decision modes can be either preemptive or nonpreemptive (also said cooperative). In the former case a running process may be blocked by the dispatcher because of the scheduling policy used, e.g. expiration of a fixed time slice, submission of a process with higher priority, particular interrupts occurring, etc. In the latter a running process is given control of the CPU until completion, or until it put itself to sleep following a request of some service, e.g. an I/O event.

Preemptive modes cause a higher overhead than non-preemptive ones, because of the multiple switches that may occur during the execution of a process, but allow in principle to achieve fairness in CPU usage, since they prevent a process from monopolising the CPU.

In the next several paragraphs the most common basic selection criteria will be presented. While hardly any actual operating systems implements them literally, it's often the case that real dispatcher designs embody a mix these basic techniques, hence a clear understanding of their relative advantages and disadvantages is important for any designer.

- *Nonpreemptive:* Nonpreemptive algorithms are designed so that once a process enters the running state (is allowed a process), it is not removed from the processor until it has completed its service time (or it explicitly yields the processor).
- *Preemptive:* Preemptive algorithms are driven by the notion of prioritized computation. The process with the highest priority should always be the one currently using the processor. If a process is currently using the processor and a new process with a higher priority enters the ready list, the process on the processor should be removed and returned to the ready list until it is once again the highest-priority process in the system.

6.4.1 First Come First Served (FCFS)

This is a nonpreemptive technique. A single queue of ready processes is maintained, and the dispatcher always picks the first one. This method does not emphasises throughput, since long processes are allowed to monopolise CPU. For the same reason, the response time with FCFS can be high, especially if there is a high variance in process execution times. It's fairly obvious that this method penalises short processes following long ones, though no starvation is possible.

A scheduling algorithm is to execute the processes in the order they arrive and to execute them to completion. In fact, this simply implements a nonpreemptive scheduling algorithm.

It is an easy algorithm to implement. When a process becomes ready it is added to the tail of ready queue. This is achieved by adding the Process Control Block (PCB) to the queue.

When the CPU becomes free the process at the head of the queue is removed, moved to a running state and allowed to use the CPU until it is completed.

The problem with FCFS is that the average waiting time can be long. Consider the following processes.

Process	***Burst time***
*P*1	27
*P*2	9
*P*3	2

*P*1 will start immediately, with a waiting time of 0 milliseconds (ms). *P*2 will have to wait 27 ms. *P*3 will have to wait 36 ms before starting. This gives us an average waiting time of 21 ms [i.e. (0 + 27 + 36) /3].

Now consider if the processes had arrived in the order *P*2, *P*3, and *P*1. The average waiting time would now be 6.6 ms [i.e. (0 + 9 + 11) /3].

This is obviously a big saving and all due to the fact the way the jobs arrived. It can be shown that FCFS is not generally minimal, with regard to average waiting time and this figure varies depending on the process burst times.

The FCFS algorithm can also have other undesirable effects. A CPU bound job may make the I/O bound (once they have finished the I/O) wait for the processor. At this point the I/O devices are sitting idle.

When the CPU bound job finally does some I/O, the mainly I/O processes use the CPU quickly and now the CPU sits idle waiting for the mainly CPU bound job to complete its I/O.

Although this is a simplistic example, you can appreciate that FCFS can lead to I/O devices and the CPU both being idle for long periods.

Consider another example with $P1 = 24$, $P2 = 3$, $P3 = 3$

Gantt chart for FCFS: 0 – 24 *P*1, 25 – 27 *P*2, 28 – 30 *P*3

Turnaround time for $P1 = 24$

Turnaround time for $P1 = 24 + 3$

Turnaround time for $P1 = 24 + 3 + 3$

Average turnaround time = $(24*3 + 3*2 + 3*1)/3$

In general we have $[n*a + (n-1)*b + ...]/n$

If we want to minimize this, *a* should be the smallest, followed by *b* and so on.

6.4.2 Shortest Job First

Using the SJF algorithm, each process is tagged with the length of its next CPU burst. The processes are then scheduled by selecting the shortest job first.

Consider these processes, *P*1..*P*4. Assume they arrived in the order *P*1..*P*4.

Process	*Burst time*	*Wait time*
*P*1	12	0
*P*2	19	12
*P*3	4	31
*P*4	7	35

If we schedule the processes in the order they arrive then the average wait time is 19.5 (78/4). If we run the processes using the burst time as a priority then the wait times will be 0, 4, 11 and 23; giving an average wait time of 9.50.

In fact, the SJF algorithm is provably optimal with regard to the average waiting time. And, intuitively, this is the case as shorter jobs add less to the average time, thus giving a shorter average.

The problem is we do not know the burst time of a process before it starts.

For some systems (notably batch systems) we can make fairly accurate estimates but for interactive processes it is not so easy. One approach is to try and estimate the length of the next CPU burst, based on the process's previous activity.

To do this we can use the following formula:

$$Tn + 1 = a\ tn + (1 - a)\ Tn$$

Where,

$$a, 0 <= a <= 1,$$

Tn stores the past history. tn contains the most recent information.

What this formula allows us to do is weight both the history of the burst times and the most recent burst time. The weight is controlled by a.

If $a = 0$ then $Tn + 1 = Tn$ and recent history (the most recent burst time) has no effect. If $a = 1$ then the history has no effect and the guess is equal to the most recent burst time.

A value of 0.5 for a is often used so that equal weight is given to recent and past history.

Shortest job first is just a special case of priority scheduling. Of course, we can use a number of different measures as priority.

Another example of setting priorities based on the resources they have previously used is as follows.

Assume processes are allowed 100 ms before the scheduler preempts it. If a process only used, say 2 ms, then it is likely to be a job that is I/O bound and it is in our interest to allow this job to run as soon as it has completed I/O—in the hope that it will go away and do some more I/O; thus making effective use of the processor as well as the I/O devices.

If a job used all its 100 ms we might want to give this job a lower priority, in the belief that we can get smaller jobs completed first before we allow the longer jobs to run.

One method of calculating priorities based on this reasoning is to use the formula:

$$1/(n/p)$$

Where n is the last CPU burst for that process. p is the CPU time allowed for each process before it is preempted (100 ms in our example).

Plugging in some real figures we can assign priorities as follows:

CPU burst last time	*Processing time slice*	*Priority assigned*
100	100	1
50	100	2
25	100	4
4	100	20
2	100	50
1	100	100

Another way of assigning priorities is to set them externally. During the day interactive jobs may be given a high priority and batch jobs are only allowed to run when there are no interactive jobs. Another alternative is to allow users who pay more for their computer time to be given higher priority for their jobs.

One of the problems with priority scheduling is that some processes may never run. There may always be higher priority jobs that get assigned the CPU. This is known as ***indefinite blocking*** or ***starvation***.

One solution to this problem is called *aging*. This means that the priority of jobs are gradually increased until even the lowest priority jobs will become the highest priority job in the system. This could be done, for example, by increasing the priority of a job after it has been in the system for a certain length of time.

6.4.3 Round Robin (RR) Scheduling

It is preemptive. A single queue of ready processes is maintained, and a fixed time quantum is assigned to each running process. After the quantum expires, the process is blocked and put at the end of the queue, and the next in the line is dispatched. This method is obviously very fair, and provides good responsiveness to short processes. The drawback is that the length of the time quantum must be carefully tuned, otherwise throughput will suffer. If it's too short, there may be excessive process switching overhead, if too long we are back to the lack of fairness problem of FCFS. This technique prevents starvation.

The processes to be run are held in a queue and the scheduler takes the first job off the front of the queue and assigns it to the CPU (so far the same as FCFS).

In addition, there is a unit of time defined (called a ***quantum***). Once the process has used up a quantum the process is preempted and a context switch occurs. The process which was using the processor is placed at the back of the ready queue and the process at the head of the queue is assigned to the CPU.

Of course, instead of being preempted the process could complete before using its quantum. This would mean a new process could start earlier and the completed process would not be placed at the end of the queue (it would either finish completely or move to a blocked state whilst it waited for some interrupt, for example, I/O).

The average waiting time using RR can be quite long. Consider these processes (which we assume all arrive at time zero).

Process	*Burst time*
P1	24
P2	3
P3	3

Assume a quantum of 4 ms is being used. Process 1 will run first and will be preempted after 4 ms. Next process 2 will run for 3 ms, followed by process 3 (for 3 ms).

Following this process 1 will run to completion, taking five quantum.

The waiting time is 17 ms (process 2 had to wait 4 ms, process 3 had to 7 ms and process 1 had to wait 6 ms), giving an average of 5.66 ms. If we compare this to SJF, the average is only 3 ms (9/3). But, the main concern with the RR algorithm is the length of the quantum. If it is too long then processes will never get preempted and we have the equivalent of FCFS.

If we switch processes after every ms then we make it appear as if every process has its own processor that runs at 1/n the speed of the actual processor. In fact, this ignores the effect of context switching. If the quantum is too small then the processor will spend large amounts of time context switching, and not processing data. Say, for example, we set the quantum to 5 ms and it takes 5 ms to execute a process switch then we are using half the CPU capability simply switching processes. A quantum of around 100 ms is often used.

6.4.4 Shortest Process Next (SPN)

This is nonpreemptive, assume that the execution time of a program can be accurately estimated in advance. Then a suitable selection criterion is to always pick the shortest process, because in this way throughput is obviously maximised. As obviously, there's a risk of starvation for long processes, and they experience sluggish response times anyway.

A difficulty with this method is that the execution time must be estimated as accurately as possible in advance: if too short a time is specified the scheduler might abort the job. Hence this method is mainly suitable in a production environment, where the same jobs are often run with about the same amount of data to process (e.g. printing paychecks for a firm every second week) so that a running average of previous execution times is likely to yield a good prediction for the next one.

6.4.5 Shortest Remaining Time Next (SRTN)

This is a preemptive version of the previous one, in which the scheduler always dispatches that ready process which has the shortest expected remaining time to completion. The dispatching decison is always made when a new process is submitted: the currently running process has obviously a smaller remaining time than all other ready ones, otherwise it wouldn't have been dispatched. But a newly submitted job may have an even shorter one, in which case the currently running one would be blocked and put in ready state.

This decreases the average turnaround time with respect to SPN, since short, newly arrived processes are given immediate attention, if their expected completion time happens to be less than the remaining time to completion of the currently running and ready processes. As with SPN, there's a risk of starvation for long processes, in presence of a constant supply of short ones.

Since all preemption decisions are made only either upon a new process submission or when a process completes, there's less overhead involved than with RR.

EXAMPLE

Assume we are presented with the following processes, which all arrive at time zero.

Process	*Burst time*
P1	9
P2	33
P3	2
P4	5
P5	14

For FCFS the process would be executed in the following order, with the following wait times.

Process	*Burst time*	*Wait time*
P1	9	0
P2	33	9
P3	2	42
P4	5	44
P5	14	49

Therefore, the average waiting time is

$$[(0 + 9 + 42 + 44 + 49)/5] = 28.80 \text{ milliseconds}$$

For SJF (nonpreempted) the processes would run as follows.

Process	*Burst time*	*Wait time*
P3	2	0
P4	5	2
P1	9	7
P5	14	16
P2	33	30

The average waiting time is

$$[(0 + 2 + 7 + 16 + 30)/5] = 11 \text{ milliseconds.}$$

For RR the jobs would execute as follows:

Process	*CPU time*
*P*1	8
*P*2	8
*P*3	2
*P*4	5
*P*5	8
*P*1	1
*P*2	8
*P*5	6
*P*2	8
*P*2	8
*P*2	1

The waiting time for each process is as follows:

$P1 : 0 + 23 = 23$

$P2 : 8 + 16 + 6 = 30$

$P3 : 16$

$P4 : 18$

$P5 : 23 + 9 = 32$

Therefore, the average waiting time is

$$[(23 + 30 + 16 + 18 + 32)/5] = 23.80$$

Executable code for processor scheduling algorithms:

```
#include<stdio.h>
#include<conio.h>
#include<stdlib.h>
Struct process
{
```

```
char id(10);
int burst;
int arrival;
int complete;
int wait;
int turn;
};
void FCFS[struct process p(),int n];
void SJF[struct process p(),int n];
void RR[struct process p(),int n];
void space(int n);
void display[struct process p(),int n];
void main()
{
int n,i,choice,c;
struct process p(5);
loop;
clrscr();
printf('Enter total processer:');
scanf('%d',&n);
for(i=0;i<n;i++)
{
printf('process ID...:');
scanf['%s',p(i).id];
printf('Burst time...:');
scanf('%d',&p(i).burst];
P(i).arrival=p(i).wait=p(i).turn=p(i).
compliete=o;
}
printf('\n 1.FCFS\n2.SJF\n3.RR\n4.Exit\n');
printf('Enter the choice:');
scanf('%d',&choice);
switch(choice)
{
case1:FCFS(p,n);
```

```
break;
cASE2:SJF(P,n);
break;
case3:RR(p,n);
break;
case4:break;
}
printf(Do u want to continue.....(1/0");
scanf('c/od;',&c);
if (c=1)
goto loop;
}
//FCFS routine
void FCFS(struct processp[],int n)
{
int i,tot=0;
for(i=0;i<n;i++)
{
tot+=p(i).burst;
p(i).complete + tot;
p(i+1).wait = tot;
p(i).turn=p(i).complete-p(i).arrival;
}
clrscr();
printf('Gantt diagram....\n');
for(i=0;i<tot+8;i++)
printf('-');
printf('\n');
printf('|');
for(i=0;i,n;i++)
{
space[p(i).burst/2];
printf['c/os',p(i).id];
space[p(i).burst/2);
```

```
printf('|');
}
printf('\n');
for(i=0;i<tot+8;i++)
{
printf('-');}
printf('\n0');
for(i=0;i<n;i++)
{
space[p(i).burst+1];
printf['c/od',p(i).complete];
}
printf('\n\n\n');
display(p,n);
}
}
//SJF routine
void SJF [struct process p(),int n]
{
struct process temp;
int i,j,;
for(i=0;i<n-1;i++)
{
if[p(i).burst>p(i).burst]
{
temp=p(i);
p(i)=p(i);
p(j)=temp;
}
}
}
fCFS(p,n);
}
//Round Robin routine
void RR[struct process p(),int n]
{
```

```
int t,i,j,k,c=0,totitr=0,itr,
    ind=0=0,comp(10);
struct oricess old(10);
struct process temp(10);
printf('Enter the time quantum.');
scanf('c/od',&t);
for(i=0;i<n;i++)
{
if{[p(i).burst%t]==0]
totitr+=p(i).burst/t;
else
totitr+=p(i).burst/t+1;
old(i)=p(i);
}
clrscr();
printf('\tGanttDiagram\n');
printf('..............................\n');
for(itr=0;itr<totitr;)
{
k=0;
for(i=0;i<n;i++)
if[p(i).burst!=0]
temp(k++)=p(i);
for(i=0;i<n;i++)
{
for(j=0;j<k;j++)
{
if{strcmp[p(i).id.temp(i).id]==0}
{
printf['%s I',p(i).id];
if[p(i).burst>=t]
{
c +=t;
p(i).complete=c;
p(i).burst-=t;
```

```
}
else
{
c +=p(i).burst;
p(i).complete=c;
p(i).burst=0;
}
comp(ind++)=p(i).complete;
}
}
p(i).turn =p(i).complete-p(i).arrival;
p(i).wait= p(i).turn-old(i).burst;
}
itr+=k;
}
for(i=0;i<n;i++)
p(i).burst=old(i).burst;
printf('\n----------\n');
for(i=0;i<ind;i++)
{
space(t);
printf[%d',comp(i)];
}
printf(\n\n');
display(p,n);
{
void display[struct prlcess p(),int n]
{
int i,twt=0,tt=0;
float avgwt,avgtt;
printf('process burst arrival complete
wait Turnaound\n');;
printf('-----------\n');
for(i=0;i<n;i++)
{
```

```
printf['%s\t\t%d\t%d\t%d\t%d\t%d\n',
p(i).id,p(i).burst,p(i).arrival,
p(i).compkete,p(i).wait,p(i).turn];
twt+=p(i).wait;
tt+=p(i).turn;
}
printf('——————————————\n\n');
avgwt=(float)twt/n;
avgtt=(float)tt/n;
printf('\tA verage waiting time;%f seconds
\n',avgwt);
printf('\t Average turnaround tme:%f secinds
\n\n',avgtt);
getch();
}
void space(int n)
{
int i;
for(i=1;i<=n;i++)
printf('');
}
```

7

Memory Management

7.1 MEMORY MANAGEMENT

The memory management subsystem is one of the most important parts of the operating system. Since the early days of computing, there has been a need for more memory than that exists physically in a system. Strategies have been developed to overcome this limitation and the most successful of these is virtual memory. Virtual memory makes the system appear to have more memory than it actually has by sharing it between competing processes as they need it.

Virtual memory does more than just make your computer's memory go further. The memory management subsystem provides, the following.

Large Address Spaces

The operating system makes the system appear as if it has a larger amount of memory than it actually has. The virtual memory can be many times larger than the physical memory in the system.

Protection

Each process in the system has its own virtual address space. These virtual address spaces are completely separate from each other and so a process running one application cannot affect another. Also, the hardware virtual memory mechanisms allow areas of memory to be protected against writing. This protects code and data from being overwritten by rogue applications.

Memory Mapping

Memory mapping is used to map image and data files into a process's address space. In memory mapping, the contents of a file are linked directly into the virtual address space of a process.

Fair Physical Memory Allocation

The memory management subsystem allows each running process in the system a fair share of the physical memory of the system.

Shared Virtual Memory

Although virtual memory allows processes to have separate (virtual) address spaces, there are times when you need processes to share memory. For example, there could be several processes in the system running the bash command shell. Rather than have several copies of bash, one in each process's virtual address space, it is better to have only one copy in physical memory and all of the processes running bash share it. Dynamic libraries are another common example of executing code shared between several processes.

Shared memory can also be used as an Inter Process Communication (IPC) mechanism, with two or more processes exchanging information via memory common to all of them.

7.2 AN ABSTRACT MODEL OF VIRTUAL MEMORY

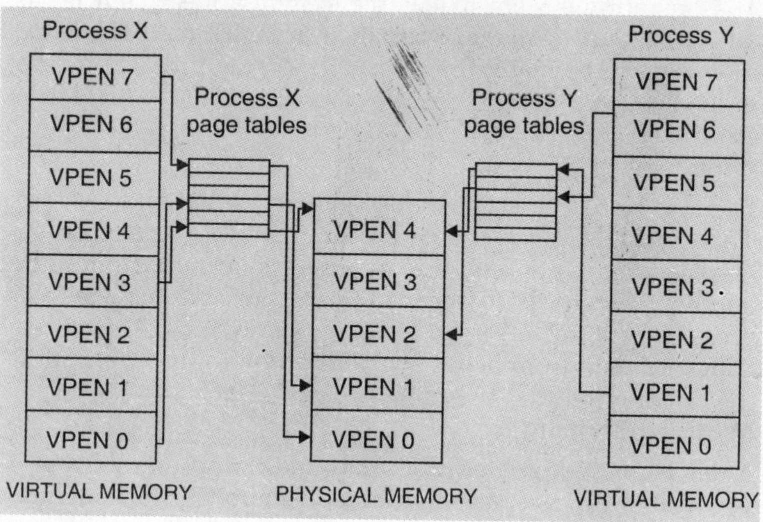

Fig. 7.1: Abstract model of virtual to physical address mapping

Before considering the methods that operating system has to support virtual memory, it is useful to consider an abstract model that is not cluttered by too much detail.

As the processor executes a program it reads an instruction from memory and decodes it. In decoding the instruction it may need to fetch or store the contents of a location in memory. The processor then executes the instruction and moves onto the next instruction in the program. In this way the processor is always accessing memory either to fetch instructions or to fetch and store data.

In a virtual memory system all of these addresses are virtual addresses and not physical addresses. These virtual addresses are converted into physical addresses by the processor based on information held in a set of tables maintained by the operating system.

To make this translation easier, virtual and physical memory are divided into handy sized chunks called *pages*. These pages are all the same size, they need not be but if they were not, the system would be very hard to administer. Each of these pages is given a unique number; the page frame number (PFN).

In this paged model, a virtual address is composed of two parts; an offset and a virtual page frame number. If the page size is 4 Kbytes, bits 11 : 0 of the virtual address contain the offset and bits 12 and above are the virtual page frame number. Each time the processor encounters a virtual address it must extract the offset and the virtual page frame number. The processor must translate the virtual page frame number into a physical one and then access the location at the correct offset into that physical page. To do this the processor uses *page tables*.

Figure 7.1 shows the virtual address spaces of two processes, process *X* and process *Y*, each with their own page tables. These page tables map each processes virtual pages into physical pages in memory. This shows that process *X*'s virtual page frame number 0 is mapped into memory in physical page frame number 1 and that process *Y*'s virtual page frame number 1 is mapped into physical page frame number 4. Each entry in the theoretical page table contains the following information:

- Valid flag. This indicates if this page table entry is valid,
- The physical page frame number that this entry is describing,
- Access control information. This describes how the page may be used. Can it be written to? Does it contain executable code?

The page table is accessed using the virtual page frame number as an offset. Virtual page frame 5 would be the 6th element of the table (0 is the first element).

To translate a virtual address into a physical one, the processor must first work out the virtual address's page frame number and the offset within that virtual page. By making the page size a power of 2 this can be easily done by masking and shifting. Looking again at Fig. 7.1 and assuming a page size of 0 × 2000 bytes (which is decimal 8192) and an address of 0 × 2194 in process *Y*'s virtual address space then the processor would translate that address into offset 0 × 194 into virtual page frame number 1.

The processor uses the virtual page frame number as an index into the process's page table to retrieve its page table entry. If the page table entry at that offset is valid, the processor takes the physical page frame number from this entry. If the entry is invalid, the process has accessed a non-existent area of its virtual memory. In this case, the processor cannot resolve the address and must pass control to the operating system so that it can fix things up.

Just how the processor notifies the operating system that the correct process has attempted to access a virtual address for which there is no valid translation is specific to the processor. However, the processor delivers it, this is known as a page fault and the operating system is notified of the faulting virtual address and the reason for the page fault.

Assuming that this is a valid page table entry, the processor takes that physical page frame number and multiplies it by the page size to get the address of the base of the page in physical memory. Finally, the processor adds in the offset to the instruction or data that it needs.

Using the above example again, process *Y*'s virtual page frame number 1 is mapped to physical page frame number 4 which starts at 0 × 8000 (4 × 0 × 2000). Adding in the 0 × 194 byte offset gives us a final physical address of 0 × 8194.

By mapping virtual to physical addresses this way, the virtual memory can be mapped into the system's physical pages in any order. For example, in Fig. 7.1 process *X*'s virtual page frame number 0 is mapped to physical page frame number 1 whereas virtual page frame number 7 is mapped to physical page frame number 0 even though it is higher in virtual memory than virtual page frame number 0. This demonstrates an interesting byproduct of virtual memory; the pages of virtual memory do not have to be present in physical memory in any particular order.

7.3 DEMAND PAGING

As there is much less physical memory than virtual memory the operating system must be careful that it does not use the physical memory inefficiently. One way to save physical memory is to only load virtual pages that are currently being used by the executing program. For example, a database program may be run to query a database. In this case not all of the database needs to be loaded into memory, just those data records that are being examined. If the database query is a search query then it does not make sense to load the code from the database program that deals with adding new records. This technique of only loading virtual pages into memory as they are accessed is known as demand paging.

When a process attempts to access a virtual address that is not currently in memory the processor cannot find a page table entry for the virtual page referenced. For example, in Fig. 7.1 there is no entry in process X's page table for virtual page frame number 2 and so if process X attempts to read from an address within virtual page frame number 2 the processor cannot translate the address into a physical one. At this point the processor notifies the operating system that a page fault has occurred.

If the faulting virtual address is invalid this means that the process has attempted to access a virtual address that it should not have. Maybe the application has gone wrong in some way, for example, writing to random addresses in memory. In this case the operating system will terminate it, protecting the other processes in the system from this rogue process.

If the faulting virtual address was valid but the page that it refers to is not currently in memory, the operating system must bring the appropriate page into memory from the image on disk. Disk access takes a long time, relatively speaking, and so the process must wait quite a while until the page has been fetched. If there are other processes that could run then the operating system will select one of them to run. The fetched page is written into a free physical page frame and an entry for the virtual page frame number is added to the process's page table. The process is then restarted at the machine instruction where the memory fault occurred. This time the virtual memory access is made, the processor can make the virtual to physical address translation and so the process continues to run.

Operating system uses demand paging to load executable images into a processes virtual memory. Whenever a command is executed, the file containing it is opened and its contents are mapped into the process's virtual memory. This is done by modifying the data structures describing this process's memory map and is known as *memory mapping*. However, only the first part of the image is actually brought into physical memory. The rest of the image is left on disk. As the image executes, it generates page faults and uses the process's memory map in order to determine which parts of the image to bring into memory for execution.

7.4 SWAPPING

If a process needs to bring a virtual page into physical memory and there are no free physical pages available, the operating system must make room for this page by discarding another page from physical memory.

If the page to be discarded from physical memory came from an image or data file and has not been written to then the page does not need to be saved. Instead it can be discarded and if the process needs that page again it can be brought back into memory from the image or data file.

However, if the page has been modified, the operating system must preserve the contents of that page so that it can be accessed at a later time. This type of page is known as a *dirty* page and when it is removed from memory it is saved in a special sort of file called the swap file. Accesses to the swap file are very long relative to the speed of the processor and physical memory and the operating system must juggle the need to write pages to disk with the need to retain them in memory to be used again.

If the algorithm used to decide which pages to discard or swap, the *swap algorithm* is not efficient then a condition known as *thrashing* occurs. In this case, pages are constantly being written to disk and then being read back and the operating system is too busy to allow much real work to be performed. If, for example, physical page frame number 1 in Fig. 7.1 is being regularly accessed then it is not a good candidate for swapping to hard disk. The set of pages that a process is currently using is called the *working set*. An efficient swap scheme would make sure that all processes have their working set in physical memory.

Linux uses a Least Recently Used (LRU) page aging technique to fairly choose pages which might be removed from the system. This scheme involves every page in the system having an age which changes as the page is accessed. The more that a page is accessed, the younger it is; the less that it is accessed the older and more stale it becomes. Old pages are good candidates for swapping.

7.5 SHARED VIRTUAL MEMORY

Virtual memory makes it easy for several processes to share memory. All memory access are made via page tables and each process has its own separate page table. For two processes sharing a physical page of memory, its physical page frame number must appear in a page table entry in both of their page tables.

Figure 7.1 shows two processes that each shares physical page frame number 4. For process *X* this is virtual page frame number 4 whereas for process *Y* this is virtual page frame number 6. This illustrates an interesting point about sharing pages: the shared physical page does not have to exist at the same place in virtual memory for any or all of the processes sharing it.

7.6 PHYSICAL AND VIRTUAL ADDRESSING MODES

It does not make much sense for the operating system itself to run in virtual memory. This would be a nightmare situation where the operating system must maintain page tables for itself. Most multi-purpose processors support the notion of a physical address mode as well as a virtual address mode. Physical addressing mode requires no page tables and the processor does not attempt to perform any address translations in this mode. The kernel is linked to run in physical address space.

Access Control

The page table entries also contain access control information. As the processor is already using the page table entry to map a process's virtual address to a physical one, it can easily use the access control information to check that the process is not accessing memory in a way that it should not.

There are many reasons why you would want to restrict access to areas of memory. Some memory, such as that containing executable code, is naturally read only memory; the operating system should not allow a process to write data over its executable code. By contrast, pages containing data can be written to but attempts to execute that memory as instructions should fail. Most processors have at least two modes of execution: *kernel* and *user*. The kernel code executing by a user or kernel data structures to be accessible except when the processor is running in kernel mode.

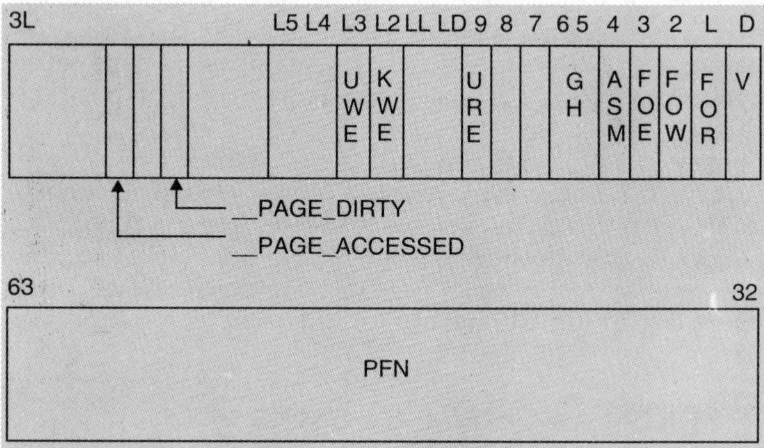

Fig. 7.2: Page table entry

The access control information is held in the PTE and is processor specific. Figure 7.2 shows the PTE. The bit fields have the following meanings:

V Valid, if set this PTE is valid,

FOE 'Fault on execute', whenever an attempt to execute instructions in this page occurs, the processor reports a page fault and passes control to the operating system,

FOW 'Fault on write', as above but page fault on an attempt to write to this page,

FOR 'Fault on read', as above but page fault on an attempt to read from this page,

ASM Address space match. This is used when the operating system wishes to clear only some of the entries from the translation buffer,

KRE Code running in kernel mode can read this page,

URE Code running in user mode can read this page,

GH Granularity hint used when mapping an entire block with a single translation buffer entry rather than many,

KWE Code running in kernel mode can write to this page,

UWE Code running in user mode can write to this page,

Page Frame Number

For PTEs with the *V* bit set, this field contains the physical Page Frame Number (page frame number) for this PTE. For invalid PTEs, if this field is not zero, it contains information about where the page is in the swap file.

The following two bits are defined and used by an operating system:

_PAGE_DIRTY

If set, the page needs to be written out to the swap file,

_PAGE_ACCESSED

Used to mark a page as having been accessed.

Caches

If you were to implement a system using the above theoretical model then it would work, but not particularly efficiently. Both operating system and processor designers try hard to extract more performance from the system. Apart from making the processors, memory and so on faster the best approach is to maintain caches of useful information and data that make some operations faster. Linux uses a number of memory management related caches.

Buffer Cache

The buffer cache contains data buffers that are used by the block device drivers.

These buffers are of fixed sizes (for example 512 bytes) and contain blocks of information that have either been read from a block device or are being written to it.

A block device is one that can only be accessed by reading and writing fixed sized blocks of data. All hard disks are block devices.

The buffer cache is indexed via the device identifier and the desired block number and is used to quickly find a block of data. Block devices are only ever accessed via the buffer cache. If data can be found in the buffer cache then it does not need to be read from the physical block device, for example, a hard disk, and access to it is much faster.

Page Cache

This is used to speed up access to images and data on disk.

It is used to cache the logical contents of a file a page at a time and is accessed via the file and offset within the file. As pages are read into memory from disk, they are cached in the page cache.

Swap Cache

Only modified (or *dirty*) pages are saved in the swap file.

So long as these pages are not modified after they have been written to the swap file then the next time the page is swapped out there is no need to write it to the swap file as the page is already in the swap file. Instead the page can simply be discarded. In a heavily swapping system this saves many unnecessary and costly disk operations.

Hardware Caches

One commonly implemented hardware cache is in the processor; a cache of Page Table Entries. In this case, the processor does not always read the page table directly but instead caches translations for pages as it needs them. These are the Translation Look-aside Buffers and contain cached copies of the page table entries from one or more processes in the system.

When the reference to the virtual address is made, the processor will attempt to find a matching TLB entry.

If it finds one, it can directly translate the virtual address into a physical one and perform the correct operation on the data. If the processor cannot find a matching TLB entry then it must get the operating system to help. It does this by signalling the operating system that a TLB miss has occurred. A system specific mechanism is used to deliver that exception to the operating system code that can fix things up. The operating system generates a new TLB entry for the address mapping. When the exception has been cleared, the processor will make another attempt to translate the virtual address. This time it will work because there is now a valid entry in the TLB for that address.

The drawback of using caches, hardware or otherwise, is that in order to save effort, an operating system must use more time and space maintaining these caches and, if the caches become corrupted, the system will crash.

7.7 PAGE TABLES

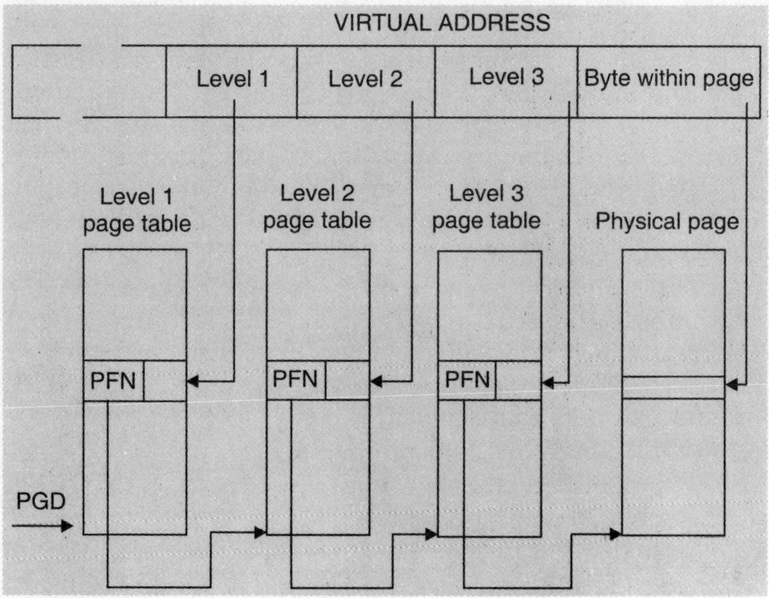

Fig. 7.3: Three level page tables

There are three levels of page tables. Each page table accessed contains the page frame number of the next level of page table. Figure 7.3 shows how a virtual address can be broken into a number of fields; each field providing an offset into a particular page table. To translate a virtual address into a physical one, the processor must take the contents of each level field, convert it into an offset into the physical page containing the page table and read the page frame number of the next level of page table. This is repeated three times until the page frame number of the physical page containing the virtual address is found. Now the final field in the virtual address, the byte offset, is used to find the data inside the page.

Each platform that operating system runs on must provide translation macros that allow the kernel to traverse the page tables for a particular process. This way, the kernel does not need to know the format of the page table entries or how they are arranged.

7.8 PAGE ALLOCATION AND DEALLOCATION

There are many demands on the physical pages in the system. For example, when an image is loaded into memory the operating system needs to allocate pages. These will be freed when the image has finished executing and is unloaded. Another use for physical pages is to hold kernel specific data structures such as the page tables themselves. The mechanisms and data structures used for page allocation and deallocation are perhaps the most critical in maintaining the efficiency of the virtual memory subsystem.

All of the physical pages in the system are described by the mem_map data structure which is a list of mem_map_t structures which is initialized at boot time. Each mem_map_t describes a single physical page in the system. Important fields (so far as memory management is concerned) are:

Count This is a count of the number of users of this page. The count is greater than one when the page is shared between many processes,

Age This field describes the age of the page and is used to decide if the page is a good candidate for discarding or swapping,

Map_nr This is the physical page frame number that this mem_map_t describes.

The free_area vector is used by the page allocation code to find and free pages. The whole buffer management scheme is supported by this mechanism and so far as the code is concerned, the size of the page and physical paging mechanisms used by the processor are irrelevant.

Each element of free_area contains information about blocks of pages. The first element in the array describes single pages, the next blocks of 2 pages, the next blocks of 4 pages and so on upwards in powers of two. The list element is used as a queue head and has pointers to the page data structures in the mem_map array. Free blocks of pages are queued here. Map is a pointer to a bitmap which keeps track of allocated groups of pages of this size. Bit N of the bitmap is set if the Nth block of pages is free.

7.8.1 Page Allocation

The page allocation code attempts to allocate a block of one or more physical pages. Pages are allocated in blocks which are powers of 2 in size. That means that it can allocate a block 1 page, 2 pages, 4 pages and so on. So long as there are enough free pages in the system to grant this request the allocation code will search the free_area for a block of pages of the size requested. Each element of the free_area has a map of the allocated and free blocks of pages for that sized block. For example, element 2 of the array has a memory map that describes free and allocated blocks each of 4 pages long.

The allocation algorithm first searches for blocks of pages of the size requested. It follows the chain of free pages that is queued on the *list* element of the free_area data structure. If no blocks of pages of the requested size are free, blocks of the next size (which is twice that of the size requested) are looked for. This process continues until all of the free_area has been searched or until a block of pages has been found. If the block of pages found is larger than that requested it must be broken down until there is a block of the right size. Because the blocks are each a power of 2 pages big then this breaking down process is easy as you simply break the blocks in half. The free blocks are queued on the appropriate queue and the allocated block of pages is returned to the caller.

For example, in Fig. 7.4 if a block of 2 pages was requested, the first block of 4 pages (starting at page frame number 4) would be broken into two 2 page blocks. The first, starting at page frame number 4 would be returned to the caller as the allocated pages and the second block, starting at page frame number 6 would be queued as a free block of 2 pages onto element 1 of the free_area array.

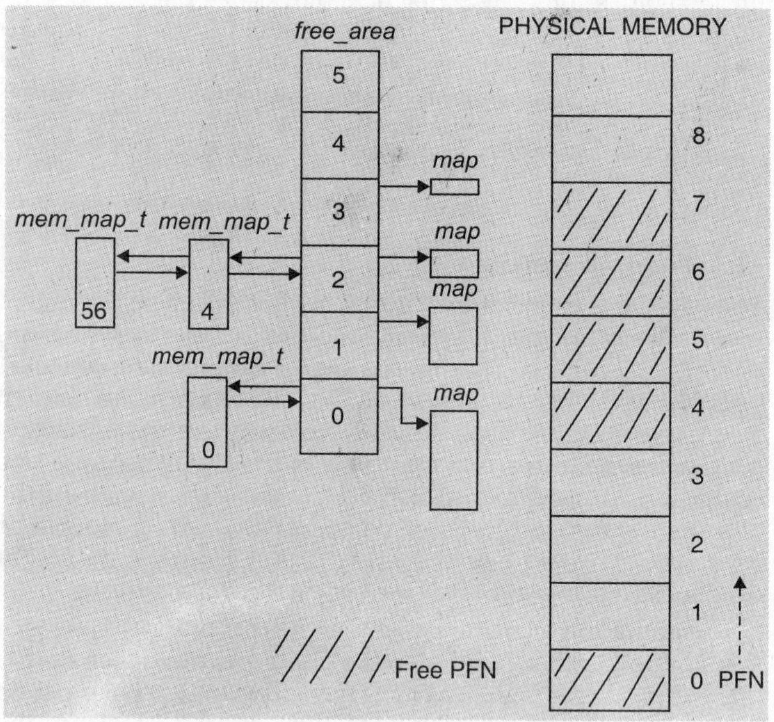

Fig. 7.4: The free_area data structure

7.8.2 Page Deallocation

Allocating blocks of pages tend to fragment memory with larger blocks of free pages being broken down into smaller ones. The page deallocation code recombines pages into larger blocks of free pages whenever it can. In fact the page block size is important as it allows for easy combination of blocks into larger blocks.

Whenever a block of pages is freed, the adjacent or buddy block of the same size is checked to see if it is free. If it is, then it is combined with the newly freed block of pages to form a new free block of pages for the next size block of pages. Each time two blocks of pages are recombined into a bigger block of free pages the page deallocation code attempts to recombine that block into a yet larger one. In this way the blocks of free pages are as large as memory usage will allow.

For example, in Fig. 7.4, if page frame number 1 were to be freed, then that would be combined with the already free page frame number 0 and queued onto element 1 of the free_area as a free block of size 2 pages.

7.9 MEMORY MAPPING

When an image is executed, the contents of the executable image must be brought into the process's virtual address space. The same is also true of any shared libraries that the executable image has been linked to use. The executable file is not actually brought into physical memory, instead it is merely linked into the process's virtual memory. Then, as the parts of the program are referenced by the running application, the image is brought into memory from the executable image. This linking of an image into a process's virtual address space is known as memory mapping.

Every process's virtual memory is represented by an mm_struct data structure (Fig. 7.5). This contains information about the image that it is currently executing (for example bash) and also has pointers to a number of vm_area_struct data structures. Each vm_area_struct data structure describes the start and end of the area of virtual memory, the process's access rights to that memory and a set of operations for that memory. These operations are a set of routines that Linux must use when manipulating this area of virtual memory. For example, one of the virtual memory operations performs the correct actions when the process has attempted to access this virtual memory but finds (via a page fault) that the memory is not actually in physical memory. This operation is the *nopage* operation. The

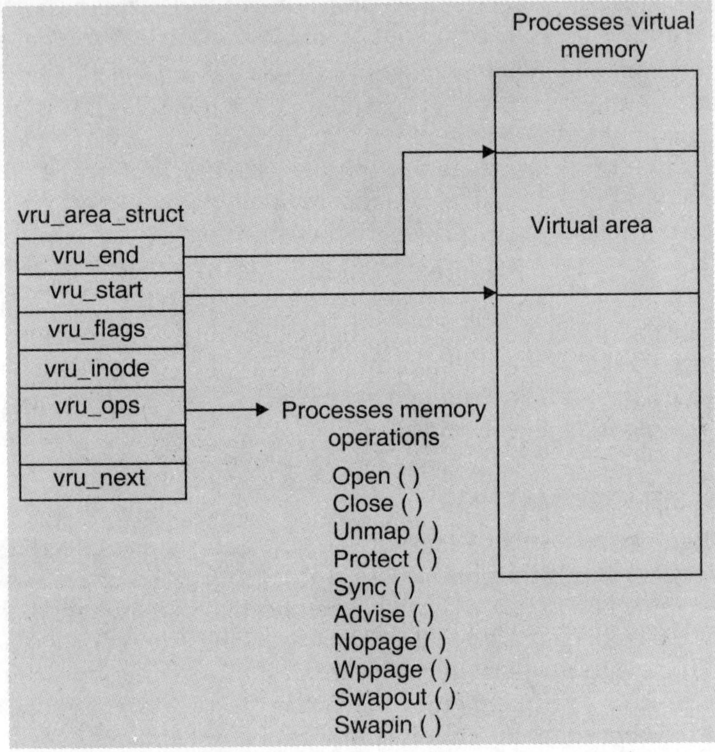

Fig. 7.5: Areas of virtual memory

nopage operation is used when Linux demand pages of an executable image into memory.

When an executable image is mapped into a process's virtual address a set of vm_area_struct data structures is generated. Each vm_area_struct data structure represents a part of the executable image; the executable code, initialized data (variables), uninitialised data and so on. Linux supports a number of standard virtual memory operations and as the vm_area_struct data structures are created, the correct set of virtual memory operations are associated with them.

7.10 DEMAND PAGING

Once an executable image has been memory mapped into a process's virtual memory it can start to execute. As only the very start of the image is physically pulled into memory it will soon access an area of virtual memory that is not yet in physical memory. When a process accesses a virtual address that does not have a valid page table entry, the processor will report a page fault to the system.

The page fault describes the virtual address where the page fault occurred and the type of memory access that caused.

Operating system must find the vm_area_struct that represents the area of memory that the page fault occurred in. As searching through the vm_area_struct data structures is critical to the efficient handling of page faults, these are linked together in an AVL (Adelson-Velskii and Landis) tree structure. If there is no vm_area_struct data structure for this faulting virtual address, this process has accessed an illegal virtual address. Operating system will signal the process, sending a SIGSEGV signal, and if the process does not have a handler for that signal it will be terminated.

System next checks the type of page fault that occurred against the types of accesses allowed for this area of virtual memory. If the process is accessing the memory in an illegal way, say writing to an area that it is only allowed to read from, it is also signalled with a memory error.

Now that operating system has determined that the page fault is legal, it must deal with it.

It must differentiate between pages that are in the swap file and those that are part of an executable image on a disk somewhere. It does this by using the page table entry for this faulting virtual address.

If the page's page table entry is invalid but not empty, the page fault is for a page currently being held in the swap file. For page table entries, these are entries which do not have their valid bit set but which have a non-zero value in their PFN field. In this case the PFN field holds information about where in the swap (and which swap file) the page is being held. How pages in the swap file are handled is described later in this chapter.

Not all vm_area_struct data structures have a set of virtual memory operations and even those that do may not have a *nopage* operation. This is because by default system will fix up the access by allocating a new physical page and creating a valid page table entry for it. If there is a *nopage* operation for this area of virtual memory, system will use it.

The *nopage* operation is used for memory mapped executable images and it uses the page cache to bring the required image page into physical memory.

However, the required page is brought into physical memory, the process's page tables are updated. It may be necessary for hardware specific actions to update those entries, particularly if the processor uses translation look aside buffers. Now that the page fault has been handled it can be dismissed and the process is restarted at the instruction that made the faulting virtual memory access.

7.11 THE PAGE CACHE

The role of the page cache is to speed up access to files on disk. Memory mapped files are read a page at a time and these pages are stored in the page cache. Figure 7.6 shows that the page cache consists of the page_hash_table, a vector of pointers to mem_map_t data structures.

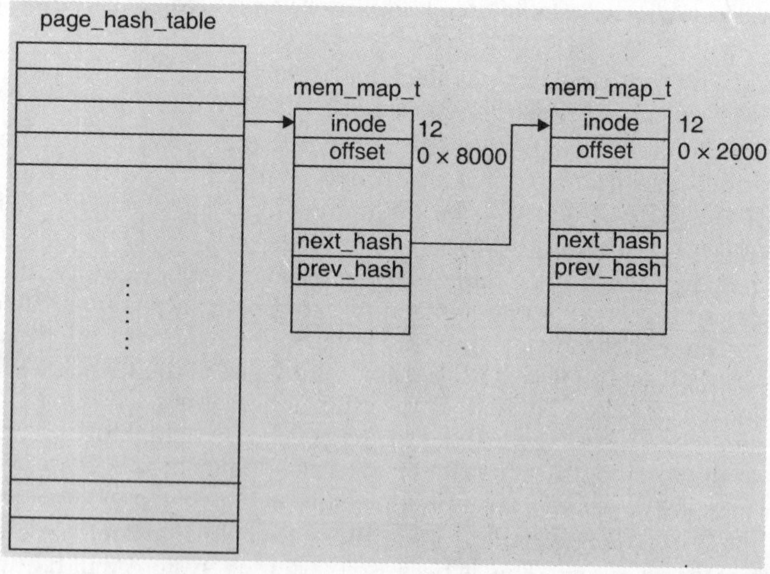

Fig. 7.6: The page cache

Each file in Linux is identified by a VFS inode data structure and each VFS inode is unique and fully describes one and only one file. The index into the page table is derived from the file's VFS inode and the offset into the file.

Whenever a page is read from a memory mapped file, for example, when it needs to be brought back into memory during demand paging, the page is read through the page cache. If the page is present in the cache, a pointer to the mem_map_t data structure representing it is returned to the page fault handling code. Otherwise the page must be brought into memory from the file system that holds the image. Operating system allocates a physical page and reads the page from the file on disk.

This single page read ahead means that if the process is accessing the pages in the file serially, the next page will be waiting in memory for the process.

Over time the page cache grows as images are read and executed. Pages will be removed from the cache as they are no longer needed, say as an image is no longer being used by any process. As operating system uses memory it can start to run low on physical pages. In this case it will reduce the size of the page cache.

7.12 SWAPPING AND DISCARDING PAGES

When physical memory becomes scarce the memory management subsystem must attempt to free physical pages. This task falls to the kernel swap daemon (*kswapd*).

The kernel swap daemon is a special type of process, a kernel thread. Kernel threads are processes have no virtual memory, instead they run in kernel mode in the physical address space. The kernel swap daemon is slightly misnamed in that it does more than merely swap pages out to the system's swap files. Its role is make sure that there are enough free pages in the system to keep the memory management system operating efficiently.

The kernel swap daemon (*kswapd*) is started by the kernel init process at startup time and sits waiting for the kernel swap timer to periodically expire.

Every time the timer expires, the swap daemon looks to see if the number of free pages in the system is getting too low. It uses two variables, *free_pages_high* and *free_pages_low* to decide if it should free some pages. So long as the number of free pages in the system remains above *free_pages_high*, the kernel swap daemon does nothing; it sleeps again until its timer next expires. For the purposes of this check the kernel swap daemon takes into account the number of pages currently being written out to the swap file. It keeps a count of these in *nr_async_pages*; this is incremented each time a page is queued waiting to be written out to the swap file and decremented when the write to the swap device has completed. *Free_pages_low* and *free_pages_high* are set at system startup time and are related to the number of physical pages in the system. If the number of free pages in the system has fallen below *free_pages_high* or worse still *free_pages_low*, the kernel swap daemon will try three ways to reduce the number of physical pages being used by the system:

- Reducing the size of the buffer and page caches,
- Swapping out system Vs shared memory pages,
- Swapping out and discarding pages.

If the number of free pages in the system has fallen below *free_pages_low*, the kernel swap daemon will try to free 6 pages before it next runs. Otherwise it will try to free 3 pages. Each of the above methods is tried in turn until enough pages have been freed. The kernel swap daemon remembers which method it was using the last time that it attempted to free physical pages. Each time it runs it will start trying to free pages using this last successful method.

After it has free sufficient pages, the swap daemon sleeps again until its timer expires. If the reason that the kernel swap daemon freed pages was that the number of free pages in the system had fallen below *free_pages_low*, it only sleeps for half its usual time. Once the number of free pages is more than *free_pages_low* the kernel swap daemon goes back to sleeping longer between checks.

The swap daemon looks at each process in the system in turn to see if it is a good candidate for swapping.

Good candidates are processes that can be swapped (some cannot) and that have one or more pages which can be swapped or discarded from memory. Pages are swapped out of physical memory into the system's swap files only if the data in them cannot be retrieved another way.

A lot of the contents of an executable image come from the image's file and can easily be re-read from that file. For example, the executable instructions of an image will never be modified by the image and so will never be written to the swap file. These pages can simply be discarded; when they are again referenced by the process, they will be brought back into memory from the executable image. Once the process to swap has been located, the swap daemon looks through all of its virtual memory regions looking for areas which are not shared or locked. It does not swap out all of the swappable pages of the process that it has selected; instead it removes only a small number of pages.

Pages cannot be swapped or discarded if they are locked in memory. The swap algorithm uses page aging. Each page has a counter (held in the mem_map_t data structure) that gives the kernel swap daemon some idea whether or not a page is worth swapping. Pages age when they are unused and rejuvinate on access; the swap daemon only swaps out old pages. The default action when a page is first allocated, is to give it an initial age of 3. Each time it is touched, its age is increased by 3 to a maximum of 20. Every time the kernel swap daemon runs it ages pages, decrementing their age by 1. These default actions can be changed and for this reason they (and other swap related information) are stored in the swap_control data structure.

If the page is old (age = 0), the swap daemon will process it further. *Dirty* pages are pages which can be swapped out. Linux uses an architecture specific bit in the PTE to describe pages this way. However, not all *dirty* pages are necessarily written to the swap file. Every virtual memory region of a process may have its own swap operation (pointed at by the vm_ops pointer in the vm_area_struct) and that method is used. Otherwise, the swap daemon will allocate a page in the swap file and write the page out to that device.

The page's page table entry is replaced by one which is marked as invalid but which contains information about where the page is in the swap file. This is an offset into the swap file where the page is held and an indication of which swap file is being used. Whatever the swap method used, the original physical page is made free by putting it back into the free_area. Clean (or rather not *dirty*) pages can be discarded and put back into the free_area for re-use.

If enough of the swappable processes pages have been swapped out or discarded, the swap daemon will again sleep. The next time it wakes it will consider the next process in the system. In this way, the swap daemon nibbles away at each processes physical pages until the system is again in balance. This is much fairer than swapping out whole processes.

7.13 REDUCING PAGE SIZE AND BUFFER CACHES

The pages held in the page and buffer caches are good candidates for being freed into the free_area vector. The Page Cache, which contains pages of memory mapped files, may contain unneccessary pages that are filling up the system's memory. Likewise the Buffer Cache, which contains buffers read from or being written to physical devices, may also contain unneeded buffers. When the physical pages in the system start to run out, discarding pages from these caches is relatively easy as it requires no writing to physical devices (unlike swapping pages out of memory). Discarding these pages does not have too many harmful side effects other than making access to physical devices and memory mapped files slower. However, if the discarding of pages from these caches is done fairly, all processes will suffer equally.

Every time the kernel swap daemon tries to shrink these caches it examines a block of pages in the mem_map page vector to see if any can be discarded from physical memory. The size of the block of pages examined is higher if the kernel swap daemon is intensively swapping; that is if the number of free pages in the system has fallen dangerously low. The blocks of pages are examined in a cyclical manner; a different block of pages is examined each time an attempt is made to shrink the memory map. This is known as the *clock* algorithm as, rather like the minute hand of a clock, the whole mem_map page vector is examined a few pages at a time.

Each page being examined is checked to see if it is cached in either the page cache or the buffer cache. You should note that shared pages are not considered for discarding at this time and that a page cannot be in both caches at the same time. If the page is not in either cache then the next page in the mem_map page vector is examined.

Pages are cached in the buffer cache (or rather the buffers within the pages are cached) to make buffer allocation and deallocation more efficient. The memory map shrinking code tries to free the buffers that are contained within the page being examined.

If all the buffers are freed, then the pages that contain them are also be freed. If the examined page is in the page cache, it is removed from the page cache and freed.

When enough pages have been freed on this attempt then the kernel swap daemon will wait until the next time it is periodically woken. As none of the freed pages were part of any process's virtual memory (they were cached pages), then no page tables need updating. If there were not enough cached pages discarded then the swap daemon will try to swap out some shared pages.

7.14 SWAPPING Vs SHARED MEMORY PAGES

System Vs shared memory is an inter-process communication mechanism which allows two or more processes to share virtual memory in order to pass information amongst themselves. It is enough to say that each area of System Vs shared memory is described by a shmid_ds data structure. This contains a pointer to a list of vm_area_struct data structures, one for each process sharing this area of virtual memory. The vm_area_struct data structures describe where in each process's virtual memory this area of System Vs shared memory goes. Each vm_area_struct data structure for this System Vs shared memory is linked together using the vm_next_shared and vm_prev_shared pointers. Each shmid_ds data structure also contains a list of page table entries each of which describes the physical page that a shared virtual page maps to.

The kernel swap daemon also uses a *clock* algorithm when swapping out System Vs shared memory pages.

Each time it runs it remembers which page of which shared virtual memory area it last swapped out. It does this by keeping two indices, the first is an index into the set of shmid_ds data structures, the second into the list of page table entries for this area of System Vs shared memory. This makes sure that it fairly victimizes the areas of System Vs shared memory.

As the physical page frame number for a given virtual page of System Vs shared memory is contained in the page tables of all of the processes sharing this area of virtual memory, the kernel swap daemon must modify all of these page tables to show that the page is no longer in memory but is now held in the swap file. For each shared page it is swapping out, the kernel swap daemon finds the page table entry in each of the sharing process's page tables (by following a pointer from each vm_area_struct data structure). If this process's page table entry for this page of System Vs shared memory is valid, it converts it into an invalid but swapped out page table entry and reduces this (shared) page's count of users by one. The format of a swapped out System Vs shared page table entry contains an index into the set of shmid_ds data structures and an index into the page table entries for this area of System Vs shared memory.

If the page's count is zero after the page tables of the sharing processes have all been modified, the shared page can be written out to the swap file. The page table entry in the list pointed at by the shmid_ds data structure for this area of System Vs shared memory is replaced by a swapped out page table entry. A swapped out page table entry is invalid but contains an index into the set of open swap files and the offset in that file where the swapped out page can be found. This information will be used when the page has to be brought back into physical memory.

7.15 SWAP CACHE

When swapping pages out to the swap files, operating system avoids writing pages if it does not have to. There are times when a page is both in a swap file and in physical memory.

This happens when a page that was swapped out of memory was then brought back into memory when it was again accessed by a process. So long as the page in memory is not written to, the copy in the swap file remains valid.

It uses the swap cache to track these pages. The swap cache is a list of page table entries, one per physical page in the system. This is a page table entry for a swapped out page and describes which swap file the page is being held in together with its location in the swap file. If a swap cache entry is non-zero, it represents a page which is being held in a swap file that has not been modified. If the page is subsequently modified (by being written to), its entry is removed from the swap cache.

When it needs to swap a physical page out to a swap file it consults the swap cache and, if there is a valid entry for this page, it does not need to write the page out to the swap file. This is because the page in memory has not been modified since it was last read from the swap file.

The entries in the swap cache are page table entries for swapped out pages. They are marked as invalid but contain information which allow it to find the right swap file and the right page within that swap file.

7.16 SWAPPING PAGES IN

The dirty pages saved in the swap files may be needed again, for example, when an application writes to an area of virtual memory whose contents are held in a swapped out physical page. Accessing a page of virtual memory that is not held in physical memory causes a page fault to occur. The page fault is the processor signalling the operating system that it cannot translate a virtual address into a physical one. In this case this is because the page table entry describing this page of virtual memory was marked as invalid when the page was swapped out. The processor cannot handle the virtual to physical address translation and so hands control back to the operating system describing as it does so the virtual address that faulted and the reason for the fault. The format of this information and how the processor passes control to the operating system is processor specific.

The processor specific page fault handling code must locate the vm_area_struct data structure that describes the area of virtual memory that contains the faulting virtual address. It does this by searching the vm_area_struct data structures for this process until it finds the one containing the faulting virtual address. This is very time critical code and a process's vm_area_struct data structures are so arranged as to make this search take as little time as possible.

Having carried out the appropriate processor specific actions and found that the faulting virtual address is for a valid area of virtual memory, the page fault processing becomes generic and applicable to all processors that Linux runs on.

The generic page fault handling code looks for the page table entry for the faulting virtual address. If the page table entry it finds is for a swapped out page, it must swap the page back into physical memory. The format of the page table entry for a swapped out page is processor specific but all processors mark these pages as invalid and put the information neccessary to locate the page within the swap file into the page table entry. Linux needs this information in order to bring the page back into physical memory.

At this point, it knows the faulting virtual address and has a page table entry containing information about where this page has been swapped to. The vm_area_struct data structure may contain a pointer to a routine which will swap any page of the area of virtual memory that it describes back into physical memory. This is its *swapin* operation. If there is a *swapin* operation for this area of virtual memory then system will use it. This is, in fact, how swapped out system Vs shared memory pages are handled as it requires special handling because the format of a swapped out system Vs shared page is a little different from that of an ordinary swapped out page. There may not be a *swapin* operation, in which case Linux will assume that this is an ordinary page that does not need to be specially handled.

It allocates a free physical page and reads the swapped out page back from the swap file. Information telling it where in the swap file (and which swap file) is taken from the invalid page table entry.

If the access that caused the page fault was not a write access then the page is left in the swap cache and its page table entry is not marked as writable. If the page is subsequently written to, another page fault will occur and, at that point, the page is marked as dirty and its entry is removed from the swap cache. If the page is not written to and it needs to be swapped out again, system can avoid the write of the page to its swap file because the page is already in the swap file.

8

Virtual Memory Management

8.1 INTRODUCTION

Virtual memory is an imaginary memory area supported by some operating systems (for example, Windows but not DOS) in conjunction with the hardware. Virtual memory can be touched of as an alternate set of memory addresses. Programs use these virtual addresses rather than real addresses to store instructions and data. When the program is actually executed, the virtual addresses are converted into real memory addresses.

The purpose of virtual memory is to enlarge the address space, the set of addresses a program can utilize. For example, virtual memory might contain twice as many addresses as main memory. A program using all of virtual memory, therefore, would not be able to fit in main memory all at once. Nevertheless, the computer could execute such a program by copying into main memory those portions of the program needed at any given point during execution.

To facilitate copying virtual memory into real memory, the operating system divides virtual memory into pages, each of which contains a fixed number of addresses. Each page is stored on a disk until it is needed. When the page is needed, the operating system copies it from disk to main memory, translating the virtual addresses into real addresses.

The process of translating virtual addresses into real addresses is called mapping. The copying of virtual pages from disk to main memory is known as paging or swapping.

8.2. CHARACTERISTICS OF PAGING AND SEGMENTATION

Two characteristics are the keys to paging and segmentation:

1. All memory references are logical addresses within a process which are dynamically converted into physical address at run time. This means that a process may be swapped (moved) in and out of main memory such that it occupies different location in memory at different times during execution.
2. A process may be broken up into a number of pieces (pages or segments) and these pieces need not be contiguously located in main memory during execution.

The biggest advantage with these two characteristics is that not whole process has to be in memory while executing, meaning those pages or segments not loaded can be brought in whenever required during execution and the ones not required can be swapped out. Those portions of a process in memory are called resident set of process. The main advantages are:

- More process can be maintained in the main memory.
  - Only some of the pieces of each process are loaded in.
  - With so many processes in main memory, it is very likely a process will be in the ready state at any particular time.
- Process size is independent of the main memory present in the system.
  - It is possible for a process to be larger than all the main memory.

8.3 LOCAL AND VIRTUAL MEMORY

There are two main types of memory that are real memory that is the main memory of a computer system and virtual memory (memory on disk) that allows for effective multi-programming and relieves the user of fixed constraints of main memory.

Virtual memory scheme is attractive. Execution of a process with large arrays of data bank may be restricted to a specific area of an array. So, there is no point in loading all the portions of the process. Occasionally, if reference for some data is made and it is not in the main memory it can be brought in. Therefore, not only more processes can be loaded in the memory but also it saves time as less swapping is required. The swapping strategy is employed by the operating system, that manages which piece to keep and which one to swap. Because, if for some reason processor gets busy in swapping in and out of these program portions, which is called thrashing the system will become very inefficient. So, it has to employ a scheme which avoids thrashing and basically this thing has given birth to the principle of locality.

The principle of locality states that, program and data references within a process tend to cluster. Hence, the assumption that only a few pieces of a process will be needed over a short period of time is valid. Also, it should be possible to make intelligent guesses about which pieces will be needed in the future, which avoid thrashing and suggests that virtual memory may work efficiently.

For virtual memory to be practical and effective, some supports are needed. First, there must be a hardware support for paging and segmentation. Secondly, operating system must include a software to manage the movement of pages and/or segments between secondary memory and main memory.

8.4 VIRTUAL MEMORY PAGING

Each process has its own page table. Each page table entry contains the frame number of the corresponding page in main memory. A bit (P) is needed to indicate whether the page is in main memory or not as shown in Fig. 8.1. The page table entry also includes a modify (M) bit. Modify bit is needed to indicate if the page has been altered since it was last loaded into main memory. If no change has been made, the page does not have to be written to the disk when it needs to be swapped out.

Virtual address

Page number	Offset

Page table entry

P	M	Other control bits	Frame number

Fig. 8.1: Memory management format for paging (P: present bit, M: modified bit)

The entire page table may take up too much main memory. Hence, the page tables are also stored in virtual memory. When a process is running, part of its page table is loaded in main memory.

8.5 VIRTUAL MEMORY SEGMENTATION

Segments may be of unequal and dynamic size. Memory references consist of (segment number, offset) form of address. This organization has a number of advantages over non-segmented address space.

- It simplifies handling of growing data structures.
- It allows programs to be altered and recompiled independently.
- It lends itself to sharing data among processes.
- It lends itself to protection.

Each process has its own segment table, and when all its segments are loaded into main memory, the segment table for a process is created and loaded into main memory. Each entry contains the length of the segment. A bit is needed to determine if segment is already in main memory (P), if it is in the memory, then the entry also includes the starting address and length of the segment. Another bit (M) is needed to determine if the segment has been modified since it was loaded in main memory as shown in Fig. 8.2.

Virtual address

Segment number	Offset

Segment table entry

P	M	Other control bits	Length	Segment base

Fig. 8.2: Memory management format for segmentation (P: present bit, M: modified bit)

8.6 PAGING AND SEGMENTATION

Both segmentation and paging have their strengths. Paging is transparent to the programmer while segmentation is visible to the programmer. In this combined scheme, each segment is broken into fixed-size pages. Figure 8.3 suggests a structure to support combined paging/segmentation. Each process is associated with a segment table and a number of page tables, one per process segment. The present and modified bits are not needed in segment table because these matters are handled at the page level.

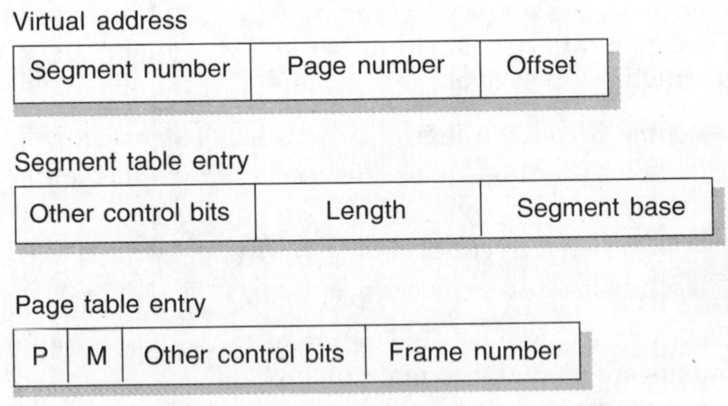

Fig. 8.3: Combined memory management format for segmentation and paging (P: present bit, M: modified bit)

8.7 OPERATING SYSTEM SOFTWARE FOR VIRTUAL MEMORY

Design of memory-management depends on the following areas of choice:

- Whether or not to use virtual memory.
- The use of paging or segmentation or both.
- The algorithms employed for various aspects of memory management.

8.7.1 Fetch Policy

The fetch policy determines when a page should be brought into memory. Two common alternatives are demand paging and prepaging.

1. ***Demand paging:*** With demand paging, a page is brought into main memory only when a reference is made to a location on the page. Typically, when a process is first started, frequency of page fault* will be high. As more pages are brought in the principle of locality will start working.
2. ***Prepaging:*** With prepaging, pages other than the one demanded by a paper fault are brought in. It is more efficient than demand paging to bring in pages that reside contiguously on the disk.

8.7.2 Placement Policy

Placement policy determines where in real memory a process piece is to reside. In segmentation systems the placement policy is an important design issue. There are policies such that, first-fit, best-fit and so on. For paging or combined (combined paging with segmentation) systems placement policy is irrelevant as the address translation hardware and the main memory access hardware will perform their job efficiently.

Replacement Policy

Replacement policy is probably the most important aspect of the Memory Management Software. This policy determines which page or piece of data is to be replaced. The objective here is to replace or remove that piece which is most likely not to be accessed in future. Principle of locality brings high correlation among the references, most policies predict based

---

* **Page fault:** This error occurs when the desired page is not in the memory and causes an interrupt signal to be sent to request the loading of the proper page into main memory.

on the past behavior. It should also be noted that the most sophisticated and elaborated policy will have greater hardware and software overheads. There are three interrelated concepts while dealing with this topic:

- How many frames are to be allocated for an active process?
- Pages considered for replacement should be limited to that particular process or it should include all the page frames in the main memory.
- Among the selected set considered for replacement which particular portion should be replaced.

Basic Replacement Algorithms

There are certain basic algorithms that are used for the selection of a page to replace.

(i) Optimal Policy

The optimal policy selects for replacement a page for which the time to the next reference is the longest. This policy results in the fewest number of page faults. But this policy is impossible to implement since it requires the operating system to have perfect knowledge of future events.

Figure 8.4 gives an example of the optimal policy. The example assumes a fixed frame allocation for this process of three frames. The execution of process requires reference to five distinct pages. The page address stream formed by executing the program is:

			2	3	2	1	5	2	4	5	3	2	5	2

which means that the first page reference is 2, the second page reference is 3, and so on. The optimal policy produces three page faults after the frame allocation has been filled.

(ii) The Least Recently Used (LRU)

This policy replaces the page in memory that has not been referenced recently (longest time). By the principle of locality, this should be the page least likely to be referenced in the near future. It almost does nearly as well as the optimal replacement policy. The problem with this approach is the difficulty in implementation. As seen in Fig. 8.4, in this example there are four page faults.

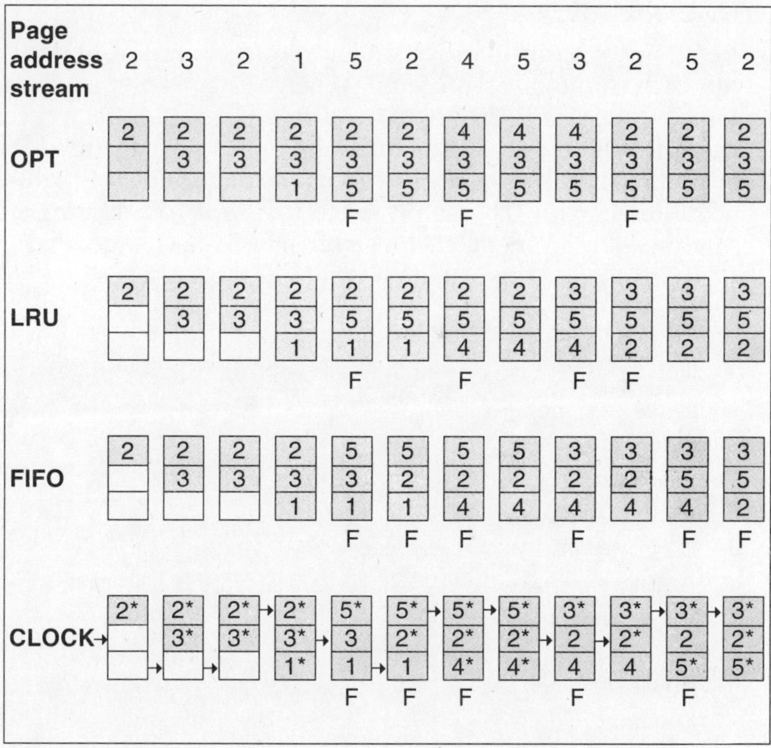

Fig. 8.4: Behaviors of four page replacement algorithms

F = page fault occurring after the frame allocation is initially filled.

(iii) First-in First-out (FIFO)

This policy treats page frames allocated to a process as a circular buffer. It is the simplest replacement policy to implement. In this scheme, the page that has been in memory the longest is replaced. But the drawback is that, these pages may be needed again very soon. Continuing to the example shown in Fig. 8.4

the FIFO policy results in six page faults. Note that LRU recognizes that pages 2 and 5 are referenced more frequently than other pages, whereas FIFO does not.

(iv) Clock Policy

The simplest form of clock policy requests an additional bit with each frame called a use bit. When a page is first loaded in memory, the use bit is set to 1. When the page is referenced (after the reference that generated the page fault), the use bit is set to 1. When it is time to replace a page, the first frame encountered with the use bit set to 0 is replaced. During the search for replacement, each use bit set to 1 is changed to 0.

This policy uses a bit called use bit to replace a page:

- Use bit is set to 1 once a page is loaded into the memory.
- The set of frame are structured into a circular buffer.
- Once a page is replaced the pointer is set to the next element (frame) of the buffer.
- Operating system starts scanning the buffer and looks for a frame with use bit 0.
- If it finds it, frame is replaced.
- If not means the bit is 1, so it sets that bit to 0 and proceeds to the next frame and so on.
- After a full circle if it has not found any frame with 0 use bit, it replaces the original position frame (from where it started).

The behavior of clock policy is illustrated in Fig. 8.4. The presence of an asterisk indicates that the corresponding use bit is equal to 1, and arrow indicates the current position of the pointer.

9

File System Interface and Implementation

9.1 FILE CONCEPT

A *file* is a container that holds information. Most of the files you use contain information (data) in some particular format—a document, a spreadsheet, a chart. The format is the particular way the data is arranged inside the file. The format of a file is known as its *data type*.

When File Manager is in one of its icon-view modes, you can identify the data type of a file by the icon used to represent the file. Each data type has a different icon.

Most application programs understand a limited number of data types. For example, a document editor probably cannot read a spreadsheet file. The desktop helps you recognize different types of files using a data type database. A data type identifies the files of a particular format and associates them with the appropriate applications. These associations mean you don't have to remember commands to accomplish frequent tasks. In most cases, when you double-click a file, the desktop will automatically launch the application that understands that file's data type. The typical file system structure is shown in Fig. 9.2.

The maximum allowable length of a file name varies from system to system. Some operating systems do not allow file names longer than 14 characters.

A *folder* is a container for files, similar to a folder in a file cabinet. In fact, File Manager uses a folder icon to represent a folder. A folder can contain other folders—sometimes called subfolders. With folders and subfolders, you can create multiple layers of organization that form a hierarchy. In other contexts, folders are often referred to as directories.

If you draw a picture of the folder hierarchy with each subfolder underneath the folder that contains it—its parent folder—and draw a line from each folder to its parent, the picture would look like an upside-down tree. Therefore, we often call the folder hierarchy a *folder tree.*

Within any single folder, each file name must be unique. However, files in different folders may have the same name.

As you navigate from folder to folder, your current location is referred to as the *current folder*.

Since files and folders are both represented in File Manager as icons, the term *object* is used to describe them both. Objects are discrete things on the desktop that you can create and manipulate.

On the desktop, applications can also be represented as objects. For example, Application Manager contains objects representing the applications available on your system.

The location of a file is often specified by listing the folders and subfolders that lead to the file—this list is called a *path*. A file's path is visible in two places in File Manager. First, it is shown in the iconic path as a string of folders. Second, it is shown in a text form in the text path line above the view area. These two areas can be turned off.

Paths and Path Names

The path to an object is a way to specify where the object is located in the file system. There are two ways to specify the path: absolute path and relative path.

Absolute Paths

A path is an *absolute path* if it begins at the root folder. The *root folder* is the single common folder on your system where the hierarchy begins. If a path begins with a slash (/), it is an absolute path specified from the root folder. For example, the following is an absolute path to the file letter 1:

/usr12/det/ letters/letter 1

Relative Paths

A path is *relative* if it describes the location of a file or folder as it relates to the current folder. If you are in a folder and you want to move down the folder tree, you don't need to type the absolute path name. You can just type the path starting with the name of the next folder in the path. If a path does not begin with a slash, it is a relative path. For example, if the current folder is /usr12/det and you want to move to the folder/usr12/det/letters/letter0, the relative path is to be used:

/letter/letter 0

Two special folder names are useful when specifying relative paths. The '.' folder (sometimes called 'dot') represents the current folder. The '..' folder (sometimes called 'dot-dot') represents the *parent* folder—the folder one level up in the folder hierarchy. For example, if your current folder is /usr12/det/letters, then the relative path to the Dtwm file becomes:

../app-defaults/*language*/Dtwm

because the file is in the /usr/dt/app-defaults/*language* folder, one level above the current folder and in the app-defaults/*language* subfolder.

9.2 FILE ACCESS METHODS

There are several ways that the information in the file can be accessed. Some systems provide only one access method for files. On other systems, many different access methods are supported, and choosing the right one for a particular application is a major design problem.

Sequential Access

Information in the file is processed in order, one record after the other. This is by far the most common mode of access of files. For example, computer editors usually access files in this fashion. A read operation reads the next portion of the file and automatically advances the file pointer. Similarly, a write appends to the end of the file and the file pointer. Similarly, a write appends to the end of the file and advances to the end of the newly written material (the new end of file). Such a file can be reset to the beginning, and, on some systems, a program may be able to skip forward or backward *n* records, for some integer *n*. This scheme is known as sequential access to a file. Sequential access is based on a tape model of a file.

Direct Access

Direct access is based on a disk model of a file. For direct access, the file is viewed as a numbered sequence of block or records. A direct access file allows arbitrary blocks to be read or written. Thus, after block 18 has been read, block 57 could be next, and then block 3. There are no restrictions on the order of reading and writing for a direct access file. Direct access files are of great use for intermediate access to large amounts of information.

The file operations must be modified to include the block number as a parameter. Thus, we have 'read *n*', where *n* is the block number, rather than 'read next', and 'write *n*', rather that 'write next'. An alternative approach is to retain 'read next' and 'write next' and to add an operation; 'position file to *n*' where *n* is the block number. Then, to effect a 'read *n*', we would issue the commands 'position to *n*' and then 'read next'.

Not all OS support both sequential and direct access for files. Some systems allow only sequential file access; others allow only direct access. Some systems require that a file be defined as sequential or direct when it is created; such a file can be accessed only in a manner consistent with its declaration.

Other Access Methods

Other access methods can be built on top of a direct access method. These additional methods generally involve the construction of an index for a file. The index contains pointers to the various blocks. To find an entry in the file, the index is searched first and the pointer is then used to access the file directly to find the desired entry. With a large file, the index itself may become too large to be kept in memory. One solution is to create an index for the index file. The primary index file would contain pointers to secondary index files, which would point to the actual data items. For example, IBM's indexed sequential access method (ISAM) uses a small master index that points to disk blocks of a secondary index. The secondary index blocks point to the actual file blocks. The file is kept sorted on a defined key. To find a particular item, we first make a binary search of the master index, which provides the block number of the secondary index. This block is read in, and again a binary search is used to find the block containing the desired record. Finally, this block is searched sequentially. In this way, any record can be located from its key by at most direct access reads.

9.3 FILE ALLOCATION METHODS

One main problem in file management is how to allocate space for files so that disk space is utilized effectively and files can be accessed quickly. Three major methods of allocating disk space are contiguous, linked, and indexed. Each method has its advantages and disadvantages. Accordingly, some systems support all three. More commonly, a system will use one particular method for all files.

9.3.1 Contiguous Allocation

The contiguous allocation method requires each file to occupy a set of contiguous address on the disk. Disk addresses define a linear ordering on the disk. Notice that, with this ordering, accessing block $b + 1$ after block b normally requires no head movement. When head movement is needed (from the last sector of one cylinder to the first sector of the next cylinder), it is only one track. Thus, the number of disk seeks required for accessing contiguous allocated files is minimal, as is seek time when a seek is finally needed. Contiguous allocation of a file is defined by the disk address and the length of the first block. If the file is n blocks long, and starts at location b, then it occupies blocks $b, b + 1, b + 2, \ldots, b + n - 1$. The directory entry for each file indicates the address of the starting block and the length of the area allocated for this file.

The difficulty with contiguous allocation is finding space for a new file. If the file to be created is n blocks long, then the OS must search for n free contiguous blocks. First-fit, best-fit, and worst-fit strategies (as discussed in Chapter 4 on multiple partition allocation) are the most common strategies used to select a free hole from the set of available holes. Simulations have shown that both first-fit and best-fit are better than worst-fit in terms of both time storage utilization. Neither first-fit nor best-fit is clearly best in terms of storage utilization, but first-fit is generally faster.

These algorithms also suffer from external fragmentation. As files are allocated and deleted, the free disk space is broken into little pieces. External fragmentation exists whēn enough total disk space exists to satisfy a request, but this space is not contiguous; storage is fragmented into a large number of small holes.

Another problem with contiguous allocation is determining how much disk space is needed for a file. When the file is created, the total amount of space it will need must be known and allocated. How does the creator (program or person) know the size of the file to be created. In some cases, this determination may be fairly simple (e.g. copying an existing file) but in general the size of an output file may be difficult to estimate.

This method requires each file to occupy a set of contiguous blocks on the disk. With the linear order of addresses on disk, i.e. both b+ block is accessed after block b. Number of disk seeks for accessing contiguous allocated file is minimum.

Contiguous allocation of file is defined by the disk addresses and length of first block (Fig. 9.1). If there are n block and start location is b the blocks occupied are $b, b + 1, b + 2, \ldots\ldots, b + n - 1, b + n$. Both sequential and direct access are supported by contiguous allocation where blocks are referred by their number.

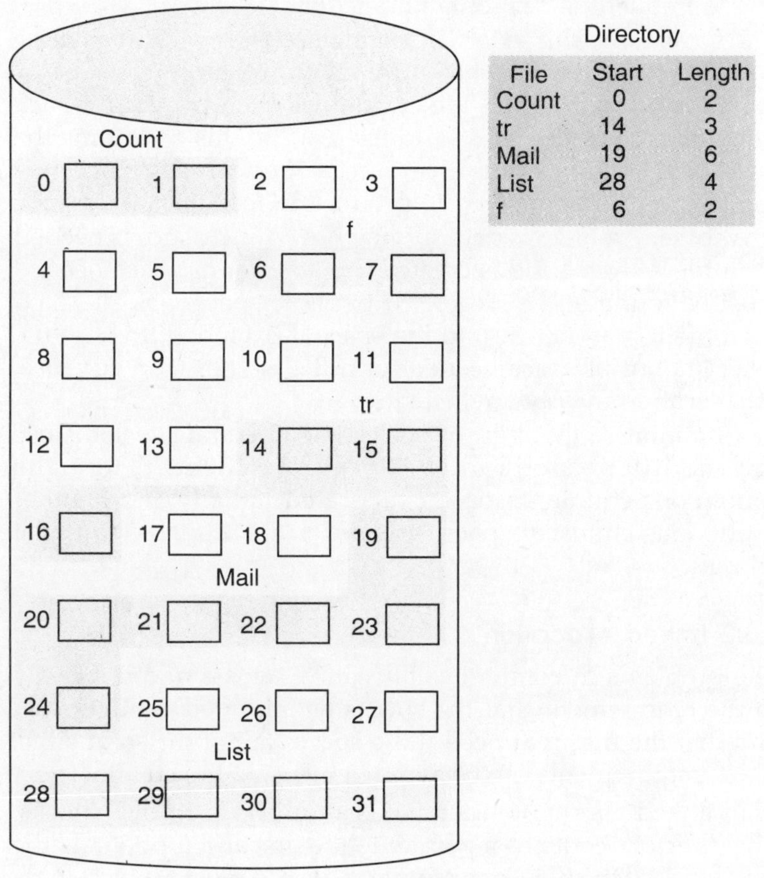

File	Start	Length
Count	0	2
tr	14	3
Mail	19	6
List	28	4
f	6	2

Fig. 9.1: Contiguous allocation of disk space

Difficulty in contiguous allocation is finding new space for a new file. Free space management determines this space allocation is an application of dynamic storage allocation. First-fit and best-fit are strategies used but first-fit is generally faster.

Problems in Contiguous Allocation

Algorithms used for dynamic storage allocation suffer from the problem of external fragmentation. This external fragmentation arises when free space is broken into chunks due to frequent allocation and deletion.

To overcome this external fragmentation repacking is done manually, i.e. copying the entire date on disk into a tape or floppy disk and freeing the entire disk then copying it back from the tape or floppy disk to the disk. So this downtime the normal system operation cannot be performed hence this compaction is not allowed in production machines.

Another problem is determining how much space is needed for a file. When a file is created the amount of space needed must be found and allocated. If too little space was allocated for a file it may not fit into the space if extended. Even if the total amount of space needed for a file is known in advance. Preallocation may be inefficient.

To minimize these drawbacks some operating systems use the modified contiguous allocation scheme. Here the contiguous chunk of space is allocated initially and another contiguous chunk of space is added to its 'extends' to initial allocation.

9.3.2 Linked Allocation

The problems in contiguous allocation can be traced directly to the requirement that the spaces be allocated contiguously and that the files that need these spaces are of different sizes. These requirements can be avoided by using linked allocation.

In linked allocation, each file is a linked list of disk blocks. The directory contains a pointer to the first and (optionally the last) block of the file. For example, a file of 5 blocks which starts at block 4, might continue at block 7, then block 16, block 10, and finally block 27. Each block contains a pointer to the next block and the last block contains a NIL pointer. The value –1 may be used for NIL to differentiate it from block 0.

With linked allocation, each directory entry has a pointer to the first disk block of the file. This pointer is initialized to nil (the end-of-list pointer value) to signify an empty file. A write to a file removes the first free block and writes to that block. This new block is then linked to the end of the file. To read a file, the pointers are just followed from block to block.

There is no external fragmentation with linked allocation. Any free block can be used to satisfy a request. Notice also that there is no need to declare the size of a file when that file is created. A file can continue to grow as long as there are free blocks. Linked allocation does have disadvantages however. The major problem is that it is inefficient to support direct access; it is effective only for sequential-access files. To find the *i*th block of a file, it must start at the beginning of that file and follow the pointers until the *i*th block is reached. Note that each access to a pointer requires a disk read.

Another severe problem is reliability. A bug in OS or disk hardware failure might result in pointers being lost and damaged. The effect of which could be picking up a wrong pointer and linking it to a free block or into another file.

Linked allocation solves all the problems of contiguous allocation. Even if the disk blocks are scattered on the disk the files can be linked. To create a new file a new entry can just be created in the directory. With this method of linked allocation each directory entry has a pointer to the first disk block of the file. This pointer is intialised to nil to represent empty file. Now the size field is also zero. Writing a file causes a free block to be searched first through free space management system and linked to end of file. A file can continue to grow as long as free blocks are available.

Reading a file is done by following the pointers from block to block.

Disadvantages of linked allocation:

- It can be used only for sequential access files. To find the *i*th block of a file the search should start from beginning of that file following the pointers to reach the *i*th block. Direct access is not supported.

- Space required for the pointers. For instance, if a pointer requires 4 bytes out of 512 byte block then 0.78% of disk space is used for pointers rather than for information.

Solution to this is to collect block into multiples called clusters and allocate clusters rather than blocks. Drawback also exists with this since only if part of cluster is used the rest of space is wasted so block is preferable here.

- Reliability is another problem. Since all files are linked through pointers if a damage occurs to one pointer then no tracing or follow-up can be done.

Linked allocation method uses the file allocation table (FAT). FAT is similar to that of a linked list. A section of disk at the beginning of each partition is set aside to contain a table. A table has one entry for each disk block, indexed with a block number. FAT table has an end-of-file value. Unused blocks are indicated by a 0 table value hence allocation of blocks to newly created file is easier.

9.3.3 Indexed Allocation

The indexed allocation method is the solution to the problem of both contiguous and linked allocation. This is done by bringing all the pointers together into one location called the index block. Of course, the index block will occupy some space and thus could be considered as an overhead of the method. In indexed allocation, each file has its own index block, which is an array of disk sector of addresses. The ith entry in the index block points to the *i*th sector of the file. The directory contains the address of the index block of a file. To read the *i*th sector of the file, the pointer in the ith index block entry is read to find the desired sector. Indexed allocation supports direct access, without suffering from external fragmentation. Any free block anywhere on the disk may satisfy a request for more space.

Linked allocation solves the problem of external fragmentation but impossible in the absence of FAT. In the absence of FAT linking cannot be done since pointers are scattered. To overcome this indexed allocation solves the problem by bringing all pointers together into a location called index block.

Each file has an index block. Index block is an array of disk block addresses. The ith entry in index block points to the *i*th block of the file. When a file is created, all pointers in the index block are set to nil. When the *i*th block is written, a block is obtained from the free space manager and its address is put into the index block entry.

Indexed allocation also suffers from wasted space. Pointers overhead of index block is greater than that of linked allocation.

If we consider that there are only one or two blocks of data then one pointer is required for each and hence much space is wasted. Now arises the question of how large the index block should be.

Every file must have an index block. So the index block must be small. If it is small thus it cannot hold pointers for large file then the following issues are to be considered:

- ***Linked scheme:*** An index block is normally one disk block. For large files it can occupy several index blocks 'next address is nil' or a pointer to another index block.
- ***Multilevel index:*** Linked representation uses a first level index block to point to a set of second level index block which points to file blocks. This is needed by o/s for block access. This approach continues to maximum file size. For instance about 10.48,576 data blocks and a maximum file size of 4 GB is accessible.
- ***Combined scheme:*** A method used in UFS allocates specified pointers of index block in file's inode. It comprises say 15 pointers in total with first 12 to direct blocks and the remaining 3 to single indirect, double indirect and triple indirect.

9.4 FREE SPACE MANAGEMENT

Since there is only a limited amount of disk space, it is necessary to reuse the space from deleted files for new files. To keep track of free disk space, the system maintains a free-space list. The free-space list records all disk blocks that are free, i.e. are not allocated to some file. To create a file, the free-space list has to be searched for the required amount of space, and allocate that space to a new file. This space is then removed from the free-space list. When a file is deleted, its disk space is added to the free-space list.

9.4.1 Bit-Vector

Frequently, the free-space list is implemented as a bit map or bit vector. Each block is represented by a 1 bit. If the block is free, the bit is 0; if the block is allocated, the bit is 1.

For example, consider a disk where blocks 2, 3, 4, 5, 8, 9, 10, 11, 12, 13, 17, 18, 25, 26, and 27 are free, and the rest of the blocks are allocated. The free-space bit map would be:

110000110000001110011111100011111...

The main advantage of this approach is that it is relatively simple and efficient to find *n* consecutive free blocks on the disk. Unfortunately, bit vectors are inefficient unless the entire vector is kept in memory for most accesses. Keeping it main memory is possible for smaller disks such as on micro-computers, but not for larger ones.

9.4.2 Linked List

Another approach is to link all the free disk blocks together, keeping a pointer to the first free block. This block contains a pointer to the next free disk block, and so on. In the previous example, a pointer could be kept to block 2, as the first free block. Block 2 would contain a pointer to block 3, which would point to block 4, which would point to block 5, which would point to block 8, and so on. This scheme is not efficient; to traverse the list, each block must be read, which requires substantial I/O time

9.4.3 Grouping

A modification of the free-list approach is to store the addresses of *n* free blocks in the first free block. The first $n - 1$ of these are actually free. The last one is the disk address of another block containing addresses of another *n* free blocks. The importance of this implementation is that addresses of a large number of free blocks can be found quickly.

9.4.4 Counting

Another approach is to take advantage of the fact that, generally, several contiguous blocks may be allocated or freed simultaneously, particularly when contiguous allocation is used. Thus, rather than keeping a list of free disk addresses, the address of the first free block is kept and the number *n* of free contiguous blocks that follow the first block. Each entry in the free-space list then consists of a disk address and a count. Although each entry requires more space than would a simple disk address, the overall list will be shorter, as long as the count is generally greater than 1.

9.5 DIRECTORY STRUCTURES

File directory structure is based on several file characteristics that determine how the file is classified and how it is handled during file manipulation operations. These characteristics are discussed in the following subsections.

Files can be classified on the basis of domain. The domain of a file determines if it is permanent, is temporary, or exists only for one particular process.

The File System maintains separate directories to record the location of PERMANENT and TEMP files. PERMANENT files are recorded in the System File Directory; and TEMP files, in the Job Temporary File Directory. A permanent or temporary file can be opened or closed with a file domain of OLD.

9.5.1 NEW Files

When you create a file, you can indicate to the File System that it is a NEW file; it did not previously exist. Space for this file has not yet been allocated. As a NEW file, only the program that creates it knows about it, and it exists only while the program is executing. When the program concludes, the file vanishes, unless you take action to retain it.

9.5.2 TEMP Files

A TEMP file is one that already exists, but only the job or session that created it knows about it. Some or all of the space for the file has been allocated, and its physical characteristics have been defined. A file in this domain is a job temporary file; it has been created for a specific purpose by its job or session. It may not be needed after the job or session ends. When the job or session concludes, the file automatically disappears, unless you take action to change it to a PERMANENT file. This is described in the 'Changing Domains' subsection below.

9.5.3 PERMANENT Files

A PERMANENT file exists as a permanent file in the File System. Its existence is not limited to the duration of its creating job or session. Any job or session can access the file when security restrictions allow. Some or all of the space for the file has been allocated, and its physical characteristics have been defined. When the job or session concludes, the file remains.

9.5.4 Effect of File Domain on Operations

You can select or change the domain disposition of a file when you close the file using the FCLOSE intrinsic. This is called the closing disposition of the file and follows these rules:

- Any file can be deleted when closed. This is the default for a NEW file.
- A NEW file can be changed to a TEMP file when closed.
- A NEW or TEMP file can be changed to PERMANENT when closed.
- A PERMANENT file can be changed to a TEMP when closed by a PM (privileged mode) user.

The File System action defaults to delete a NEW file, temporarily keep a TEMP file, and save a PERMANENT file. The way in which subsystems use files affects these defaults. You can specify a closing disposition with a FILE command that overrides how the program or subsystem closes the file.

The FCLOSE intrinsic is called for every file on which an HPFOPEN or FOPEN has been performed. The File System ensures that an opened file is automatically closed at program termination, without requiring an explicit statement. However, a subsystem must explicitly call FCLOSE to ensure that the action taken will be as specified in your program.

Determining file disposition at close time can have consequences on running programs (especially in batch mode). For example, a program can open a NEW file by default, write data to the file, and attempt to save the file as OLD. A directory error (for example, a duplicate file name) can be detected only at close time; and data is lost, unless you have used one of the following methods to check for or avoid the situation:

- Create a NEW file by using BUILD before executing the program in which the file is opened as an OLD file.
- Delete the previous copy of the file before the run.
- Rename the existing file by using FRENAME.

The File System closes files when it terminates a program, without requiring the program to explicitly close them. This allows no recourse for accidentally losing data. It is a recommended programming practice, when the content of a file is important, to write the program to properly handle closing disposition.

The CREATE domain of HPFOPEN creates a NEW file and makes it PERMANENT when closed. It eliminates the need to HPFOPEN or FOPEN it as a NEW file, HPFCLOSE or FCLOSE it as a PERMANENT file, and open it with HPFOPEN or FOPEN again as an OLD file.

9.5.5 Changing Domains

A file's domain can be changed. Any disc file can be made permanent or can be deleted after it has served its purpose. You can use the disposition parameter of the FCLOSE intrinsic to specify a different domain for a file as it closes. You can use the FILE command to change the domain of a file; specifying the DEL, TEMP or SAVE parameter determines the disposition of a file when it is closed after its next use. The DEL parameter deletes a file after its next use. The TEMP parameter changes the domain of a NEW file to TEMP when it is closed. The SAVE parameter changes the domain of a NEW or TEMP file to PERMANENT when it is closed. You can change the domain of a file from TEMP to PERMANENT without opening and closing the file by using the SAVE command. This command prompts you for the lockword if the file has one.

9.6 FILE SPECIFICATIONS

File specifications allow you to identify a file. This is necessary in order to:

- Locate it in the directory structure.

- Refer to it from a command or program.
- Determine how to handle it during file manipulations such as opening and closing.
- Transfer it during I/O.

The File System uses several designations and classifications to facilitate file identification. The use of file designators and classes allows the File System to recognize a file so that commands and programs can reference it. MPE/iX allows you to designate a name for a file in several ways.

This designation differs from PERMANENT only in the fact that first the Job Temporary File Directory and then the System Permanent File Directory are searched for the file name. OLD files are described in the 'Closing a File' subsection. There is no File System directory for files that exist only to their creating process (NEW files).

The structure of the directories and the relationship among them are the main areas where file systems tend to differ, and it is also the area that has the most significant effect on the user interface provided by the file system. The most common directory structures used by multi-user systems are:

- Single-level directory
- Two-level directory
- Tree-structured directory
- Acyclic directory

9.6.1 Single-Level Directory

In a single-level directory system, all the files are placed in one directory. This is very common on single user OSs. A single-level directory has significant limitations, however, when the number of files increases or when there is more than one user. Since all files are in the same directory, they must have unique names. If there are two users who call their data file 'test', then the unique name rule is violated. Although file names are generally selected to reflect the content of the file, they are often quite limited in length. Even with a single user, as the number of files increases, it becomes difficult to remember the names of all the files in order to create only files with unique names.

9.6.2 Two-Level Directory

In the two-level directory system, the system maintains a master block that has one entry for each user. This master block contains the addresses of the directory of the users.

There are still problems with two-level directory structure. This structure effectively isolates one user from another. This is an advantage when the users are completely independent, but a disadvantage when the users want to cooperate on some task and access files of other users. Some systems simply do not allow local files to be accessed by other users.

9.6.3 Tree-Structured Directories

In the tree-structured directory, the directories themselves are files. This leads to the possibility of having sub-directories that can contain files and sub-subdirectories. An interesting policy decision in a tree-structured directory structure is how to handle the deletion of a directory. If a directory is empty, its entry in its containing directory can simply be deleted. However, suppose the directory to be deleted is not empty, but contains several files, or possibly sub-directories. Some systems will not delete a directory unless it is empty.

Thus, to delete a directory, someone must first delete all the files in that directory. If these are any sub-directories, this procedure must be applied recursively to them, so that they can be deleted also. This approach may result in a insubstantial amount of work. An alternative approach is just to assume that, when a request is made to delete a directory, all of that directory's files and sub-directories are also to be deleted.

9.6.4 Acyclic-Graph Directories

The acyclic directory structure is an extension of the tree-structured directory structure. In the tree-structured directory, files and directories starting from some fixed directory are owned by one particular user. In the acyclic structure, this prohibition is taken out and thus a directory or file under directory can be owned by several users.

9.7 FILE SYSTEM—MOUNTING

The process of incorporating a file system into the existing directory structure is known as mounting the file system. The file system can be on a disk or disks connected directly to your system, that is, a *local* file system, or it can be part of a *remote* NFS file system, and it can be on either a non-LVM disk or a logical volume.

Mounting a file system associates it with a directory in the existing file system tree. Prior to mounting, the files, although present on the disk, are not accessible to users; once mounted, the file system becomes accessible.

The directory in the existing file system where the file is attached is known as the mount point or mount directory for the new file system, and the files in the added file system become part of the existing file system hierarchy.

The mount point should be an empty subdirectory on the existing file system. If you mount a file system onto a directory that already has files in it, those files will be hidden and inaccessible until you unmount the file system. If you try to mount the file system onto a directory whose files are in use, the mount will fail.

9.7.1 Mounting Local File Systems

To mount a local file system:

1. Choose an empty directory to serve as the mount point for the file system. Use the mkdir command to create the directory if it does not currently exist. For example, enter:

   ```
   mkdir /directory1
   ```

2. Mount the file system using the mount command. Use the block device file name that contains the file system. You will need to enter this name as an argument to the mount command. For example, enter:

   ```
   mount /dev/vg01/lvol1 /directory1
   ```

9.7.2 Mounting Remote File Systems

You can use either SAM or the mount command to mount file systems located on a remote system.

Before you can mount file systems located on a remote system, NFS software must be installed and configured on both local and remote systems. Refer to *Installing and Administering NFS* for information.

For information on mounting NFS file systems using SAM, see SAM's online help.

To mount a remote file system using HP-UX commands:

1. You must know the name of the host machine and the file system's directory on the remote machine.
2. Establish communication over a network between the local system (that is, the 'client') and the remote system. (The local system must be able to reach the remote system via whatever hosts database is in use.) [See *named* (1 M) and *hosts* (4)]. If necessary, test the connection with/usr/sbin/ping; see *ping* (1 M).
3. Make sure the file/etc./exports on the remote system lists the file systems that you wish to make available to clients (that is, to 'export') and the local systems that you wish to mount the file systems.

   For example, to allow machines called rolf and egbert to remotely mount the/usr file system, edit the file/etc./exports on the remote machine and include the line:

   /usr rolf egbert

4. Execute/usr/sbin/exports -a on the remote system to export all directories in /etc./exports to clients.
5. Mount the file system on the local system, as in:

   mount-F nfs remotehost:/remote_dir /local_dir

9.8 FILE SHARING

'File sharing' is not a new concept; file sharing tools have been available nearly as long as the Internet. However, new types of file sharing tools—and their uses—have recently become the center of a great deal of media attention. There are three basic models of file sharing: system-native file sharing, client-server file sharing and peer-to-peer file sharing.

- ***System-native file sharing:*** This type of file sharing is built into the operating system, originally intended for sharing files (and often printers) with other users in the local network, and not intended for sharing files with others across the Internet.

- ***Client-server file sharing:*** This model covers web pages, email, FTP, and other types of file sharing where the data is stored in a central location (the server) and sent separately to each user who requests it (the clients). This model is the most commonly used type of file sharing on the Internet.
- ***Peer-to-peer file sharing:*** Peer-to-peer file sharing doesn't rely on a single central server. Any two users (the clients in the above model) can exchange data with each other directly, rather than having one user upload files to the server and the other user download files from the server.

9.9 FILE SYSTEM STRUCTURE

9.9.1 Logical File System—Overview

The *logical file system* is the level of the file system at which users can request file operations by system call. This level of the file system provides the kernel with a consistent view of what might be multiple physical file systems and multiple file system implementations. As far as the logical file system is concerned, file system types, whether local, remote, or strictly logical, and regardless of implementation, are indistinguishable.

A consistent view of file system implementations is made possible by the virtual file system abstraction. This abstraction specifies the set of file system operations that an implementation must include in order to carry out logical file system requests. Physical file systems can differ in how they implement these predefined operations, but they must present a uniform interface to the logical file system. A list of file system operators can be found at requirements for a File System Implementation.

Each set of predefined operations implemented constitutes a virtual file system. As such, a single physical file system can appear to the logical file system as one or more separate virtual file systems.

Virtual file system operations are available at the logical file system level through the *virtual file system switch*. This array contains one entry for each virtual file system, with each entry holding entry point addresses for separate operations. Each file system type has a set of entries in the virtual file system switch.

The logical file system and the virtual file system switch support other operating system file-system access semantics. This does not mean that only other operating system file systems can be supported. It does mean, however, that a file system implementation must be designed to fit into the logical file system model. Operations or information requested from a file system implementation need be performed only to the extent possible.

Logical file system can also refer to the tree of known path names in force while the system is running. A virtual file system that is mounted onto the logical file system tree itself becomes part of that tree. In fact, a single virtual file system can be mounted onto the logical file system tree at multiple points, so that nodes in the virtual subtree have multiple names. Multiple mount points allow maximum flexibility when constructing the logical file system view.

9.9.2 Logical File System—Component Structure

The logical file system is divided into the following components:

- *System calls:* Implement services exported to users. System calls that carry out file system requests do the following:
  - Map the user's parameters to a file system object. This requires that the system call component use the v-node (virtual node) component to follow the object's path name. In addition, the system call must resolve a file descriptor or establish implicit (mapped) references using the open file component.
  - Verify that a requested operation is applicable to the type of the specified object.
  - Dispatch a request to the file system implementation to perform operations.
- ***Logical file system file routines:*** Manage open file table entries and per-process file descriptors. An open file table entry records the authorization of a process's access to a file system object. A user can refer to an open file table entry

through a file descriptor or by accessing the virtual memory to which the file was mapped. The logical file system routines are those kernel services, such as **fp_ioctl** and **fp_select**, that begin with the prefix **fp_**.

- *v-nodes:* Provide system calls with a mechanism for local name resolution. Local name resolution allows the logical file system to access multiple file system implementations through a uniform name space.

9.9.3 File Organization Module (The Basic I/O Supervisor)

The FOM is responsible for the instigation and termination of the I/O. It will also select the correct device on the basis of a file and keep a note of the files a process has active. Disk scheduling is handled by this routine, as well as secondary memory space allocation. I/O buffers too will be created and supervised.

Only parts of this section made it to the implementation design stage. The following is an explanation of a few of the routines designed for this module.

- Select Device
- Clear FAT
- Read FAT
- Write FAT
- Allocate (From free list)
- Return (To free list)

Select Device will determine, from the application and file, to/from which device the file must be accessed. This could be the backing storage, CD-Rom or Tape. Access to the correct device driver is decided upon by this identification. On making a file request the file name would be parsed and the device inferred from the volume on which the file was resident. This information would be stored on the OFT to speed access when further file requests were processed. **Clear FAT**, **Read FAT** and **Write FAT** provide a means to manipulate the File Allocation Table. As this is a simple array data structure, it will ensure the simplicity of the algorithm. Clear FAT provides a means to initialize the structure at boot time. A simple sequential traversal of the structure will be sufficient. Read FAT will be comprised of a direct access to the structure based upon the directory address for the start of the file on the FAT. Read FAT will not alter the contents of the FAT. Write FAT makes changes as and when the file is altered. Additional records may cause another disk block to be allocated by the Free Space Manager and therefore, necessitating the generation of a new FAT entry.

Allocate and **Return** are Free Space Manager invocation routines. **Allocate** will return a value from the FSM module upon which a disk write may be based. On the deletion of a file the new free space will be recorded by calling the Return function.

9.10 FILE SYSTEM PROTECTION

When designing file systems, one of the main considerations is how to protect sharable files. Sometimes this is avoided by not permitting sharing of files and hence, protection is quite easy to implement, or make all files public and provide complete sharing. However, neither of this is acceptable to users. There are files that users want to share and there are some which only a group of users should be allowed to access. The solution to this is to allow limited sharing, i.e. users can share but to a limited extent only. Protection is achieved by limiting the type of file access which can be made. Access is permitted or denied depending upon several factors, one of which is the type of access requested. Several operations on files can be controlled. Some of these are:

- *Read:* Read a file.
- *Write:* Write a file.
- *Execute:* Load and execute a file.
- *Append:* Append information at the end of a file.
- *Delete:* Free the space allocated to a file.

The most common implementation of the file systems allow the owners of the file to do operations 1–5, whereas other users can only invoke those operations that do not modify the file, e.g. file read. However, in some systems, e.g. UNIX, the user can change the access control of a file such that he can let anybody access (modification allowed) the file or he can completely deny any user (including himself) access to a file.

The three most popular implementations of file protection are the following:

File naming: This depends upon the inability of a user to access a file he cannot name. This can be implemented by allowing only users to see the files they have created. But since most file systems allow only a limited number of characters for file names, there is no guarantee that two users will not use the same file names.

Passwords: This scheme associates a password to each file. If a user does not know the password associated to a file then he cannot access it. This is a very effective way of protecting files but for a user who owns many files, and constantly changes the password to make sure that nobody accesses these files will require that users have photographic memories.

Access control: An access list is associated to each file or directory. The access list contains information on the type of users and accesses that they can do on a directory or file. An example is the following access list associated with a UNIX file or directory:

drwxrwxrwx

The d indicates that this is an access list for a directory, the first rwx indicates that it can be read, written, and executed by the owner of the file, the second rwx is an access information for users belonging to the same group as the owner (somewhere on the system is a list of users belonging to same group as the owner), and the last rwx for all other users. The rwx can be changed to just *r*—indicating that it can only be read, or —*w*—for write, only *x*—for execute only.

9.11 FILE SYSTEM IMPLEMENTATION

Disk provides bulk of secondary storage on which file system is maintained. Storing multiple files has two characteristics:

1. They can be rewritten.
2. Direct access of any block of information on disk is possible.

For providing efficient and convenient access to disk, o/s imposes file systems to store, locate or retrieve data. There are two different design problems as:

1. Defining how the file system should look to user.

2. Creating algorithms and data structure to map logical file system to physical storage devices.

On-disk and in-memory structures are used to implement a file system.

On-disk structures containing booting information, number of blocks, location and free blocks, directory structure.

On-disk structures include:

- A boot control block (BCB)-contain info needed for booting. If number of o/s is three in disk this BCB is empty. In UFS this is called boot block and in NTFS it is called partition boot sector.
- A partition control block (PCB) has number of blocks in the partition, size of block, free-block count, free-block pointer, free FCB count and FCB pointers. In UFS it is called superblock and in NTFS it is called master file table.
- A directory structure to organize files.
- FCB-files details including file permission, ownership, size and location of data block. In UFS, it is called inode.

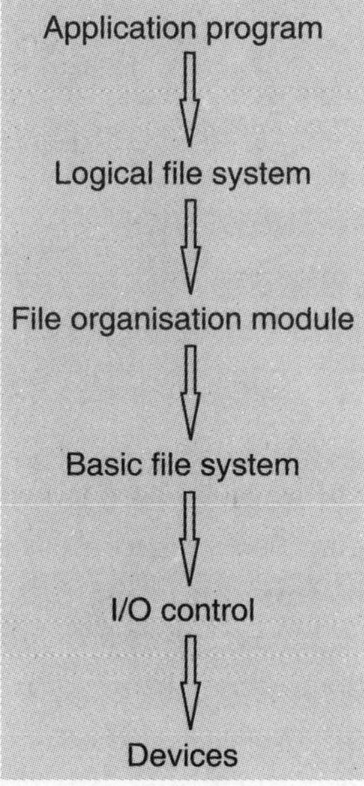

Fig. 9.2: Layered file system

In-memory structures are used for both file-system management and performance via caching. It includes:

- An in-memory partition table containing info about each partition.
- Disk structure to hold directory information of recently accessed directories.
- System wide open file table to hold a copy of FCB (Fig. 9.3) of each open file.
- Perprocess open file table has pointer to particular entry as well as other information.

A typical FCB has the following structure:

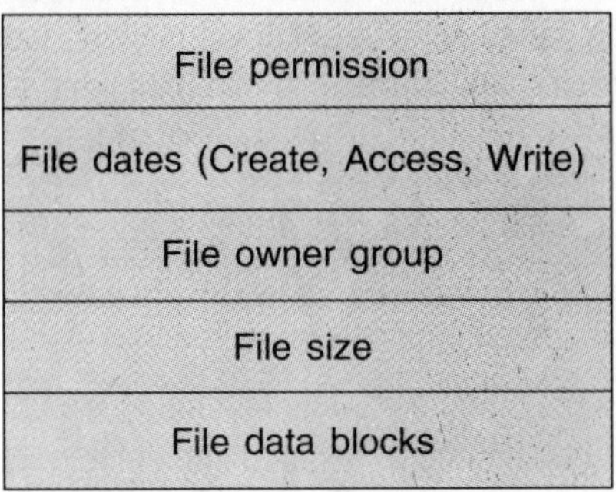

Fig. 9.3: File control block

9.12 DIRECTORY IMPLEMENTATION

Directory allocation also and directory management also have a large effect on efficiency, performance and reliability. The tradeoffs involved in these algorithms are given below.

9.12.1 Linear List

- Simplest method to implement a directory.
- Linear list of file names with pointers to data blocks.
- Directory entry to this linear list needs a linear search to find a particular entry which is a disadvantage.
- This is simple but time-consuming for execution.
- This can be used to decrease the time to delete a file.
- To add a file—search the whole directory if this name exists.
- To delete a file—search the file's location and free that space.

9.12.2 Hash Table

- Hash table takes a value computed from the file name and returns a pointer to the file name in linear list.
- This decreases the directory search time.
- Collision may occur when two file names hash to the same location.

10

Networking and Distributed Systems

10.16 Middleware
- Distributed Object Middleware
- Challenges
- Architectural Model
- Object Model
- Interfaces
- Naming and Binding
- Remote Method Invocation
- Services

10.17 CORBA

10.18 Synchronisation and Coordination
- Time and Clock
- Coordination and Multicast
- Coordination and Elections
- Transactions
- Concurrency in Transactions
- Distributed Transactions
- Security in Distributed Systems
- Naming
  - Basic Concepts
  - System Names Versus Human Names
  - Name Resolution
  - Naming Service
  - Name Caches
- Distributed File Systems
  - File Access Semantics
  - Stateful Vs Stateless Servers
  - Replication
  - Caching
  - Case Study
    - Network File System
    - Andrew File System
    - Coda
    - Google File System
    - Sprite System

10.1 INTRODUCTION

What is a computer network?

A network is any collection of independent computers that communicate with one another over a shared network medium. A computer network is a collection of two or more connected computers. When these computers are joined in a network, people can share files and peripherals such as modems, printers, tape backup drives or CD-ROM drives. When networks at multiple locations are connected using services available from phone companies, people can send e-mail, share links to the global Internet, or conduct video conferences in real time with other remote users. As companies rely on applications like electronic mail and database management for core business operations, computer networking becomes increasingly more important.

Every network includes:

- At least two computers server or client workstation.
- Networking Interface Card (NIC).
- A connection medium, usually a wire or cable, although wireless communication between networked computers and peripherals is also possible.
- Network operating system software, such as Microsoft Windows NT or 2000, Novell NetWare, Unix and Linux.

10.2 NETWORK TOPOLOGIES

In networking, the term topology refers to the layout of connected devices on a network. It is the logical 'shape' of the network wiring. This *logical* shape does not necessarily correspond to the actual *physical* layout of the devices on the network. For example, the computers on a home LAN may be arranged in a circle, but it would be highly unlikely to find an actual ring topology there.

'Logical' means how it looks as a pure design concept, rather than how it actually looks physically, e.g. the topology pictures you will see have nice straight lines between bits of the network, they don't try to show all the corners that need to be turned and holes that have to be drilled in a real cable installation.

Each topology has its advantages and disadvantages: usually related to cost, complexity, reliability and traffic 'bottlenecks'.

The 5 topologies are: Bus ... Ring ... Star ... Tree ... Mesh.

Bus Topology

Many devices connect to a single cable 'backbone'. If the backbone is broken, the entire segment fails. Bus topologies are relatively easy to install and don't require much cabling compared to the others.

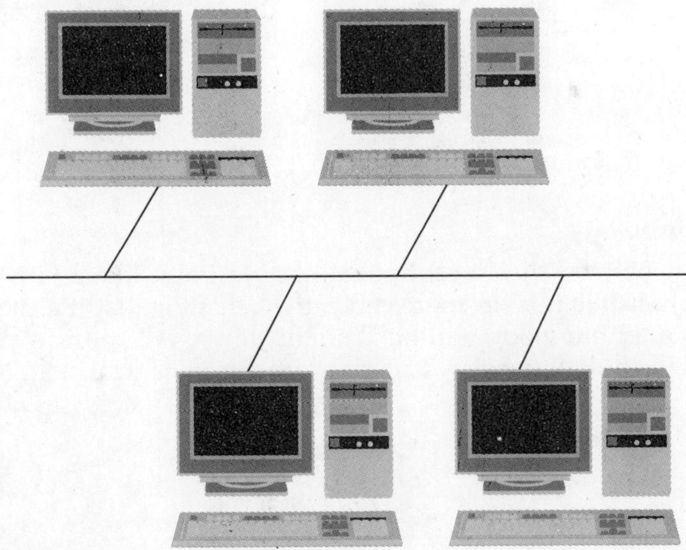

Ring Topology

In a ring network, every device has exactly two neighbours for communication purposes. All messages travel through a ring in the same direction. Like the bus topology, a failure in any cable or device breaks the loop and will take down the entire segment. A disadvantage of the ring is that if any device is added to or removed from the ring, the ring is broken and the segment fails until it is reconstructed. It is also considerably more expensive than other topologies.

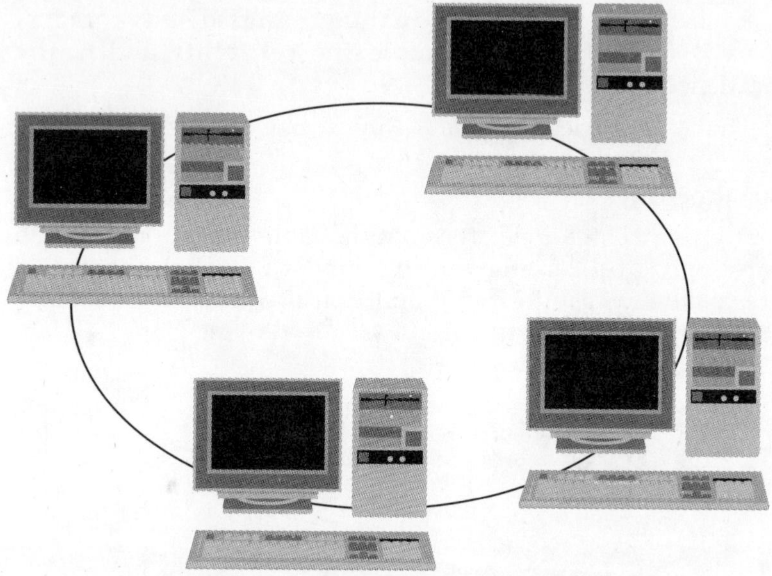

Star Topology

A star network has a central connection point like a hub or switch. While it takes more cable, the benefit is that if a cable fails, only one node will be brought down. All traffic starts from the hub of the star. The central site is in control of all the

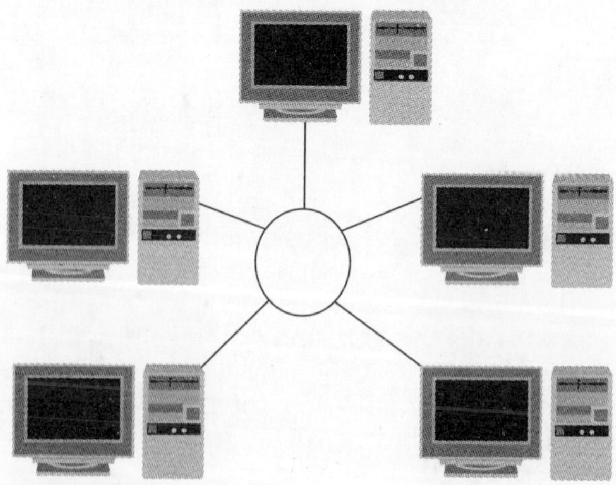

nodes attached to it. The central hub is usually a fast, self-contained computer and is responsible for routing all traffic to other nodes. The main advantages of a star network is that one malfunctioning node does not affect the rest of the network. However, this type of network can be prone to bottleneck and failure problems at the central site.

Tree Topology

Also known as the 'Hierarchical topology', the tree topology is a combination of bus and star topologies. They are very common in larger networks. A typical scenario is: a file server is connected to a backbone cable (e.g. coaxial) that runs through the building, from which switches are connected, branching out to workstations.

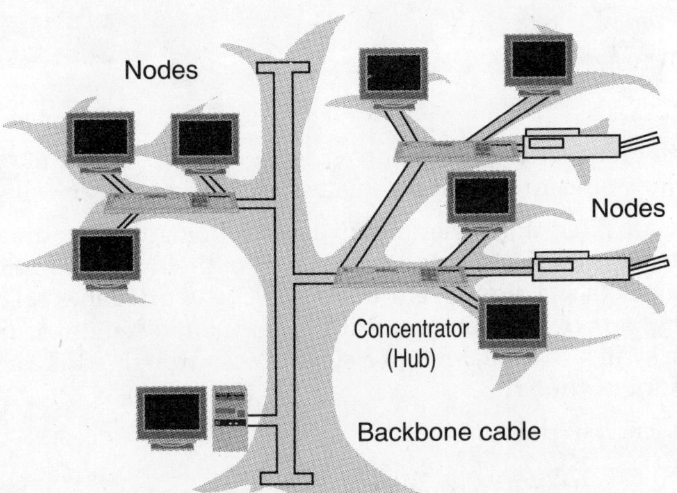

Mesh Topology

In the topologies shown above, there is only one possible path from one node to another node. If any cable in that path is broken, the nodes cannot communicate.

Mesh topology uses lots of cables to connect every node with every other node. It is very expensive to wire up, but if any cable fails, there are many other ways for two nodes to communicate. Some WANs, like the Internet, employ mesh

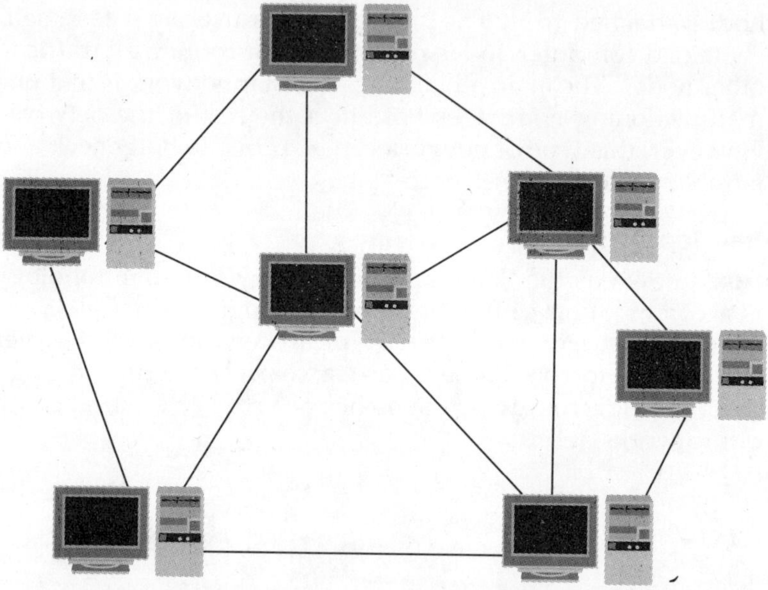

routing. In fact, the Internet was deliberately designed like this to allow sites to communicate even during a nuclear war.

A consideration in setting up a tree topology using Ethernet protocol is the 5–4–3 rule. One aspect of the Ethernet protocol requires that a signal sent out on the network cable reaches every part of the network within a specified length of time. Each switch or repeater that a signal goes through adds a small amount of time.

This leads to the rule that:

- Between any two nodes on the network there can only be a maximum of 5 segments,
- Connected through 4 repeaters/switches, and
- If the segments use coaxial cable, only 3 of them may be populated (trunk) segments .

This rule does not apply in Ethernet networks where all fibre optic cabling or a combination of a fibre backbone with UTP cabling is used. If there is a combination of fibre optic backbone and UTP cabling, the rule is simply translated to 7–6–5 rule.

10.3 TYPES OF NETWORKS

LANs (Local Area Networks)

A network is any collection of independent computers that communicate with one another over a shared network medium. LANs are networks usually confined to a geographic area, such as a single building or a college campus. LANs can be small, linking as few as three computers, but often link hundreds of computers used by thousands of people. The development of standard networking protocols and media has resulted in worldwide proliferation of LANs throughout business and educational organizations.

WANs (Wide Area Networks)

Wide area networking combines multiple LANs that are geographically separate. This is accomplished by connecting the different LANs using services such as dedicated leased phone lines, dial-up phone lines (both synchronous and asynchronous), satellite links, and data packet carrier services. Wide area networking can be as simple as a modem and remote access server for employees to dial into, or it can be as complex as hundreds of branch offices globally linked using special routing protocols and filters to minimize the expense of sending data sent over vast distances.

Internet

The Internet is a system of linked networks that are worldwide in scope and facilitate data communication services such as remote login, file transfer, electronic mail, the World Wide Web and newsgroups.

With the meteoric rise in demand for connectivity, the Internet has become a communications highway for millions of users. The Internet was initially restricted to military and academic institutions, but now it is a full-fledged conduit for any and all forms of information and commerce. Internet websites now provide personal, educational, political and economic resources to every corner of the planet.

Intranet

With the advancements made in browser-based software for the Internet, many private organizations are implementing intranets. An intranet is a private network utilizing Internet-type tools, but available only within that organization. For large organizations, an intranet provides an easy access mode to corporate information for employees.

MANs (Metropolitan Area Networks)

This refers to a network of computers within a city.

VPN (Virtual Private Network)

VPN uses a technique known as tunneling to transfer data securely on the Internet to a remote access server on your workplace network. Using a VPN helps you save money by using the public Internet instead of making long-distance phone calls to connect securely with your private network. There are two ways to create a VPN connection, by dialing an Internet service provider (ISP), or connecting directly to Internet.

10.4 CATEGORIES OF NETWORKS

Network can be divided into two main categories:

- Peer-to-peer.
- Server-based.

In peer-to-peer networking there are no dedicated servers or hierarchy among the computers. All of the computers are equal and therefore, known as peers. Normally each computer serves as client/server and there is no one assigned to be an administrator responsible for the entire network.

Peer-to-peer networks are good choices for needs of small organizations where the users are allocated in the same general area, security is not an issue and the organization and the network will have limited growth within the foreseeable future.

The term client/server refers to the concept of sharing the work involved in processing data between the client computer and the most powerful server computer.

The client/server network is the most efficient way to provide:

- Databases and management of applications such as spreadsheets, accounting, communications and document management.
- Network management.
- Centralized file storage.

The client/server model is basically an implementation of distributed or cooperative processing. At the heart of the model is the concept of splitting application functions between a client and a server processor. The division of labour between the different processors enables the application designer to place an application function on the processor that is most appropriate for that function. This lets the software designer optimize the use of processors—providing the greatest possible return on investment for the hardware.

Client/server application design also lets the application provider mask the actual location of application function. The user often does not know where a specific operation is executing. The entire function may execute in either the PC or server, or the function may be split between them. This masking of application function locations enables system implementers to upgrade portions of a system over time with a minimum disruption of application operations, while protecting the investment in existing hardware and software.

10.5 NETWORK ARCHITECTURES

Ethernet

Ethernet is the most popular physical layer LAN technology in use today. Other LAN types include Token Ring, Fast Ethernet, Fiber Distributed Data Interface (FDDI), Asynchronous Transfer Mode (ATM) and LocalTalk. Ethernet is popular because it strikes a good balance between speed, cost and ease of installation. These benefits, combined with wide acceptance in the computer marketplace and the ability to support virtually all popular network protocols, make Ethernet an ideal networking technology for most computer users today. The Institute for Electrical and Electronic Engineers (IEEE) defines the Ethernet standard as IEEE Standard 802.3. This standard defines rules for configuring an Ethernet network as well as specifying how elements in an Ethernet network interact with one another. By adhering to the IEEE standard, network equipment and network protocols can communicate efficiently.

Fast Ethernet

For Ethernet networks that need higher transmission speeds, the Fast Ethernet standard (IEEE 802.3 u) has been established. This standard raises the Ethernet speed limit from 10 Megabits per second (Mbps) to 100 Mbps with only minimal changes to the existing cable structure. There are three types of Fast Ethernet: 100 BASE-TX for use with level 5 UTP cable, 100 BASE-FX for use with fiber-optic cable, and 100BASE-T4 which utilizes an extra two wires for use with level 3 UTP cable. The 100 BASE-TX standard has become the most popular due to its close compatibility with the 10 BASE-T Ethernet standard. For the network manager, the incorporation of Fast Ethernet into an existing configuration presents a host of decisions. Managers must determine the number of users in each site on the network that need the higher throughput, decide which segments of the backbone need to be reconfigured specifically for 100 BASE-T and then choose the necessary hardware to connect the 100 BASE-T segments with existing 10 BASE-T segments. Gigabit Ethernet is a future technology that promises a migration path beyond Fast Ethernet so the next generation of networks will support even higher data transfer speeds.

Token Ring

Token Ring is another form of network configuration which differs from Ethernet in that all messages are transferred in a unidirectional manner along the ring at all times. Data is transmitted in tokens, which are passed along the ring and viewed by each device. When a device sees a message addressed to it, that device copies the message and then marks that message as being read. As the message makes its way along the ring, it eventually gets back to the sender who now notes that the message was received by the intended device. The sender can then remove the message and free that token for use by others.

FDDI

FDDI (Fiber-Distributed Data Interface) is a standard for data transmission on fiber optic lines in a local area network that can extend in range up to 200 km (124 miles). The FDDI protocol is based on the token ring protocol. In addition to being large geographically, an FDDI local area network can support thousands of users.

10.6 COMMUNICATION PROTOCOLS

Network protocols are standards that allow computers to communicate. A protocol defines how computers identify one another on a network, the form that the data should take in transit, and how this information is processed once it reaches its final destination. Protocols also define procedures for handling lost or damaged transmissions or 'Packets'. TCP/IP (for UNIX, Windows NT, Windows 95 and other platforms), IPX (for Novell NetWare), DECnet (for networking Digital Equipment Corp. computers), AppleTalk (for Macintosh computers), and NetBIOS/NetBEUI (for LAN Manager and Windows NT networks) are the main types of network protocols in use today.

Although each network protocol is different, they all share the same physical cabling. This common method of accessing the physical network allows multiple protocols to peacefully coexist over the network media, and allows the builder of a network to use common hardware for a variety of protocols. This concept is known as 'Protocol Independence'.

10.7 TCP/IP NETWORKS

TCP/IP-based networks play an increasingly important role in computer networks. Perhaps one reason for their appeal is that they are based on an open specification that is not controlled by any vendor.

What is TCP/IP?

TCP stands for Transmission Control Protocol and IP stands for Internet Protocol. The term TCP/IP is not limited just to these two protocols, however. Frequently, the term TCP/IP is used to refer to a group of protocols related to the TCP and IP protocols such as the User Datagram Protocol (UDP), File Transfer Protocol (FTP), Terminal Emulation Protocol (TELNET), and so on.

The Origins of TCP/IP

In the late 1960s, DARPA (the Defense Advanced Research Project Agency), in the United States, noticed that there was a rapid proliferation of computers in military communications. Computers, because they can be easily programmed, provide flexibility in achieving network functions that is not available with other types of communications equipment. The computers then used in military communications were manufactured by different vendors and were designed to interoperate with computers from that vendor only. Vendors used proprietary protocols in their communications equipment. The military had a multi-vendor network but no common protocol to support the heterogeneous equipment from different vendors.

10.8 THE OSI MODEL

Open System Interconnection (OSI) reference model has become an international standard and serves as a guide for networking. This model is the best known and most widely used guide to describe networking environments. Vendors design network products based on the specifications of the OSI model. It provides a description of how network hardware and software work together in a layered fashion to make communications possible. It also helps with trouble shooting by providing a frame of reference that describes how components are supposed to function.

There are seven to get familiar with and these are the physical layer, data link layer, network layer, transport layer, session layer, presentation layer and the application layer.

- Physical layer is just that the physical parts of the network such as wires, cables, and there media along with the length. Also this layer takes note of the electrical signals that transmit data throughout system.

- Data link layer, this layer is where we actually assign meaning to the electrical signals in the network. The layer also determines the size and format of data sent to printers, and other devices. Also I don't want to forget that these are also called nodes in the network. Another thing to consider in this layer will also allow and define the error detection and correction schemes that insure data was sent and received.
- Network layer, this layer provides the definition for the connection of two dissimilar networks.
- Transport layer, this layer allows data to be broken into smaller packages for data to be distributed and addressed to other nodes (workstations).
- Session layer, this layer helps out with the task to carry information from one node (workstation) to another node (workstation). A session has to be made before we can transport information to another computer.
- Presentation layer, this layer is responsible to code and decode data sent to the node.
- Application layer, this layer allows you to use an application that will communicate with say the operation system of a server. A good example would be using your web browser to interact with the operating system on a server such as Windows NT, which in turn gets the data you requested.

10.9 DISTRIBUTED SYSTEMS—INTRODUCTION

Distributed system is a collection of independent computers that appear to its users as a single coherent system. In networked environment the multiplicity of system components exists through the abstractions provided by the operating system and other software. Also a distributed system can be called as a collection of independent computers that are used jointly to perform a single task or to provide a single service. Some examples of distributed system are collection of web servers implementing HTTP protocol. That jointly provide the distributed database of hypertext and multimedia documents that is said to be world wide web. When compared to the centralized systems, distributed systems are preferred for both economic and technical reasons as reasons may be cost, performance, scalability, inherent distribution, reliability, security, software complexity.

10.10 PRINCIPLES OF DISTRIBUTED SYSTEM

There are several key principles underlying all distributed systems. As such, any distributed system can be described based on how those principles apply to that system.

- System architecture
- Communication
- Synchronisation
- Replication and consistency
- Fault tolerance
- Security
- Naming

Most distributed systems are based on a particular model, for describing distribution and communication. Some of these models are:

- Shared memory
- Distributed objects
- Distributed file system
- Shared documents
- Distributed coordination
- Agents

10.11 HARDWARE AND SOFTWARE ARCHITECTURES

The main characteristic of distributed system is that it includes independent computers (hardware) and task/service provided (software), where the former is implemented in multi-computers and the latter is implemented as distributed operating system or middleware.

10.11.1 Multicomputers

A multicomputer consists of separate computing nodes connected to each other over a network as illustrated in the Fig. 10.1.

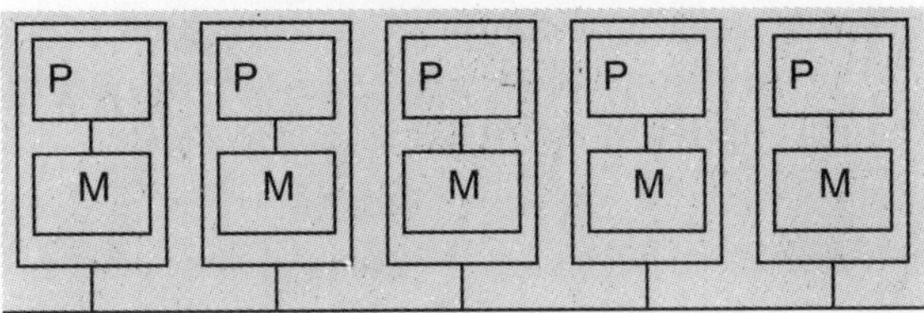

Fig. 10.1: Multicomputers

Multicomputers differ from each other in three main ways.

1. ***Node resources:*** This includes the processors, amount of memory, amount of secondary storage, etc. available on each node.
2. ***Network connection:*** The network connection between the various nodes can have a large impact on the functionality and applications that such a system can be used for. A multicomputer with a very high bandwidth network is more suitable for applications that actively share data over the nodes and modify large amounts of that shared data.
3. ***Homogeneity:*** A homogeneous multicomputer is one where all the nodes are the same, that is they are based on the same physical architecture, e.g. processor, system bus, memory, etc. A heterogeneous multicomputer is one where the nodes are not expected to be the same.

One common characteristic of all types of multicomputers is that the resources on any particular node cannot be directly accessed by any other node. All access to remote resources ultimately takes the form of requests sent over the network to the node where that resource resides.

10.11.2 Distributed Operating System (Fig. 10.2)

A distributed operating system is an operating system that is built, from the ground up, to provide distributed services. These services may include distributed shared memory, assignment of tasks to processors, masking of failures, distributed storage, interprocess communication, transparent sharing of resources, distributed resource management, etc. A key property of a distributed operating system is that it strives for a very high level of transparency, ideally providing a single system image.

Distributed operating systems generally assume a homogeneous multicomputer. They are also generally more suited to LAN environments than to WAN environments.

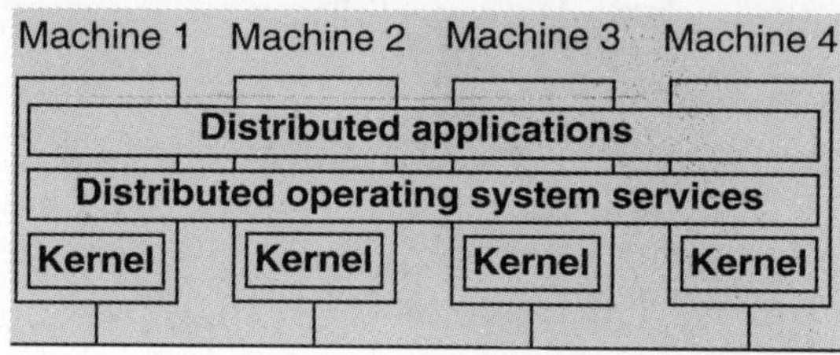

Fig. 10.2: Distributed operating system

Middleware (Fig. 10.3)

The goal of middleware is to create system independent interfaces for distributed applications.

Middleware consists of a layer of services added between those of a regular network operating system and the actual applications. A network OS is a regular OS enhanced with network services such as sockets, remote login, remote file transfer, etc. These services facilitate the implementation of distributed applications and attempt to hide the heterogeneity (both hardware and software) of the underlying system architectures. The principle aim of middleware is raising the

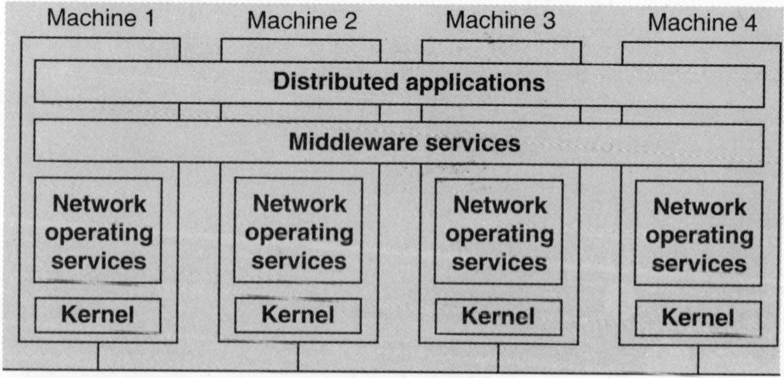

Fig. 10.3: Middleware

level of abstraction for distributed programming. This is achieved in three ways:

1. Communication mechanisms that are more convenient and less error-prone than basic message passing;
2. Independence from OS, network protocol, programming language, etc. and
3. Standard services (such as a naming service, transaction service, security service, etc.).

To make the integration of these various services easier, and to improve transparency and system independence, middleware is usually based on a particular paradigm, or model, for describing distribution and communication. Providing such a model automatically provides an abstraction for programmers to follow, and provides direction for how to design and set up the distributed applications. Middleware is generally implemented as a set of libraries and tools that enable fitting of distributed computing capabilities to existing programming languages. Such systems typically use a central mechanism of the host language like the procedure call or method invocation.

Since an important goal of middleware is to hide the heterogeneity of the underlying systems, middleware systems often try to offer a complete set of services so that clients do not have to rely on underlying OS services directly. This provides transparency for programmers writing distributed applications using the given middleware. As such, current systems exhibit an unhealthy tendency to include more and more functionality in basic middleware and its extensions, which leads to a huge number of bloated interfaces.

10.12 PROBLEMS AND CHALLENGES IN DISTRIBUTED SYSTEMS

Distributed systems also face some challenges. They are:

- Transparency.
- Scalability.
- Dependability.
- Performance.
- Flexibility.

These challenges can also be seen as the goals of a distributed system.

Transparency

Transparency is the concealment from the user and the application programmer of the separation of the components of a distributed system. Transparency is a strong property that is often difficult to achieve. There are a number of different forms of transparency including the following:

- ***Access transparency:*** Local and remote resources are accessed in same way.
- ***Location transparency:*** Users are unaware of the location of resources.
- ***Migration transparency:*** Resources can migrate without name change.
- ***Replication transparency:*** Users are unaware of the existence of multiple copies of resources.
- ***Failure transparency:*** Users are unaware of the failure of individual components.
- ***Concurrency transparency:*** Users are unaware of sharing resources with others.

Note that complete transparency is not always desirable due to the trade-offs with performance and scalability, as well as the problems that can be caused when confusing local and remote operations. Furthermore complete transparency may not always be possible since nature imposes certain limitations on how fast communication can take place in wide-area networks.

Scalability

Scalability is important in distributed systems, and in particular in wide area distributed systems, and those expected to experience large growth. According to Neumann a system is scalable if it can handle the addition of users and resources without suffering a noticeable loss of performance or increase in administrative complexity.

Adding users and resources causes a system to grow. This growth has three dimensions:

- *Size:* A distributed system can grow with regards to the number of users or resources (e.g. computers) that it supports. As the number of users grows the system may become overloaded. Likewise as the number of resources managed by the system grows the administration that the system has to perform may become too overwhelming for it.

- *Geography:* A distributed system can grow with regards to geography or the distance between nodes. An increased distance generally results in greater communication delays and the potential for communication failure. Another aspect of geographic scale is the clustering of users in a particular area. While the whole system may have enough resources to handle all users, when they are all concentrated in a single area, the resources available there may not be sufficient to handle the load.
- *Administration:* As a distributed system grows, its various components (users, resources, nodes, networks, etc.) will start to cross administrative domains. This means that the number of organisations or individuals that exert administrative control over the system will grow. In a system that scales poorly with regards to administrative growth this can lead to problems of resource usage, reimbursement, security, etc.

A claim often made for newly introduced distributed systems is that they are scalable. These claims of scalability are often unintentionally not founded because they focus on very limited aspects of scalability. Although this is a valid, the scalability with respect to users or geographic distribution is not considered. The key approach in designing and building a scalable system is decentralisation. Generally this avoids centralisation in any form since it can cause performance bottlenecks. In particular a scalable distributed system must avoid centralising: components (server), database, algorithms. When designing algorithms for distributed systems the following design rules can help avoid centralisation:

- Do not require any machine to hold complete system state.
- Allow nodes to make decisions based on local information.
- Algorithms must survive failure of nodes.
- No assumption of a global clock.

Approaches to avoiding centralisation and improving scalability includes:

1. Hiding communication delays introduced by wide area networks.
2. Distributing data over various machines to reduce the load placed on any single machine.
3. Creating replicas of data and services to reduce the load on any single machine. Furthermore, by allowing distribution of data, the management of, and responsibility over, data can be kept within any particular administrative domain, thus helping to improve administrative scalability as well.

Dependability

Although distributed systems provide the potential for higher availability due to replication, the distributed nature of services means that more components have to work properly for a single service to function. Hence, there are more potential points of failure and if the system architecture does not take explicit measures to increase reliability, there may actually be a degradation of availability. Dependability requires consistency, security and fault tolerance.

Performance

Any system should achieve maximum performance, but in the case of distributed systems this is an important challenge, since it directly connects with some other desirable properties. In particular, transparency, security, dependability and scalability can easily be related to performance.

Flexibility

A flexible distributed system can be configured to provide exactly the services that a user or programmer needs. A system with this kind of flexibility generally provides a number of key properties.

'Extensibility' allows one to add or replace system components in order to extend or modify system functionality.

'Openness' means that a system provides its services according to standard rules regarding invocation syntax and semantics. Openness allows multiple implementations of standard components to be produced. This provides choice and flexibility.

'Interoperability' ensures that systems implementing the same standards (and possibly even those that do not) can interoperate.

An important concept with regards to flexibility is the separation of policy and mechanism. A mechanism provides the infrastructure necessary to do something while a policy determines how that something is done. Component-based architectures are inherently more flexible than monolithic architectures, which makes them particularly attractive for distributed systems.

10.13 COMMON MISTAKES IN DISTRIBUTED SYSTEMS

When developing the distributed applications for the first time developers typically make a number of false assumptions. All of these assumptions hold for nondistributed systems, but typically do not hold for distributed systems.

- The network is reliable.
- The network is secure.
- Everything is homogeneous.
- The topology does not change.
- Latency is zero.
- Bandwidth is infinite.
- Transport cost is zero.
- There is one administrator.

Making these assumptions invariably leads to difficulties in achieving the desired goals for distributed systems. For example, assuming that the network is reliable will lead to trouble when the network starts dropping packets. Likewise assuming zero latency will undoubtedly lead to scalability problems as the application grows geographically, or is moved to a different kind of network.

10.14 SYSTEM ARCHITECTURE

A distributed system is composed of software components, processing nodes and networks. When building a distributed system, the software is under the designer's control. Depending on the scale of the system, the hardware can also be specified within the design or if already exists has to be taken as it is.

The key, however, is that the software components must be distributed over the hardware components in some way.

The software of distributed systems are fairly complex—especially in large distributed systems and its components are spread over many machines. It is important, therefore, to understand the organization of the system. The software architecture of distributed systems deals with how software components are organised and how they communicate with each other. Typical software architectures include the layered, object-oriented, data-centered, and event-based architectures. Once the software components are initialised and placed on real machines, then the actual system architecture is considered. A few such architectures are discussed here. These architectures are distinguished from each other by the method of process communication.

10.14.1 Client-Server

The Client-Server architecture is the most common and widely used model for process communication. As shown in the Fig. 10.4 one process takes on the role of a server, while all other processes take the roles of clients. The server process provides a service and the clients are customers of that service. A client sends a request to a server, the request is processed at the server and a reply is returned to the client.

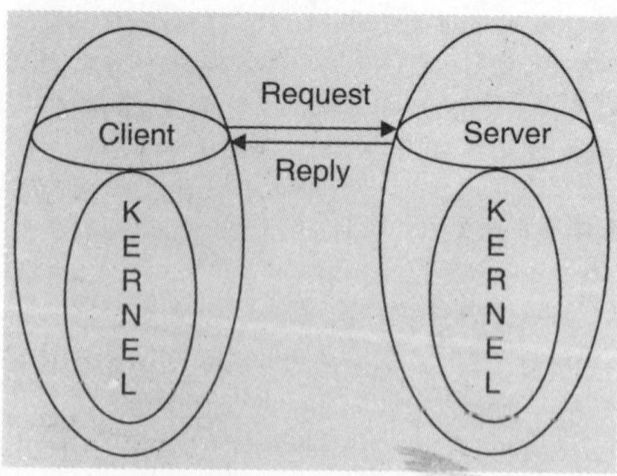

Fig. 10.4: Client-server architecture

A typical client-server application can be decomposed into three logical parts:

- Interface part,
- Application logic part,
- Data part.

Implementations of the client-server architecture vary with regards to how the parts are separated over the client and server. A thin client implementation will provide a minimal user interface layer, and leave everything else to the server. Whereas a fat client implementation will include all of the user interface and application logic in the client, and only rely on the server to store and provide access to data. Implementations in between will split up the interface or application logic parts over the clients and server in different ways.

10.14.2 Vertical Distribution (Multi-Tier)

One among the client-server architectures, the vertical distribution, or multi-tier architecture as shown in Fig. 10.5 below distributes the server functionality over multiple servers. A client request is sent to the first server. During processing of the request this server will request the services of the next server, who will do the same, until the final server is reached.

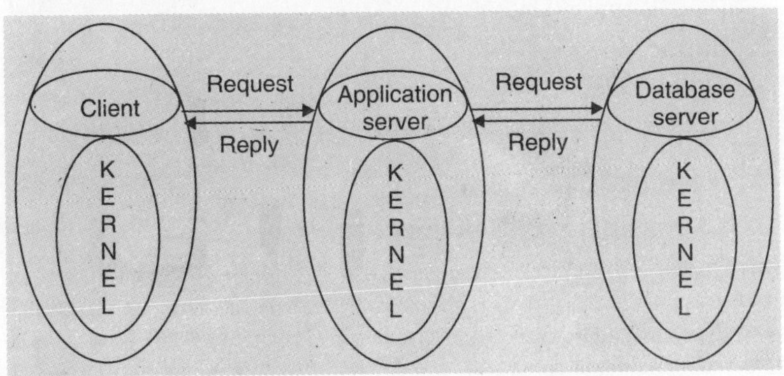

Fig. 10.5: Vertical distribution (multi-tier)

In this way the various servers become clients of each other as shown in Fig. 10.6. Here the communication in multi-tier architecture is revealed. Each server is responsible for a different step (or tier) in the fulfillment of the original client request.

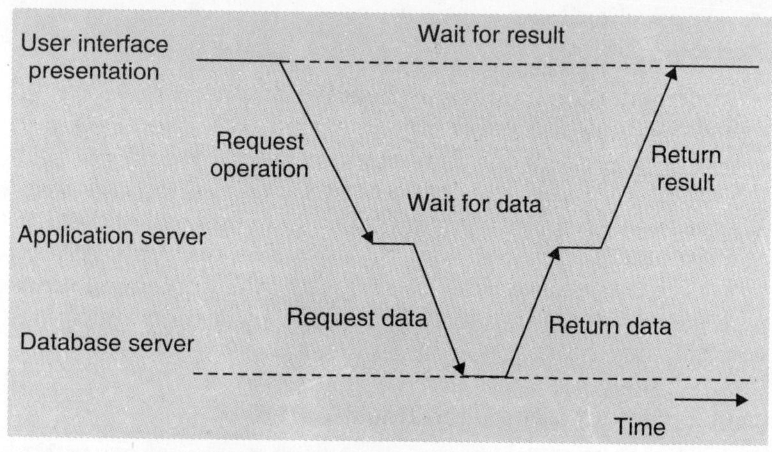

Fig. 10.6: Communication in multi-tier architecture

Splitting up the server functionality like this is beneficial to a system's scalability as well as its flexibility. Scalability is improved because the processing load on each individual server is reduced and the whole system can, therefore, accommodate more users. Regarding flexibility this architecture allows the internal functionality of each server to be modified as long as the interfaces provided remain the same.

10.14.3 Horizontal Distribution

Splitting up of server's functionality over multiple computers is done in vertical distribution whereas the horizontal distribution replicates the server's functionality over multiple computers. In this case each server machine contains a complete copy of all hosted web pages and client requests are passed on to the servers in a round robin fashion. The horizontal distribution architecture is generally used to improve scalability and reliability (Fig. 10.7).

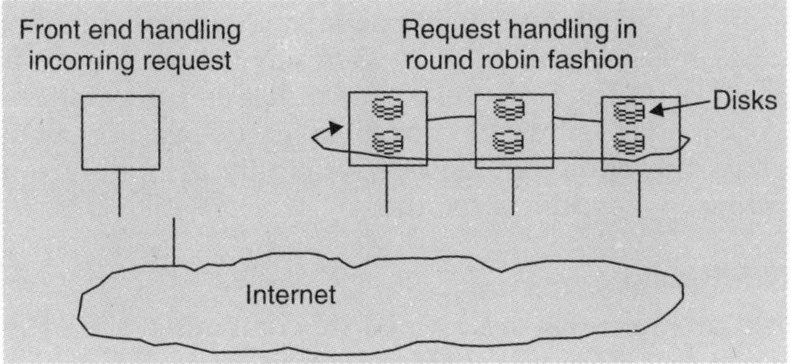

Fig. 10.7: Horizontally distributed web server

10.14.4 Peer-to-Peer

In the horizontal distribution model different processes play different roles in the communication architecture, but the peer-to-peer (P2P) architecture takes an opposite approach. Here all processes play the same role and hence are called peers to each other. Here each process acts as both server and client. File-sharing applications are examples of P2P model. In these applications users start up a program that they use to search for and download files from other users. At the same time, however, the program also handles search and download requests from other users.

With the potentially huge number of participating nodes in a peer-to-peer network, it becomes practically impossible for a node to keep track of all other nodes in the system and the information they offer. To reduce the problem, the nodes form an overlay network, in which nodes form a virtual network among themselves and only have direct knowledge of a few other nodes. When a node wishes to send a message to other node it must first locate that node by propagating a request along the links in the overlay network. Once the destination node is found, the two nodes can communicate directly.

There are two key types of overlay networks, based on the architecture and its maintenance. In all cases a node in the network will maintain a list of neighbors. A node's partial view consists of a random list of other nodes. In order to keep the network connected all nodes as they join and leave, the network periodically exchange their partial views with neighbors, creating a new neighbor list for themselves from time to time. As long as nodes both push and pull this information the network tends to stay well connected. In the case of structured overlays the choice of a node's neighbors is determined according to a specific structure.

10.14.5 Hybrid

Hybrid architectures are formed by combining one or more architectures (discussed above) in different ways. Some of the networks involving hybrid architecture are:

Superpeer networks: In this architecture a few superpeers form a peer-to-peer network, while the regular peers are clients to a superpeer. This hybrid architecture maintains some of the advantages of a peer-to-peer system, but simplifies the system by having only the superpeers managing the index of the regular peers, or acting as brokers, e.g. Skype.

Edge-server networks: In edge-server networks, as the name implies, servers are placed at the 'edge' of the Internet, for example at internet service providers (ISPs) or close to enterprise networks. Client nodes (e.g. home users or an enterprise's employees) then access the nearby edge servers instead of the original server (which may be located far away). This architecture is typically well suited for large-scale content-distribution networks.

Collaborative distributed systems: In collaborative distributed systems, peers typically support each other to deliver content in a peer-to-peer like architecture, while they use a client server architecture for the initial setup of the network. In BitTorrent for example, nodes requesting to download a file from a server first contact the server to get the location of a tracker. The tracker then tells the nodes the locations of other nodes, from which chunks of the content can be downloaded concurrently. Nodes must then offer downloaded chunks to other nodes and are registered with the tracker, so that the other nodes can find them.

10.15 COMMUNICATION IN A DISTRIBUTED SYSTEM

The means of communication between processes is a uniprocessor environment, and in a distributed system (i.e. a multicomputer environment) remains similar. The main dfference is that in a distributed system processes running on separate computers cannot directly access each other's memory. But processes in a distributed system can still communicate through either shared memory or message passing.

Distributed Shared Memory

Because distributed processes cannot access each other's memory directly, using shared memory in a distributed system requires special mechanisms that emulate the presence of directly accessible shared memory. This is called distributed shared memory (DSM). The idea behind DSM is that processes on separate computers all have access to the same virtual address space. The memory pages that make up this address space actually reside on separate computers. Whenever a process on one of the computers needs to access a particular page, it must find the computer that actually hosts that page and request the data from it.

Message Passing

Message passing in a distributed system is similar to communication using messages in a non-distributed system. The main difference being that the only mechanism available for the passing of messages is network communication.

At its core, message passing involves two operations send ( ) and receive ( ). Although these are very simple operations, there are many variations on the basic model. For example, the communication can be connectionless or connection oriented. Connection oriented communication requires that the sender and receiver first create a connection before send ( ) and receive ( ) can be used.

There are a number of important issues to consider when dealing with processes that communicate using message passing, which are described in the next section. Besides these variations in the message passing model, there are also issues involved with communicating between processes on heterogeneous computers. This brings up issues such as data representation and dealing with pointers, which will be discussed in more detail later.

10.15.1 Communication Modes

There are a number of alternative ways, or modes, in which communication can take place. It is important to know and understand these different modes, because they are used to describe the different services that a communication subsystem offers to higher layers. A first distinction is between the two modes data-oriented communication and control-oriented communication. In the first mode, communication serves solely to exchange data between processes. Although the data might trigger an action at the receiver, there is no explicit transfer of control implied in this mode. The second mode, control-oriented communication, explicitly associates a transfer of control with every data transfer. Data-oriented communication is clearly the type of communication used in communication via shared address space and shared memory, as well as message passing. Control-oriented communication is the mode used by abstractions such as remote procedure call, remote method invocation, active messages, etc. Note that low-level communication mechanisms are generally data-oriented, while the higher level ones are control-oriented.

Communication operations can be synchronous or asynchronous.

- In synchronous communication the sender of a message blocks until the message has been received by the intended recipient.
- Synchronous communication is usually even stronger than this in that the sender often blocks until the receiver has processed the message and the sender has received a reply. In asynchronous communication, on the other hand, the sender continues execution immediately after sending a message. Another possible alternative involves the buffering of communication. In the buffered case, a message will be stored if the receiver is not able to pick it up immediately. In the unbuffered case the message will be lost.

Communication can be transient and persistent.

- In transient communication a message will only be delivered if a receiver is active. If there is no active receiver process then an undeliverable message will simply be dropped.

- In persistent communication, however, a message will be stored in the system until it can be delivered.

There are also varying degrees of reliability of the communication. With reliable communication errors are discovered and fixed transparently. This means that the processes can assume that a message that is sent will actually arrive at the destination. With unreliable communication messages may get lost and processes have to deal with it.

10.15.2 Communication Abstractions

In the previous discussion it was assumed that all processes explicitly are assumed to send and receive messages. Although this style of programming is effective and works, it is not always easy to write correct programs using explicit message passing.

In the same way that higher level programming languages make programming easier by providing abstractions over the assembly language, hence communication abstractions make programming in distributed systems easier. Some of the abstractions hide the fact that communication is taking place. While other abstractions do not attempt to hide communication, all abstractions have in common that they hide the details of the communication taking place.

10.15.2.1 Remote Procedure Call (RPC)

RPC replaces the explicit message passing model with the model of executing a procedure call on a remote node. A programmer using RPC simply performs a procedure call, while behind the scenario messages are transferred between the client and server machines. In theory the following steps are involved in performing RPC.

1. Client program calls client stub routine (normal procedure call).
2. Client stub packs parameters into message data structure (marshalling).
3. Client stub performs send ( ) syscall and blocks.
4. Kernel transfers message to remote kernel.
5. Remote kernel delivers to server stub procedure, blocked in receive ( ).

6. Server stub unpacks message, calls service procedure (normal procedure call).
7. Service procedure returns to stub, which packs result into message.
8. Server stub performs send ( ) syscall.
9. Kernel delivers to client stub.
10. Client stub unpacks result (unmarshalling).
11. Client stub returns to client program (normal return from procedure).

A server that provides remote procedure call services defines the available procedures in a service interface. A service interface is generally defined in an interface definition language (IDL), which is a simplified programming language, sufficient for defining data types and procedure signatures but not for writing executable code. The IDL service interface definition is used to generate client and server stub code. The stub code is then compiled and linked in with the client program and service procedure implementations respectively.

More modern RPC frameworks are based on XML as a data format and are defined to operate on top of widely used standard network protocols such as HTTP. This simplifies integration with web servers and is useful when transparent operation through firewalls is desired, e.g. of such frameworks are XML-RPC. As mentioned earlier there are issues involved with communicating between processes on heterogeneous architectures. These include different representations of data, different byte orderings, and problems with transferring pointers or pointer-based data structures. One of the tasks that RPC frameworks hide from programmers is the packing of data into messages (marshalling) and unpacking data from messages (unmarshalling). Marshalling and unmarshalling are performed in the stubs by code generated automatically from IDL compilers and stub generators. An important part of marshalling is converting data into a format that can be understood by the receiver. Generally, differences in format can be handled by defining a standard network format into which all data is converted. However, this may be wasteful if two communicating machines use the same internal format, but that format differs from the network format. To avoid this problem, an alternative is to indicate the format used in the transmitted message and rely on the receiver to apply conversion where required.

Because pointers cannot be shared between remote it is necessary to flatten, or serialise, all pointer-based data structures when they are passed to the RPC client stub. At the server stub, these serialised data structures must be unpacked and recreated in the recipient's address space. Unfortunately this approach presents problems with aliasing and cyclic structures. Another approach to deal with pointers involves the server sending a request for the referenced data to the client every time a pointer is encountered. In general the RPC abstraction assumes synchronous, or blocking communication. This means that clients invoking RPCs are blocked and made to work until the procedure has been executed remotely and a reply is returned. Although this is often the desired behaviour, sometimes the waiting is not necessary. In this case it is better for the RPC to return as soon as the server acknowledges receipt of the message. This is called an asynchronous RPC.

The information is important to the client, but since it is not needed right away the client does not want to wait. In this case it is best if the server performs an asynchronous call to the client when the results are available. This is known as 'deferred synchronous RPC'. A final issue is how a client stub knows where to send the RPC message. In a regular procedure call the address of the procedure is determined at compile time, and the call is then made directly. In RPC this information is acquired from a binding service that allows registration and lookup of services. A binding service typically provides an interface similar to the following:

- Register (name, version, handle, UID).
- Deregister (name, version, UID).
- Lookup (name, version) ! (handle, UID).

Here handle is some physical address (IP address, process ID, etc.) and UID is used to distinguish between servers offering the same service. Moreover, it is important to include version information since the flexibility requirement for distributed system requires us to deal with different versions of the same software in a heterogeneous environment.

10.15.2.2 Remote Method Invocation (RMI)

When using RPC, programmers must explicitly specify the server on which they want to perform the call. Furthermore, it is complicated for a server to keep track of the different state belonging to different clients and their invocations. These problems with RPC lead to the remote method invocation (RMI) abstraction. The transition from RPC to RMI is, at its core, a transition from the server metaphor to the object metaphor. When using RMI, programmers invoke methods on remote objects. The object metaphor associates all operations with the data that they operate on, meaning that state is encapsulated in the remote object and much easier to keep track of. Furthermore, the concept of remote object, improves location transparency: once a client is bound to a remote object, it no longer has to worry about where that object is located. Also, objects in a model can be passed as arguments or received as results in RMI. This helps to relieve many of the problems associated with passing pointers in RPC. Although, technically, RMI is a small evolutionary step from RPC, the model of remote and distributed objects is very powerful.

In addition to the new failure modes, the use of threads can lead to problems when accessing global program variables. Moreover, some forms of arguments like varargs in C do not lend themselves well to the static generation of marshalling code.

Furthermore, RPC and RMI involve many more software layers than local system calls and also incur network latencies. Both form potential performance bottlenecks. The code must, therefore, be carefully optimised and should use lightweight network protocols. Moreover, since copying often dominates the overhead, hardware support can help. This includes DMA directly to/from user buffers and scatter gather network interfaces that can compose a message from data at different addresses on the fly. Finally, issues of concurrency control can show up in subtle ways that, again, break the illusion of executing a local operation.

10.15.2.3 Message-Oriented Communication

Due to the dangers of RPC and RMI, and the fact that those models are generally limited to synchronous (and transient) communication, alternative abstractions are often needed. The message-oriented communication abstraction is one of these and does not attempt to hide the fact that communication is taking place. Instead its goal is to make the use of flexible message passing easier. Message-oriented communication is based around the model of processes sending messages to each other. Underlying message-oriented communication has two orthogonal properties. Communication can be synchronous or asynchronous, and it can be transient or persistent. Whereas RPC and RMI are generally synchronous and transient, message-oriented communication systems make many other options available to programmers.

Message-oriented communication is provided by message-oriented middleware (MOM). Besides providing many variations of the send ( ) and receive ( ) primitives, MOM also provides infrastructure required to support persistent communication. The send ( ) and receive ( ) primitives offered by MOM also abstract from the underlying operating system or hardware primitives. As such, MOM allows programmers to use message passing without having to be aware of what platforms their software will run on, and what services those platforms provide. As part of this abstraction MOM also provides marshalling services. Furthermore, as with most middleware, MOM also provides other services that make building distributed applications easier.

MPI (Message Passing Interface) is an example of a MOM that is geared toward high-performance transient message passing. MPI is a message passing library that was designed for parallel computing. It makes use of available networking protocols, and provides a huge array of functions that basically perform synchronous and asynchronous send ( ) and receive ( ).

Communication in a message queuing system is largely asynchronous. The basic queue interface is very simple. There is a primitive to append a message onto the end of a specified queue, and a primitive to remove the message at the head of a specific queue. These can be blocking or nonblocking. All messages contain the name or address of a destination queue.

Messages can only be added to and retrieved from local queues. Senders place messages in source queues, while receivers retrieve messages from destination queues. The underlying system is responsible for transferring messages from source queues to destination queues. This can be done simply by fetching messages from source queues and directly sending them to machines responsible for the appropriate destination queues. Or it can be more complicated and involve relaying messages to their destination queues through an overlay network of routers. If in an application a sender A sends a message to an application on receiver B it places the message in its local source queue, from where it is forwarded through routers R1 and R2 into the receiver's destination queue.

Another form of message-oriented communication is event-based communication. Event-based communication is implemented through the propagation of events and generally associated with publish/subscribe systems. In a publish/subscribe system a sender process publishes events which may carry data, while a receiver process subscribes to certain events. The middleware then ensures that the receiver processes only receive events to which they subscribed.

10.15.2.4 Group Communication

Group communication provides a departure from the point-to-point style of communication. In this model of communication a process can send a single message to a group of other processes. Group communication is often referred to as broadcast and multicast. It is often used to send requests to a group of replicas, or to send updates to a group of servers containing the same data. It is also used for service discovery as well as event notification.

Issues involved with implementing and using group communication are similar to those involved with regular point-to-point communication. This includes reliability and ordering. The issues are made more complicated because now there are multiple recipients of a message and different combinations of problems may occur.

A widely implemented example of group communication is IP multicast. The IP multicast specification has existed for a long time, but it has taken a while for implementations to make their way into the routers and gateways. An increasingly important form of group communication is gossip-based communication, which is often used for data dissemination. This technique relies on epidemic behaviour like diseases spreading among people. One variant is rumour spreading, which resembles the way in which rumours spread in a group of people. In this form of communication, a node *A* that receives some new information will contact an arbitrary other node *B* in the system to push the data to that node. If node *B* did not have the data previously, nodes *A* and *B* will continue to contact other nodes and push the data to them. If, however, node *B* already had the bit of data, then node *A* stops spreading the data with a certain probability.

10.16 MIDDLEWARE

Middleware consists of a layer of services added between those of a regular network OS and the actual applications. These services facilitate the implementation of distributed applications and attempt to hide the heterogeneity of the underlying system architectures (both hardware and software). Middleware is usually based on a particular paradigm, or model, for describing distribution and communication. Providing such a paradigm automatically provides an abstraction for programmers to follow, and provides direction for how to design and set up the distributed applications.

The greatest advantage is that it runs in user space and can provide independence from OS, network protocol, programming language, etc. Unfortunately, this independence means that a lot of standard OS services must be re-implemented by the middleware, leading to an overabundance of features and bloat. One direction that current middleware is taking is to increase flexibility (and reduce bloat) by focusing on adaptation and reflection.

The most popular (and widely used) middleware abstraction is that of distributed objects. Besides distributed objects, other abstractions include RPC, transaction processing, message passing, events, shared data spaces and web services. In this lecture we focus on distributed object-based middleware and (event-based) publish/subscribe middleware.

10.16.1 Distributed Object Middleware

Remote method invocation (RMI) is an extension of the RPC model of communication to objects. Whereas RPC involves the invocation of procedures on remote servers, RMI involves the invocation of methods on remote objects.

The main advantage of RMI over RPC is the fact that it combines state and operations on that state into a single entity, an object. Thus, whereas operations in RPC are directly associated with a server, operations in RMI are only associated with an object. This means that the actual location of the object (e.g. the server on which it is hosted) is transparent to the client invoking its methods. This transparency applies not only to the object's location, but also encompasses replication and migration transparency. Encapsulating state in an object also allows the (server) programmer to keep track of related state more easily than in the RPC model. Similarly the distributed object model allows concurrent access to related state to be synchronised more easily (that is, with less programmer effort) than with the RPC model.

The popularity of the distributed object model is largely due to the fact that there is a natural mapping between the common distributed-systems model of communicating entities (e.g. client and server, resource and user, etc.) and the distributed object model of communicating objects. By encapsulating state and operations on that state, objects also provide a natural unit of replication and migration. Furthermore, object boundaries also provide a good place to impose security restrictions and perform auditing. An object-based model also provides a familiar abstraction to programmers and allows the use of many existing object-based tools and techniques for designing systems and applications.

10.16.2 Challenges

The main challenge in designing a distributed object based middleware system is to provide transparency. It provides location, migration and replication transparency. A greater challenge is to provide failure transparency. Remote method invocation can fail in ways that local method invocation cannot. Moreover, trying to mask the possibility of these kinds of failures is not always a good idea. A distributed object system must deal with these kinds of failures. In particular the system must deal with partial failures, that is failures of some components of the system (e.g. network, a server, etc.) that make it unclear where the fault occurred. Another main challenge of designing a distributed object system is scalability: making sure that the system can deal with growth. The system must deal with growth in the number of clients an object has, the number of objects deployed in the system, and the distance between clients and objects. Performance and flexibility are also important challenges. When designing distributed object based applications it is also important that the distributed nature of the application be taken into account from the beginning. Due to the communication delays and possibilities for partial failures, as well as scalability concerns, taking a non-distributed object-based design and implementing it with distributed objects retrospectively is a recipe for failure.

10.16.3 Architectural Model

A typical distributed object architecture is presented in Fig. 10.8. In this architecture a client process invokes methods on a proxy object in its address space. The proxy object marshals the invocation and with the help of the runtime system sends the invocation request onto the object server. At the server the

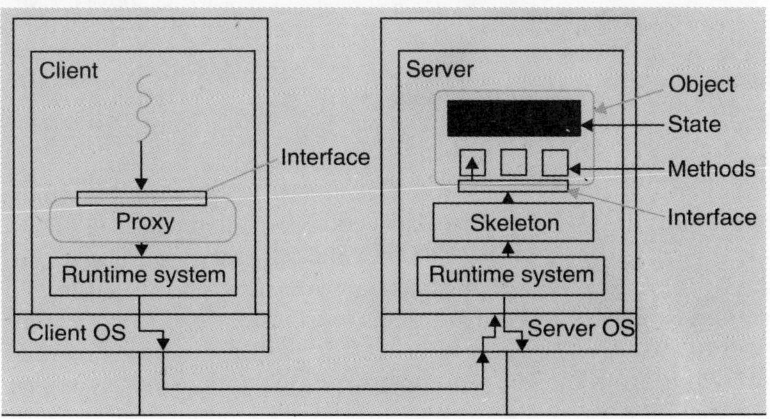

Fig. 10.8: A typical distributed object architecture

runtime system dispatches the request to an appropriate object skeleton who is responsible for unmarshaling the request and invoking the appropriate methods on a local object instance. Results are returned in a similar fashion.

10.16.4 Object Model

A distributed object system typically distinguishes between classes and objects, where a class defines a type, and an object is an instance of a particular class. A class generally defines an interface that specifies the methods that objects of that class will implement. An object is referred to using an object reference.

There are two types of object references:

1. ***Local references:*** Which are valid within a single address space.
2. ***Global (or remote) references:*** Which are valid across address spaces and machines. Most distributed object systems provide passive objects. These are objects that have no own thread of control associated with them. Some systems also provide active objects, which do have their own thread of control.

Most systems offer both persistent and transient objects. Transient objects are those that exist only as long as they are referenced by some client (and the object server that they are hosted on exists), persistent objects, on the other hand, exist until they are explicitly destroyed (even surviving restarts of their hosting object server).

Distributed object systems offer two styles of method invocation. With static method invocation proxy object code is compiled (or linked) into the client code and methods are invoked on the proxy as normal. At the server side, the object server has the skeleton and object code compiled in and skeleton and object invocations proceed normally. With dynamic method invocation the client does not have proxy code compiled in and must create invocation requests dynamically. This involves determining the object interface at runtime and using this information to build an invocation request. At the server side the skeleton invocation must similarly be created at runtime using information about the actual object implementation.

10.16.5 Interfaces

A distributed object's functionality is defined by the interfaces that it exports, i.e. provides to clients. This interface defines the methods that an object implements. In many systems an object may export more than one interface, this ability is generally provided through composition of interfaces. Some systems also allow inheritance of interfaces. Because interfaces can evolve over time many systems allow interfaces to be explicitly versioned. Note that interfaces generally define only the syntax of method invocations and not the semantics.

As with RPC, interfaces are defined using an interface definition language (IDL). The IDL for distributed object systems is usually richer than that for RPC system, in particular it allows the specification of classes (i.e. types of objects) class attributes, public methods, exceptions, and other data types (for example, arrays, records, etc.).

Client Side

In order to use a distributed object a client must first bind to that object. This results in the creation of a proxy object in the client's address space. After binding, the client can perform regular local method invocations on the new proxy object. The proxy is responsible for marshaling the invocations and sending them off to the remote object server hosting the object that the proxy is bound to. In this way, a proxy is equivalent to an RPC stub that contains extra information about the location of the destination object server and object. A client must use a different proxy object for every separate distributed object that it wishes to access. Proxy object code is usually generated from an IDL interface specification and linked in with the client code. As mentioned, dynamic method invocation makes it possible for clients to invoke methods on objects whose interfaces are not known at compile time. The runtime system (RTS) at the client side provides any services necessary for the proxy to communicate with the object server. The RTS also provides some services directly to the client. These include operations for initialising the system, operations for binding to objects, and operations for manipulating object references, e.g. translating from local to global and vice versa.

Server Side

The object server's main task is to host object implementations and to allow remote invocation of methods. As mentioned earlier, an object contains state and implements methods that operate on that state. An object that implements the methods defined by a particular interface is said to implement or export that interface. An object implementation is accessed through a skeleton, which is similar to an RPC server stub. Like proxy code, skeleton code is usually generated from an IDL interface definition and linked into the object server (along with the object implementation code). Through dynamic skeletons it is also possible for an object server to host objects whose interfaces were not known at compile time. The RTS at the server side is responsible for receiving method invocation requests from clients and dispatching them to the appropriate skeleton. The RTS is also responsible for implementing a server's invocation policies. These are policies that determine how a method invocation takes place. Examples of policies include single-threaded invocation, multi-threaded invocation, transient object invocation, persistent object invocation, dynamic object creation, etc. The tasks of the RTS are often split up into a core RTS and an object adapter. The core RTS takes care of communication and basic dispatching, while the object adapter takes care of invocation policies, dynamic skeleton invocation, object creation, dispatching to specific objects, etc. The object adapter is also responsible for providing object wrappers for legacy code, i.e. programs that were not built to work with a particular distributed object system.

10.16.6 Naming and Binding

A local object reference is usually implemented as a local pointer to a proxy object. A remote object reference, on the other hand, must include enough information to allow clients in any address space to create a proxy and allow that proxy to find and connect to the appropriate object server hosting the object implementation. There are many different ways to implement remote ORs. In one implementation, a remote OR may, for example, contain a server address, object id, and a reference to a proxy object implementation. In another implementation it may contain an abstract reference to the object which must be resolved by a separate service. An example of such a reference is a human-friendly name or a globally unique number. An important characteristic of a remote OR is that it can be sent to, and used by, other processes. In order to use a remote OR, a client must first bind to the object referenced by it. The binding operation maps a remote OR to a local OR. It involves the creation of a proxy object in the client's address space and the locating of the object server hosting the referenced object. Most distributed object systems provide both ORs and names, which are human-friendly references to objects, i.e. they can easily be read and remembered by humans. In order to use a name to bind to an object, that name must first be resolved into an OR. This name resolution is generally performed by a separate name service. Note that named objects are generally also persistent objects.

10.16.7 Remote Method Invocation

The standard approach to remote method invocations in distributed object systems is to provide synchronous invocations. A synchronous RMI proceeds similar to a synchronous RPC. One difference between RPC and RMI is that it may be necessary for the object adapter to first create an instance of the object before the method invocation can proceed at the object server. Some distributed object systems (including CORBA) also provide alternative RMI invocation models, including asynchronous invocations, deferred synchronous invocations, invocations on persistent objects, as well as event and callback-based invocations. In the latter two, invocations are performed on functions provided by the client, rather than on the object. Remote method invocation provides an abstraction of communication for users of distributed object systems. While this shields users from the various underlying communication concerns, communication remains an important concern for the designers and implementers of distributed object systems. Generally distributed object systems are implemented according to the client server model. They make use of reliable and connection oriented point-to-point communication. Some distributed object systems also make use of group communication. Because of RMI's remote character, compounded with the possibilities of partial failure, different RMI implementations may provide different invocation semantics (i.e. guarantees about how often a method will actually be invoked on the object at the object server) in the face of failure. A method invoked on a local object is always executed exactly once. Due to the possibilities of failures, retransmissions of message, and loss of replies, such a guarantee cannot be made for remote method invocations. Overall, there are four types of invocation semantics:

Exactly-once: This is the optimal case as realised by a local invocation.

At-most-once: If the invoker receives a result, the method was executed exactly once; if the invoker catches an exception, the method was executed either once or not at all.

At-least-once: If the invoker receives a result, the method was executed at least once; if the invoker catches an exception, it cannot make any assumptions.

May be: The invoker cannot make any assumptions.

10.16.8 Services

The distributed object systems provide a host of services to make the building of distributed applications easier. These services include:

Naming and location: Services for mapping between names and object references and resolving remote object references to locations, i.e. addresses.

Directory: Services for finding objects that provide required services.

Concurrency: Services for providing concurrency control, e.g. implementing locks that span method invocations on several objects.

Event notification: Services that provide event notification to clients and objects.

Resource management: Services that can be used to manage distributed resources. This includes distributed garbage collection as well as the management of persistent objects.

Transaction: Services that provide the possibility to group method invocations into transaction that can possibly be rolled back on failures.

Fault tolerance: Services that help objects and clients deal with possible failures. This may include services that replicate state for safe keeping, as well as providing exception handling and propagation mechanisms, and failure recovery mechanisms.

Security: Services that help implement secure objects. This includes services that provide authentication of communicating parties, authorization and access control, integrity of communication and verification of data, auditing and logging of events, nonrepudiation, privacy, and protection from malicious code.

10.17 CORBA

Corba is an example of a widely used distributed object system. Besides Corba, other widely used remote object systems include Com/Dcom Net remoting, Java RMI and DCE.

Distributed Shared Objects

In Remote Object Model the object is hosted on a single object server and clients invoke methods on the object by sending invocation requests to that server. A key property of this model is that the object state is stored only at the object server, there are no copies of the state at any other servers or clients. A different approach to distributed objects is the distributed shared object (DSO) model. In this model an object's state can be replicated or partitioned over multiple locations. Furthermore state can be stored at both clients and object servers. Methods may be executed at any of the locations where the object's state is stored. By adding the concept of replication to the distributed object model, the DSO model provides the benefits of greater scalability (through decentralisation and replication), but also introduces many of the problems involved with replication and consistency.

Distributed Shared Object Model

In this DSO there are four processes bound to the object. Each process contains an instance of the object's local representative (LR) in its address space, and each LR exports the object interface. In this example, each of these LRs contains a copy of the object state. It does not distinguish between clients and object servers. In the DSO model the main difference between the two is that clients invoke methods directly on the LR, while in an object server method invocations are only performed as a result of request messages received over the network.

The DSO model distinguishes between two types of LRs, a stateless LR and a stateful LR. A stateless LR does not contain any object state, it is essentially equivalent to a proxy object. A stateful LR, on the other hand, does contain a copy of the object state (it can contain either the whole state or a part of the state). In contrast to the remote-object model, a DSO client can host either statefull or stateless LRs.

Object Server

In the DSO model the object server is a server dedicated to hosting LRs. The object server's main task is to provide an address space for LRs and provide LRs with access to local resources such as network access, local storage, etc. As with object servers in the remote-object model, DSO object servers can also provide support for dynamically creating LRs, as well as for persistent LRs. The object server provides mechanism required to implement security and fault tolerance. It is important to note that, in contrast to the remote-object model, LRs hosted by an object server do not necessarily have to be statefull. Likewise LRs hosted by clients do not necessarily have to be stateless.

Binding and Location

In order to have access to a DSO a client must bind to that object. This causes an instance of an LR to be created in the client's address space. After the LR is created it connects to (all or some of) the object's other LRs, i.e. the LRs in other address spaces. Because the object's state can be stored by many other LRs, it is not immediately clear which LRs a newly created LR should contact. Generally this decision is made with the help of an external location service. This is a service that maps an object reference to a particular location, e.g. network address and port. While in the remote object case mapping results in a single location, in the DSO case this mapping may result in a set of locations (for the various LRs). Another issue involved with binding is finding the LR code to load and instantiate. This code can be compiled into the client, or may be retrieved from an implementation repository service. When an LR has been instantiated and has contacted appropriate other LRs it may be necessary to load a copy of the object state from some of the other LRs. Which LRs provide this state, what state the LR requires and how the state is transferred depend on the implementation of the DSO model.

Replication and Consistency

Because the DSO model allows state to be replicated the issues discussed in the previous lecture on replication and consistency play an important role in DSO systems. In particular a DSO system must provide mechanisms for keeping replicated state consistent. This means that the system must implement a consistency policy and a consistency protocol. There is also the issue of state migration: can LRs be migrated to different servers, and can state be migrated between different LRs? The various LRs may also take on different roles in the system. For example, some LRs can take on the roles of permanent replicas, while others take on the roles of server-initiated and client-initiated replicas. A final issue with regards to replication and DSOs is that of replicated invocations. This is a particularly relevant issue if replicated DSOs can hold and use references to other replicated DSOs.

10.18 SYNCHRONISATION AND COORDINATION

Coordination refers to coordinating the actions of separate processes relative to each other and allowing them to agree on global state (such as values of a shared variable). Synchronisation is coordination with respect to time, and refers to the ordering of events and execution of instructions in time. Examples of synchronisation include ordering distributed events in a log file and ensuring that a process performs an action at a particular time. Examples of coordination include ensuring that processes agree on what actions will be performed, e.g. money will be withdrawn from the account. Synchronisation and coordination play an important role in most distributed algorithms. Some distributed algorithms are used to achieve synchronisation and coordination, while others assume the presence of synchronisation or coordination mechanisms. Discussions of distributed algorithms generally assume one of two timing models for distributed systems. The first is a synchronous model, where the time to perform all actions, communication delay, and clock drift on all nodes, are bounded. In asynchronous distributed systems there are no such bounds. Most real distributed systems are asynchronous, however, it is easier to design distributed algorithms for synchronous distributed systems. Algorithms for asynchronous systems are always valid on synchronous systems, however, the converse is not true.

10.18.1 Time and Clock

Time is an important concept when dealing with synchronisation and coordination. In particular it is often important to know when events occurred and in what order they occurred. In a non-distributed system dealing with time is trivial as there is a single shared clock. All processes see the same time. In a distributed system, on the other hand, each computer has its own clock. Because no clock is perfect each of these clocks has its own skew, which causes clocks on different computers to drift and eventually become out of sync. There are several notions of time that are relevant in a distributed system. First of all, internally a computer clock simply keeps track of ticks that can be translated into physical time (hours, minutes, seconds, etc.). This physical time can be global or local. Global time is a universal time that is the same for everyone and is generally based on some form of absolute time. Currently Coordinated Universal Time (UTC), which is based on oscillations of the Cesium-133 atom, is the most accurate global time. Besides global time, processes can also consider local time. In this case the time is only relevant to the processes taking part in the distributed system (or algorithm). This time may be based on physical or logical clocks.

(a) Physical Clocks

Physical clocks keep track of physical time. In distributed systems that rely on actual time it is necessary to keep individual computer clocks synchronised. The clocks can be synchronised to global time (external synchronisation), or to each other (internal synchronisation). Cristian's algorithm and the Network Time Protocol (NTP) are examples of algorithms developed to synchronize clocks to an external global time source (usually UTC). The Berkeley Algorithm is an example of an algorithm that allows clocks to be synchronised internally. Cristian's algorithm requires clients to periodically synchronise with a central time server (typically a server with a UTC receiver). One of the problems encountered when synchronizing clocks in a distributed system is that unpredictable communication latencies can affect the synchronisation. For example, when a client requests the current time from the time server, by the time the server's reply reaches the client the time will have changed. The client must, therefore, determine what the communication latency was and adjust the server's response accordingly. Cristian's algorithm deals with this problem by attempting to calculate the communication delay based on the time elapsed between sending a request and receiving a reply. The Network Time Protocol is similar to Cristian's algorithm in that synchronisation is also performed using time servers and an attempt is made to correct for communication latencies. NTP is not centralised and is designed to work on a wide-area scale. As such, the calculation of delay is somewhat more complicated. Furthermore, NTP provides a hierarchy of time servers, with only the top layer containing UTC clocks. The NTP algorithm allows client-server and peer-to-peer (mostly between time servers) synchronisation. It also allows clients and servers to determine the most reliable servers to synchronise with. NTP typically provides accuracies between 1 and 50 msec depending on whether communication is over a LAN or WAN. Unlike the previous two algorithms, the Berkeley algorithm does not synchronise to a global time. Instead, in this algorithm, a time server polls the clients to determine the average of everyone's time. The server then instructs all clients to set their clocks to this new average time. Note that in all the above algorithms a clock should never be set backward. If time needs to be adjusted backward, clocks are simply slowed down until time 'catches up'.

(b) Logical Clocks

For many applications, the relative ordering of events is more important than actual physical time. In a single process the ordering of events (e.g. state changes) is trivial. In a distributed system, however, besides local ordering of events, all processes must also agree on ordering of causally related events, e.g. sending and receiving of a single message. Given a system consisting of N processes pi, $i \in (1, \ldots, N)$, we define the local event ordering $\rightarrow i$ as a binary relation, such that, if pi observes e before $\acute{e}$, we have $e \rightarrow_i \acute{e}$. Based on this local ordering, we define a global ordering as a happened before relation $e \rightarrow$, as proposed by Lamport. The relation $\rightarrow$ is the smallest relation, such that

1. $e \rightarrow_i \acute{e}$ implies $e \rightarrow \acute{e}$,
2. for every message m, send (m) $\rightarrow$ receive (m), and
3. $e \rightarrow \acute{e}$ and $\acute{e} \rightarrow \acute{e}'$ implies $e \rightarrow \acute{e}'$ (transitivity).

The relation $\rightarrow$ is almost a partial order (it lacks reflexivity). If $a \rightarrow b$, then we say a causally affects b. We consider unordered events to be concurrent.

(c) Lamport Clocks

Lamport's logical clocks can be implemented as a software counter that locally computes the happened-before relation $\rightarrow$. This means that each process pi maintains a logical clock Li. Given such a clock, Li (e) denotes a Lamport time stamp of event e at pi and L (e) denotes a time stamp of event e at the process it occurred at. Processes now proceed as follows:

1. Before time stamping a local event, a process pi executes $Li: = Li + 1$.
2. Whenever a message m is sent from pi to pj:
   - Process pi executes $Li := Li + 1$ and sends the new Li with m.
   - Process pj receives Li with m and executes $Lj := \max(Lj, Li) + 1$. Receive (m) is annotated with the new Lj.

In this scheme, $a \rightarrow b$ implies $L(a) < L(b)$, but $L(a) < L(b)$ does not necessarily imply $a \rightarrow b$.

In some situations (e.g. to implement distributed locks) a partial ordering on events is not sufficient and a total ordering is required. In these cases, the partial ordering can be completed to total ordering by including process identifiers. Given local time stamps *Li* (*e*) and *Lj* (*é*), we define global time stamps *hLi* (*e*), ii and *hLj* (*e*), ji. We, then, use standard lexicographical ordering, where *hLi* (*e*), *ii* < *hLj* (*e*), *ji iff Li* (*e*) < *Lj* (*e*), or *Li* (*e*) = *Lj* (*e*) and *i* < *j*.

(d) Vector Clocks

The main shortcoming of Lamport's clocks is that *L* (*a*) < *L* (*b*) does not imply $a \rightarrow b$; hence, we cannot deduce causal dependencies from time stamps. The root of the problem is that clocks advance independently or via messages, but there is no history as to where advance comes from. This problem can be solved by moving from scalar clocks to vector clocks, where each process maintains a vector clock *Vi*. *Vi* is a vector of size *N*, where *N* is the number of processes. The component *Vi* (*j*) contains the process *pi*'s knowledge about *pj*'s clock. Initially, we have *Vi* (*j*): = 0

For *i*, *j* ∈ (1, . . . , *N*). Clocks are advanced as follows:

1. Before *pi* timestamps an event, it executes *Vi* (*i*): = *Vi* (*i*) + 1.
2. Whenever a message *m* is sent from *pi* to *pj*:
   - Process *pi* executes *Vi* (*i*): = *Vi* (*i*) + 1 and sends *Vi* with *m*.
   - Process *pj* receives *Vi* with *m* and merges the vector clocks *Vi* and *Vj* as follows:

$$Vj\,(k) = \begin{cases} \max\left[vj\,(k), vi\,(k)\right] + 1, \text{ if } j = k \text{ (as in scalar clocks)} \\ \max\left[vj\,(k), vi\,(k)\right], \text{ otherwise.} \end{cases}$$

This last part ensures that everything that subsequently happens at *pj* is now causally related to everything that previously happened at *pi*.

Under this scheme, we have, for all *i*, *j*, *Vi* (*i*) *Vj* (*i*), (i.e. *pi* always has the most up-to-date version of its own clock); moreover, $a \rightarrow b$ iff *V* (*a*) < *V* (*b*), where

- *V* = *V′* iff *V* (*i*) = *V′* (*i*) for all i ∈ (1, . . . , *N*),
- *V V′* iff *V* (*i*) *V′* (i) for all *i* ∈ (1, . . . , *N*),
- *V* > *V′* iff *V V′* ∈ *V* 6 = *V′*; and
- $V_k V'$ iff *V* 6 > *V′* ∈ *V′* 6 > *V*

10.18.2 Coordination and Multicast

Group communication is a model of communication where a process can send a single message to a group of other processes. When such a message is sent to a predefined group of recipients it is referred as multicast. Since a multicast is sent out to a specific group, it is important to have agreement on the membership of that group. Some terminologies to be dealt with are:

1. Static group membership where membership does not change at run time and dynamic group membership where membership changes overtime.
2. In open group anyone can send a message to the group whereas in closed group only group members can send message to the group.

   The two key properties of multicast are:

(a) ***Reliability***: Message delivery guarantees are to be considered here. The two delivery guarantees that can be provided are guarantee that if the message is delivered to any member of the group it is guaranteed to be delivered to all members of the group. A weaker guarantee that if a message is delivered to any non-failed members of the group it will be delivered to all non-failed members of the group.

(b) ***Ordering***: Guarantee are considered based upon the order in which they are delivered to group members. This requires synchronic action between the group members to ensure that everyone delivers received messages in an appropriate order.

The four typical multicast ordering guarantees: basic (no guarantee), FIFO, causal, and total order. A multicast sender performs a single multicast send operation msend (g, m) specifying the recipient group and the message to send. This operation is provided by a multicast middleware. When it is invoked, it eventually results in the invocation of an underlying unicast send (m) operation to each member of the group. At each recipient, when a message arrives, the OS delivers the message to the multicast middleware. The middleware is responsible for reordering received messages to comply with the required ordering model and then delivering [mdeliver (m)] the message to the recipient process.

Multicast implementations do not typically follow this model directly. An open group can easily be implemented in terms of a closed group by having the sender send (i.e. unicast) its message to a single member of the group who then multicasts the message onto the group members.

In basic multicast there are no ordering guarantees. Messages may be delivered in any order. The stricter orderings can be implemented making use of basic multicast to send messages to all group members. This means that any suitable basic-multicast implementation, such as IP multicast, can be used to implement the following.

- FIFO multicast guarantees that message order is maintained per sender. This means that messages from a single sender are always delivered in the same order as they were sent. FIFO multicast can be implemented by giving each group member a local send counter and a vector of the counters received from the other group members. The send counter is included with each message sent, while the receive vector is used to delay delivery of messages until all previous messages from a particular sender have been delivered.
- The causal message delivery guarantee requires that order is maintained between causally related sends. Recall that a message B is causally related to a message A (A happens before B) if A is received at the sender before B is sent. In this case all recipients must have causally related messages delivered in the happened before order. There is no ordering requirement for concurrent messages.
- Causal multicast can be implemented using a vector clock at each group member. This vector is sent with each message and is used to track causal relationships. A message is queued at a receiver until all previous (i.e. happened before) messages have been successfully delivered.
- Totally-ordered multicast guarantees that all messages will be delivered in the same order at all group members. There are various approaches to implementing totally-ordered multicast. Two such approaches are: a sequencer-based approach, and an agreement-based approach.
  1. The sequencer-based approach requires the involvement of a centralised sequencer which can be either a separate

node, or one of the group members. In this case, all messages are assigned a sequence number by the sequencer, with all recipients delivering messages in the assigned sequence order.

2. The agreement-based approach is decentralised, and requires all group members to vote on a sequence number for each message. In this approach each process keeps a local sequence number counter. After receiving a message each process replies to the sender with a proposed sequence number which is the value of its counter. The sender chooses the largest proposed sequence number and informs all the group members. Each group member then assigns the sequence number to the message and sets its counter to the maximum of the counter's current value and the sequence number. Messages are delivered in their sequence number order. Totally-ordered multicast is often combined with reliable multicast to provide atomic multicast.

10.18.3 Coordination and Elections

Various algorithms require a set of peer processes to elect a leader or coordinator. In the presence of failure, it can be necessary to determine a new leader if the present one fails to respond. Provided that all processes have a unique identification number, leader election can be reduced to finding the non-crashed process with the highest identifier. Any algorithm to determine this process needs to meet the following two requirements:

1. *Safety:* A process either doesn't know the coordinator or it knows the identifier of the process with largest value.
2. *Liveness:* Eventually, a process crashes or knows the coordinator.

Bully Algorithm

The following algorithm was proposed by Garcia-Molina and uses three types of messages:

- *Election:* Announce election.
- *Answer:* Response to an election.
- *Coordinator:* Elected coordinator announces itself.

A process begins an election when it notices through a timeout that the coordinator has failed or receives an election message. When starting an election, a process sends election message to all higher-numbered processes. If it receives no answer within a predetermined time limit, the process that started the election decides that it must be coordinator and sends a coordinator message to all other processes. If an answer arrives, the process that triggered an election, waits a predetermined period of time for a coordinator message. A process that receives an election message can immediately announce that it is the coordinator if it knows that it is the highest numbered process. Otherwise, it itself starts a sub-election by sending election message to higher-numbered processes. This algorithm is called the bully algorithm because the highest numbered process will always be the coordinator.

Ring Algorithm

An alternative to the bully algorithm is to use a ring algorithm. In this approach all processes are ordered in a logical ring and each process knows the structure of the ring. There are only two types of messages involved: election and coordinator. A process starts an election when it notices that the current coordinator has failed, e.g. because requests to it have timed out. An election is started by sending an election message to the first neighbor on the ring. The election message contains the node's process identifier and is forwarded on around the ring, with each process adding its own identifier to the message. When the election message reaches the originator, the election is complete. Based on the contents of the message that originator process determines the highest numbered process and sends out a coordinator message specifying this process as the winner of the election.

10.18.4 Transactions

A transaction can be regarded as a set of server operations that are guaranteed to appear atomic in the presence of multiple clients and partial failure. The concept of a transaction originates from the database community as a mechanism to maintain the consistency of databases. Transaction management is built around two basic operations:

1. Begin Transaction
2. End Transaction.

An End Transaction operations causes the whole transaction to either Commit or Abort. For this discussion, the operations performed in a transaction are Read and Write. Transactions have the ACID property:

Atomic: All-or-nothing, once committed the full transaction is performed, if aborted, there is no trace left;

Consistent: Concurrent transactions will not produce inconsistent results;

Isolated: Transactions do not interfere with each other, i.e. no intermediate state of a transaction is visible outside; (this is also called the serialisable property);

Durable: All-or-nothing property must hold even if server or hardware fails.

Flat Vs Nested Transactions

If a significant amount of state is altered in a single transaction, an abort shortly before the transaction would have been completed can imply a significant wasted effort and, if this occurs repeatedly, seriously degrade the performance of a system. Nested transactions subdivide a complex transaction into many smaller sub-transactions. As a result, if a single sub-transaction fails, the work that went into the others is not necessarily wasted. Generally, a parent transaction may commit even if some child transactions abort. However, if a parent transaction aborts, it forces all child transactions to abort. As a result, child transactions can abort at any time, but they cannot commit until the parent transaction is ready to commit. An example of this is booking a trip that involves a number of separate flights. Because booking individual parts of the trip may be difficult enough, if any single flight cannot be booked it may still be desirable to commit the rest of the transaction and try to find an alternative for the failed (or aborted) part later (as a separate transaction).

Transaction Implementation

Two general strategies exist for the implementation of transactions:

Private workspace: All tentative operations are performed on a shadow copy of the server state, which is atomically swapped with the main copy on Commit or discarded on Abort.

Writeahed log: Updates are performed in-place, but all updates are logged and reverted when a transaction Aborts.

10.18.5 Concurrency in Transactions

It is often necessary to allow transactions to occur simultaneously (for example, to allow multiple travel agents to simultaneously reserve seats on the same flight). Due to the consistency and isolation properties of transactions concurrent transaction must not be allowed to interfere with each other. Concurrency control algorithms for transactions guarantee that multiple transactions can be executed simultaneously while providing a result that is the same as if they were executed one after another.

A key concept when discussing concurrency control for transactions is the serialisation of conflicting operations. Recall that conflicting operations are those operations that operate on the same data item and whose combined effects depend on the order they are executed in. We define a schedule of operations as an interleaving of the operations of concurrent transactions. A legal schedule is one that provides results that are the same as though the transactions were serialized, i.e. performed one after another. This leads to the concept of serial equivalence. A schedule is serially equivalent if all conflicting operations are performed in the same order on all data items. For example, given two transactions *T*1 and *T*2 in a serially equivalent schedule, then of all the pairs of conflicting operations the first operation will be performed by *T*1 and the second by *T*2 (or vice versa: of all the pairs the first is performed by *T*2 and the second by *T*1). There are three types of concurrency control algorithms for transactions: those using locking, those using timestamps and those using optimistic algorithms.

Locking

The locking algorithms require that each transaction obtains a lock from a scheduler process before performing a read or a write operation. The scheduler is responsible for granting and releasing locks in such a way that legal schedules are produced. The most widely used locking approach is two-phase locking (2 PL). In this approach a lock for a data item is granted to a process if no conflicting locks are held by other processes (otherwise the process requesting the lock blocks until the lock is available again). A lock is held by a process until the operation it was requested for has been completed. Furthermore once a process has released a lock, it can no longer request any new locks until its current transaction has been completed. This results in a growing phase of the transaction where locks are acquired, and a shrinking phase where locks are released. While this approach results in legal schedules, it can also result in deadlock when conflicting locks are requested in reverse orders. This problem can be solved either by detecting and breaking deadlocks or by adding timeouts to the locks (when a lock times out then the transaction holding the lock is aborted). Another problem is that 2PC can lead to cascaded aborts. If a transaction (*T*1) reads the results of a write of another transaction (*T*2) that is subsequently aborted, then the first transaction (*T*1) will also have to be aborted. The solution to this problem is called strict two-phase locking and allows locks to be released only at commit or abort time.

Timestamp Ordering

A different approach to creating legal schedules is to timestamp all operations and ensure that operations are ordered according to their timestamps. In this approach each transaction receives a unique timestamp and each operation receives its transaction's timestamp. Each data item also has three timestamps: the timestamp of the last committed write, the timestamp of the last read and the timestamp of the last tentative (noncommittal) write. Before executing a write operation the scheduler ensures that the operation's timestamp is both greater than the data item's write timestamp and greater than or equal to the data item's read timestamp. For read operations the operation's timestamp must be greater than the data item's write timestamps (both committed and tentative). When scheduling conflicting operations the operation with a lower timestamp is always executed first.

Optimistic Control

Both locking and timestamping incur significant overhead. The optimistic approach to concurrency control assumes that no conflicts will occur, and therefore, only tries to detect and resolve conflicts at commit time. In this approach a transaction is split into three phases, a working phase (using shadow copies), a validation phase and an update phase. In the working phase operations are carried out on shadow copies with no attempt to detect or order conflicting operations. In the validation phase the scheduler attempts to detect conflicts with other transactions that were in progress during the working phase. If conflicts are detected then one of the conflicting transactions are aborted. In the update phase, assuming that the transaction was not aborted, all the updates made on the shadow copy are made permanent.

10.18.6 Distributed Transactions

In contrast to transactions in the sequential database world, transactions in a distributed setting are complicated because a single transaction will usually involve multiple servers. Multiple servers may involve multiple services and files stored on different servers. To ensure the atomicity of transactions, all servers involved must agree whether to Commit or Abort. Moreover, the use of multiple servers and services may require nested transactions, where a transaction is implemented by way of multiple other transactions, each of which can independently Commit or Abort. Transactions that span multiple hosts include one host that acts as the coordinator, which is the host that handles the initial Begin Transaction. This coordinator maintains a list of workers, which are the other servers involved in the transaction. Each worker must be aware of the identity of the coordinator. The responsibility for ensuring the atomicity of an entire transaction lies with the coordinator, which needs to rely on a distributed commit protocol.

Two-Phase Commit

This protocol ensures that a transaction commits only when all workers are ready to commit, which, for example, corresponds to validation in optimistic concurrency. As a result a distributed commit protocol requires at least two phases:

1. ***Voting phase:*** All workers vote on commit; then the coordinator decides whether to commit or abort.
2. ***Completion phase:*** All workers commit or abort according to the decision of the coordinator. This basic protocol is called two-phase commit (2 PC).

Figure 10.9 displays the state transition diagram implemented by the coordinator in the 2 PC protocol. It starts by sending CanCommit messages to all workers, which answer

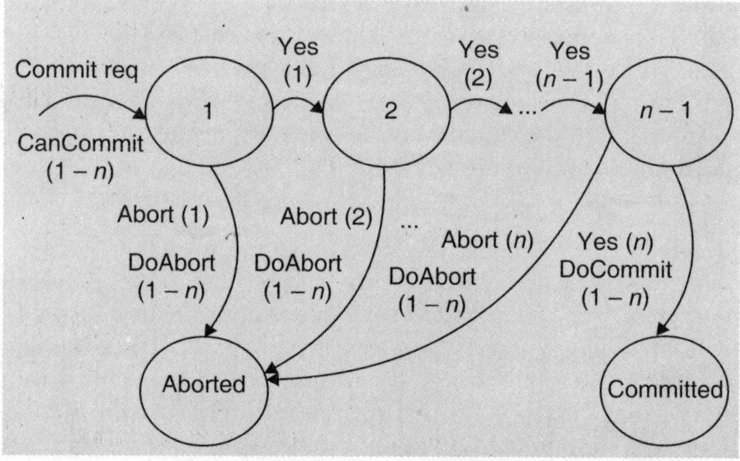

Fig. 10.9: State transition diagram of simple 2 PC coordinator

with either a yes or abort message. If yes messages are received from all workers, the coordinator sends a DoCommit message to all workers, which then implement the Commit. However, if any of the workers replies with abort instead of yes, the coordinator sends a DoAbort message to all workers to trigger a collective Abort.

The behaviour of the coordinator is complemented by that of the workers, of which the state transition diagram is displayed in Fig. 10.10. A worker on receiving a CanCommit message answers with either a yes or abort message, depending

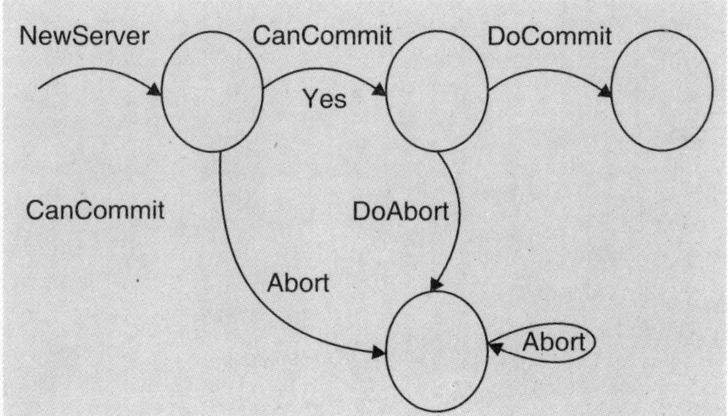

Fig. 10.10: State transition diagram of simple 2 PC worker

on the workers internal state. Afterward, it commits or aborts depending on the instructions from the coordinator. The only extra case is where the worker is in an abort cycle and immediately answers a CanCommit with an abort. In a distributed system, either a host or the network can fail. If a host fails in the 2 PC protocol, then, after being restarted, it aborts all transactions. More involved is the treatment of communication failures and, in particular, timeouts. Figures 10.11 and 10.12 depict extended state transactions diagrams for the coordinator and worker, respectively, that explicitly take timeouts into account. Whenever a worker that is ready to commit when receiving a CanCommit message times out while waiting for the decision from the coordinator, it sends a special GetDecision message that triggers the coordinator to resend the decision on whether to Commit or Abort. These messages are handled by the coordinator once the decision between committing and aborting has been made. Moreover, the coordinator resends CanCommit messages if a worker does not issue a timely reply.

These two simple 2 PC protocols have two main limitations:

- Once a node has voted with yes, it cannot retract this decision—for example, if it subsequently crashes. Hence, each node has to ensure that, after having sent a yes, it can eventually complete the transaction (possibly by logging the required state update to persistent storage).

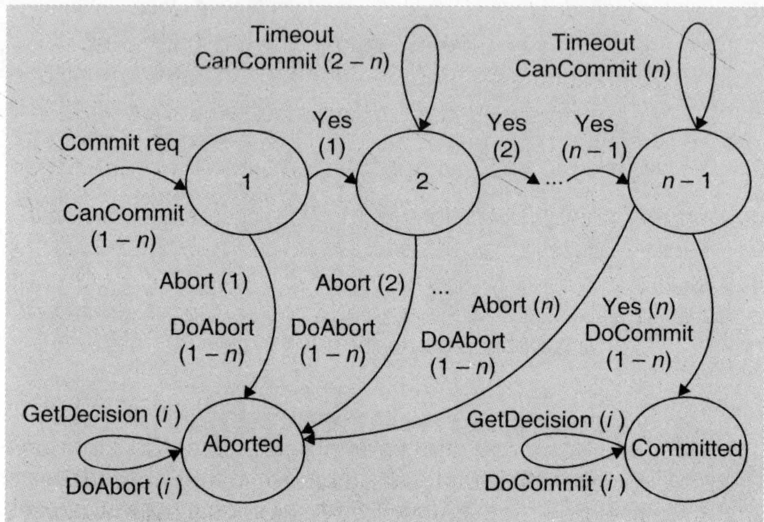

Fig. 10.11: State transition diagram of 2 PC coordinator with timeouts

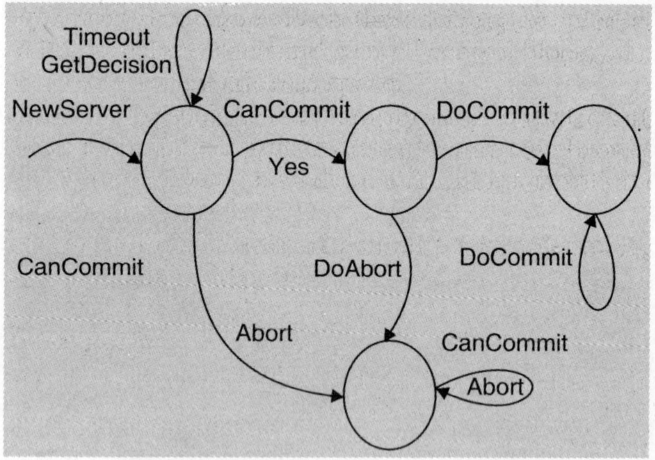

Fig. 10.12: State transition diagram of 2 PC worker with timeouts

- If the coordinator crashes, it blocks all workers. This can be avoided by moving to a decentralised three-phase commit protocol.

Distributed Nested Transactions

Distributed nested transactions are realised by letting sub-transactions commit provisionally, whereby they report a provisional commit list that contains all provisionally committed sub-transactions to the parent. If the parent aborts, it aborts all transactions on the provisional commit list. Otherwise, if the parent is ready to commit, it lets all sub-transactions commit. The actual transition from provisional to final commit needs to be via a 2 PC protocol, as a worker may crash after it has already provisionally committed. Essentially, when a worker receives a CanCommit message, there are two alternatives:

1. If it has no recollection of the sub-transactions involved in the committing transaction, it votes abort, as it must have recently crashed.
2. Otherwise, it saves the information about the provisionally committed sub-transaction to a persistent store and votes yes.

10.18.7 Security in Distributed Systems

An important aspect of dependability in distributed systems relates to security. There are two security related aspects of dependability: confidentiality and integrity. In a system that offers confidentiality, information will only be disclosed to (and services will only be provided to) authorised parties. A system that provides integrity will ensure that alterations (to data or services) can only be made in an authorised way. Furthermore, improper alterations will be detectable and recoverable.

Confidentiality and integrity are generally provided through a combination of secure communication and authorisation. Secure communication is concerned with providing a secure communication channel between entities (such as users and processes) in a distributed system. A secure channel provides confidentiality in that data sent over such a channel will not be disclosed to unauthorised third parties. Likewise the integrity of data being sent over secure channels is protected because it cannot be tampered with by unauthorised third parties. Authorisation is concerned with allowing entities to only access those resources that they are entitled to access. This requires determining the identity of entities in the system and keeping track of which resources they are allowed to access, as well as monitoring which resources they attempt to access and preventing access to unauthorised resources. By definition authorisation is required for both confidentiality and integrity.

(i) Threats

Confidentiality and integrity are not difficult to achieve in a system where no one attempts to perform unauthorised actions. Security becomes important when entities (inside or outside the system) do attempt to perform unauthorised actions (such as accessing or modifying data). The goal of security in a distributed system is to protect the services and data against security threats. We distinguish between four types of security threats. All these include some form of data falsification.

Interception: An unauthorised party attempts to gain access to a service or data. Examples of interception include eavesdropping, breaking into a system, and copying data.

Interruption: Services or data become unavailable, unusable, destroyed, etc. Examples of interruption threats include denial of service attacks, deletion of data, and corruption of data.

Modification: Unauthorised changing of data or tampering with a service so that the service no longer adheres to its specifications. Examples of this include intercepting and changing transmitted data (e.g. changing the parameters of an RPC call) and changing a program so that it performs differently than originally intended, e.g. logs user data.

Fabrication: Generation of additional data or activity that would normally not exist. Examples of fabrication include adding an entry to a password database and replaying previously sent messages.

(ii) Attacks

We distinguish between two forms of attacks: active attacks and passive attacks. Passive attacks are mainly based on observation without altering data or compromising services, they represent the interception and interruption forms of security threats. The simplest form of attack is browsing, which implies the non-destructive examination of all accessible data. This leads to the need for confidentiality and the need-to-know principle. Related is the leaking of information via authorised accomplices, which leads to the confinement problem. More indirect are attempts to infer information from traffic analysis, code breaking, and so on.

In contrast, active attacks alter or delete data and may cause service to be denied to authorised users. They represent the modification and fabrication forms of security threats. Typical active attacks attempt to modify or destroy files. Communication related active attacks attempt to modify the data sent over a communication channel.

Attacking the communication channel: Because of its networked nature, the communication channel presents a particularly important vulnerability in distributed systems. As such, many of the threats faced by distributed systems come in the form of attacks on their communication channels. We distinguish between five different types of attacks on communication channels.

Eavesdropping attacks involve obtaining copies of messages without authorisation. This could, for example, involve sniffing passwords being sent over the network.

Masquerading attacks involve sending or receiving messages using the identity of another principal without their authority. In a typical masquerading attack the attacker sends messages to the victim with the headers modified so that it looks like the messages are being sent by a trusted third party.

Message tampering attacks involve the interception and modification of messages so that they have a different effect than what was originally intended. One form of the message tampering attack is called the man-in-the-middle attack. In this attack the attacker intercepts the first message in an exchange of keys and is able to establish a secure channel with both the original sender and intended receiver. By placing itself in the middle the attacker can view and modify all communication over that channel. Replay attacks involve resending intercepted messages at a later time in order to cause an action to be repeated. This kind of attack can be effective even if communication is authenticated and encrypted. Denial of service attacks involves the coding of a channel with messages so that access is denied to others.

1. Mechanisms

In order to deal with security threats a distributed system must have appropriate mechanisms in place. The four main mechanisms used to protect against security threats are:

Encryption (cryptography): Transforms data into something an attacker cannot understand. Encryption prevents entities from being able to read or write data that they are not authorised to read or write. Note that they may still be able to access the data, but they cannot do anything with it. Encryption techniques also help to determine if data has been modified.

Authentication: Verifies the claimed identity of an entity (a user, server, client, etc.). In order to determine if an entity is authorised to access particular data or services it is necessary to know who the entity is. Examples of authentication mechanisms include passwords, chip cards and biometric identification.

Authorisation: Determines what actions an authenticated entity is authorised to perform. Authorisation mechanisms are responsible for tracking who is authorised to access what, tracking who is attempting to access what, and preventing unauthorised access to data and services.

Auditing: Traces which entities access what. Although auditing does not directly protect against security threats by preventing attacks, it is necessary in order to determine what went wrong when an attack could not be prevented.

Two lesser mechanisms can also help to improve security if they are used in combination with the above mechanisms, however, on their own they provide little benefit besides a false sense of security.

Obscurity: Counting on system details being unknown. Obscuring the actual system implementation details makes finding weaknesses and attacking the system harder. Important to note here is that the underlying mechanisms must be secure for obscurity to work. Simply expecting a system to be secure because its inner workings are obscured provides very weak protection. As soon as details about the system become known, the security gained by obscurity becomes worthless.

Intimidation: Counting on fear to keep a system safe. This approach often manifests itself as tough laws against 'cybercrime', and the threat of real world punishments. It is always a good idea to have a good security system in place, even if there is a high level of intimidation.

2. Policy

Implementing security is always a question of tradeoffs. In particular it is important to consider that the cost (in terms of money, effort, performance penalty, decreased scalability, etc.) of the security mechanisms deployed should not overshadow the value of the data and services protected. As such, it is generally not necessary for a system to be protected against all possible security threats. Instead it is necessary to determine a security policy and design the security of a system according to this policy. A security policy is a statement of security requirements. It describes the actions that the entities in a system are allowed to take and the actions that are prohibited. It also states which threats the system must be protected against.

3. Design Issues

There are a number of issues that must be taken into account when designing a secure distributed system. The first issue is the focus of control. This addresses the question of what the system protects against. In particular the system can protect against invalid operations, unauthorised invocations, and unauthorised users. In the first case the security mechanisms will focus on the protection of data in the system and ensure the integrity of the data, e.g. making sure that no operation leaves the data in an inconsistent state. In the second case the security will focus on specifying which operations can be performed and by whom. Depending on granularity the security could, for example, be at the method, interface, or object level. Finally the third approach focuses on the users of the systems and the roles they fulfill. Security is, therefore, based on the authorisation of users and their roles to access data and services.

The second design issue is the layering of security mechanisms. In a distributed system security mechanisms can be implemented at many different levels, including the application level, the middleware level, the network level, the OS level and the hardware level. What level the mechanisms are implemented at depends on how much trust is placed in the software (or hardware) at that level (and the levels above it). For example, if the security mechanisms are placed in the OS, then the applications must trust the OS and the middleware with their data. On the other hand, if the security mechanisms are built into the application itself then the trust does not have to be placed in the middleware, OS, or network hardware.

Closely related to the previous issue, the issue of distributing security mechanisms deals with minimizing the trusted computing base (TCB). The TCB of a system consists of those parts of a system that must be trusted in order for the system to be secure. In other words, the TCB is that part of the system that is able to compromise security. Ideally the TCB should be as small as possible. Sometimes this may require having to implement key middleware or OS services by the user themselves to prevent the whole middleware or OS from becoming part of the TCB. It may also be necessary to physically separate security sensitive services from other parts of the system so that those other parts do not become part of the TCB.

Finally, an important issue (not just with regards to security) is simplicity. Simplicity of a system contributes to trust. The simpler a system is, the easier it is to understand, and the more trustworthy it becomes. Unfortunately it is generally difficult to build a simple and secure system, since security mechanisms usually add much complexity to systems.

(iii) Kerberos

Kerberos is a commercial authentication system developed at MIT. It is based on Needham-Schroeder protocol and integrates symmetric key encryption, distribution and authentication into commercial computer systems. It requires a secure central server, but allows for an insecure network (so, never transmits cleartext passwords) and insecure workstations (workstations are shared between users so user passwords are held on workstations only for very short periods). Moreover, it does not hold system keys on workstations. The central server, called the key distribution centre (KDC) contains:

→ an authentication service *A*, which knows all user logins and their passwords (secret keys) as well as identity and key of *T*, and

→ a ticket granting service *T*, which knows all servers and their secret keys.

The Kerberos protocol has three phases:

1. Login session setup (user authentication).
2. Server session setup (establishing secure channel to server).
3. Client-server RPC.

The whole protocol is illustrated in Fig. 10.13.

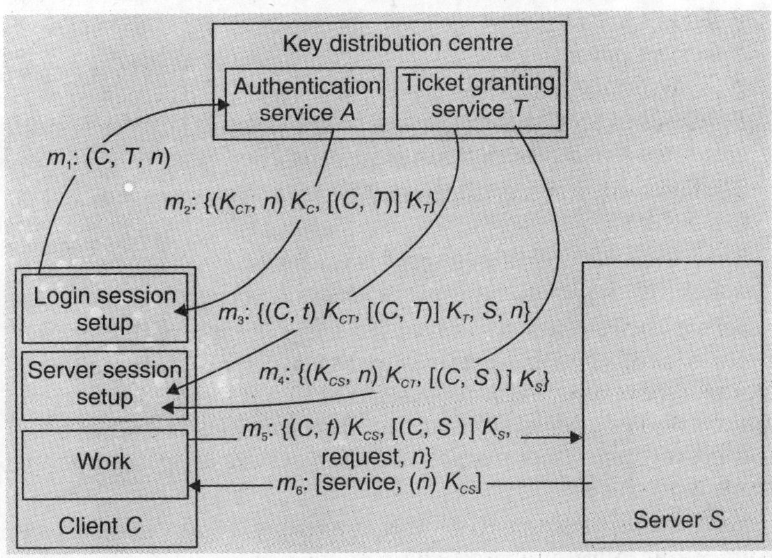

Fig. 10.13: Kerberos protocol

Kerberos user authentication: At login, the local login session setup component proceeds as follows:

1. Prompts user for login, *C*, and password, *KC*;
2. Sends *C*, nonce *n*, and request for server ticket to *A*;
3. A replies with certified session key *KCT* for communication with *T* and
   Ticket (*C*, *T*) = (*C*, *T*, *t*1, *t*2, *KCT*), valid between *t*1 and *t*2

4. User's password is used to decrypt certificate (KCT, *n*) *KC*, this authenticates the user.
5. User's password is erased.

The ticket can now be used to obtain server keys from *T*. When the ticket times out, users must re-authenticate. The nonce protects against replay attacks pretending to be from *A* and security is achieved via a shared secret, namely user's password.

Kerberos server session setup: When a user wants to communicate with server S, the server session setup component proceeds as follows:

1. Sends to *T*:
   - Authenticator (*C*, *t*) encrypted with joint key *KCT*.
   - Ticket (*C*, *T*).
   - Server name *S*.
   - New nonce *n*.
2. *T* authenticates the ticket, recovering joint key *KCT*, and validates the authenticator (and thus client *C*).
3. Replies with key certificate (*KCS*, *n*) *KCT* and server ticket [(*C*, *S*)] *KS*.
4. *C* verifies key certificate and now possesses key *KCS* and ticket [(*C*, *S*)] KS to communicate with server.

Servers only use a session key during the interval specified in the ticket. The timestamp in the authenticator protects against replay attacks pretending to be C and the nonce protects against replay attacks pretending to be from *T*. A ticket is only needed to open a connection, but the server keeps a timeout value with the key.

Kerberos client-server RPC: When a user *C* requests a service from *S*, the following protocol is used:

1. *C* sends to *S*:
   - Authenticator (*C*, *t*) encrypted with joint key *KCS*.
   - Ticket (*C*, *S*).
   - Request.
   - New nonce *n*.
2. *S* authenticates the ticket, recovers the joint key *KCS*, and validates the authenticator (and thus client *C*).
3. Replies with the result and the encrypted nonce.

Finally, *C* verifies the once.

(iv) Protection

Once a principal has been authenticated it is necessary to determine what actions that principal is allowed to perform and to enforce any restrictions placed on it. Restricting actions and enforcing those restrictions allows resources to be protected against abuse. When discussing protection of resources we often refer to access rights, which are the rights required to access a given resource. Protection of resources requires, on the one hand, the ability to verify and enforce access rights and, on the other hand, the ability to grant and revoke access rights. The former will be referred to as access control, while the latter will be authorisation. Note that the three terms, protection, access control and authorisation are often used interchangeably to refer to the same thing, i.e. protection. Underlying the discussion of protection lies the concept of protection domains. A protection domain is an abstraction that represents an execution environment for processes and defines the access rights that processes executing in that environment have. These access rights are defined as object-rights pairs (where an object is a resource in the system). Generally a protection domain is associated with a single principal, that is, it contains all the access rights that that principal possesses. Any process started by that principal will then execute in that protection domain and have the access rights defined therein. It is also common to define protection domains for groups and roles. In this case all processes that belong to a particular group or that have a particular role will be executed in the associated protection domains. The standard approach to determining the access permissions of a given authenticated subject to a given object is an access control matrix. The rows of the matrix define a subject's protection domain and the columns an object's accessibility. The access control matrix is a dynamic data structure in that it frequently changes. The change can be permanent, such as that caused by Unix's chmod command, or temporary, such as that caused by Unix's setuid bit on executable files. Because the matrix is very sparse and has many repeated entries, it is usually not stored explicitly. Before we discuss the two alternatives for implementing the access matrix, let us briefly review some design considerations in a protection system. Later we will evaluate the implementations based on these design considerations. We consider the following points:

Propagation of rights: Can someone act as an agent's proxy? That is, can one subject's access rights be delegated to another subject?

Restriction of rights: Can a subject propagate a subset of their rights (as opposed to all of their rights)?

Amplification of rights: Can an unprivileged subject perform some privileged operations [i.e. (temporarily) extend their protection domain]?

Revocation of rights: Can a right, once granted, be removed from a subject?

Determination of object accessibility: Who has which access rights on a particular object?

Determination of a subject's protection domain: What is the set of objects that a particular subject can access?

(v) Implementation of the Access Matrix

An efficient representation of the access matrix can be achieved by representing it either by column or row. A column-wise representation that associates access rights with objects is called an access control list (ACL). Row-wise representations that associate access rights with subjects are based on capabilities.

Access Control Lists

Each object may be associated with an access control list (ACL), which corresponds to one column of the access matrix, and is represented as a list of subject-rights pairs. When a subject tries to access an object, the set of rights associated with that subject is used to determine whether access should be granted. This comparison of the accessing subject's identity with the subjects mentioned in the ACL requires prior authentication of the subject. ACL-based systems usually support a concept of group rights (granted to each agent belonging to the group) or domain classes. When a large number of objects provide the same rights to a set of subjects, these subjects may be combined into a group, thus reducing the size of the ACL.

To reduce the number of groups needed, a system may have the ability to denote negative rights, so that exceptions can be easily expressed. In practice, to keep the ACL small, existing systems simplify ACLs to a fixed-size list, e.g. UNIX's user-group-others or VMS' system-owner-group-world.

The properties of ACLs, with respect to the previously listed design considerations, are as follows:

- ***Propagation:*** The owner of an object can add to or modify entries to the ACL, e.g. owner can chmod,
- ***Restriction:*** Anyone who has the right to modify the ACL can restrict access. Amplification: ACL entries can include protected-invocation rights, e.g. setuid,
- ***Revocation:*** Access rights can be revoked by removing or modifying ACL entries,
- ***Object accessibility:*** The ACL itself represents an object's accessibility,
- ***Protection domain:*** Hard (if not impossible) because the ACLs of all objects in the system must be inspected.

Capabilities

As an alternative to ACLs, subjects may be associated with a list of the access rights that they possess. In this case, a list of a subject's access rights is called a capabilities list, which also defines a protection domain. Each capability in a capability list can confer a single or a set of rights on an object. Some of these rights may be negative rights. A capability implicitly refers to a single object and can, therefore, be used as an object reference. Because capabilities also implicitly specify access rights for an object, they can be thought of as keys 2 that give access to objects. The possession of a capability can be regarded as sufficient evidence of access permission to the associated object.

The main technical problem in a capability-based system is protecting capabilities against forgery and theft. In return, because a capability alone is sufficient to prove the right for object access there is no need for explicit authentication of subjects upon object access. As a result, the system does not need to trust any intermediary, such as a remote OS kernel.

The properties of capabilities, with respect to the previously listed design considerations, are as follows:

- *Propagation:* Is achieved by simply copying a capability,
- *Restriction:* May be supported by means of derived capabilities,
- *Amplification:* Requires special amplification capabilities,
- *Revocation:* Can be difficult and depends on exactly how capabilities are represented,
- *Object accessibility:* Is hard (if not impossible) because it requires the inspection of every subject's capabilities,
- *Protection domain:* A capability list represents a protection domain.

Limitations of Access Matrix Model

Lock-key models, which combine ACLs and capabilities, try to overcome some of the disadvantages of the separate models. In these models an object has a lock (ACL) and a subject has a key (capability). Access is only permitted if both match. Note that the use of an access matrix does not provide complete protection. In particular it cannot prevent an authorised subject from accessing a resource on behalf of another unauthorized subject. This is called the confinement problem. Information can be leaked via storage channels (e.g. via files) legitimate channels (e.g. during normal communication), or covert channels (e.g. by modulating resource usage) which is very difficult to prevent. These problems can only be tackled by strictly limiting information flow. We generally distinguish between access-matrix based models that provide discretionary security, where the user has control (discretion) over who may access their data and security depends on users being trustworthy and sensible, and mandatory access control where security policies are enforced system-wide.

10.18.8 Naming

Most computer systems manage wide collections of entities such as, files, users, hosts, networks, and so on. These entities are referred to by users of the system and other entities by various kinds of names. For largely historical reasons, different entities are often named using different naming schemes. We say that they exist in different name spaces. From time to time a new system design attempts to integrate a variety of entities into a homogeneous name space, and then also attempts to provide a uniform interface to these entities. For example, a central concept of Unix systems is the uniform treatment of files, devices, sockets and so on. Some systems also introduce a /proc file system, which maps processes to names in the file system and supports access to process information through this file interface. In addition, Linux provides access to a variety of kernel data structures via the proc file system. In general 'all resources are named and accessed like files in a forest of hierarchical file systems'.

10.18.8.1 Basic Concepts

A name is the fundamental concept underlying naming. We define a name as a string of bits or characters that is used to refer to an entity. An entity in this case is any resource, user, process, etc. in the system. Entities are accessed by performing operations on them, the operations are performed at an entity's access point. An access point is also referred to by a name, we call an access point's name an address. Entities may have multiple access points and may, therefore, have multiple addresses. Furthermore an entity's access points may change over time (that is an entity may get new access points or lose existing ones), which means that the set of an entity's addresses may also change.

We distinguish between a number of different kinds of names. A pure name 1 is a name hat consists of an uninterrupted bit pattern that does not encode any of the named entity's attributes. A nonpure name, on the other hand, does encode entity attributes (such as an access point address) in the name. An identifier is a name that uniquely identifies an entity. An identifier refers to at most one entity and an entity is referred to by at most one identifier. Furthermore an identifier can never be reused, so that it will always refer to the same entity. Identifiers allow for easy comparison of entities; if two entities have the same identifier then they are the same entity. Pure names that are also identifiers are called pure identifiers. Location independent names are names that are independent of an entity's address. They remain valid even if an entity moves or otherwise changes its address. Note that pure names are always location independent, though location independent names do not have to be pure names.

10.18.8.2 System Names Versus Human Names

Related to the purity of names is the distinction between system-oriented and human-oriented names. Human-oriented names are usually chosen for their mnemonic value, whereas system-oriented names are a means for efficient access to, and identification of objects.

Taking into account the desire for transparency human-oriented names would ideally be pure. In contrast, system-oriented names are often nonpure which speeds up access to repeatedly used object attributes. We can characterise these two kinds of names as follows:

- System-oriented names are usually fixed size numerals (or a collection thereof); thus they are easy to store, compare, and manipulate, but difficult for the user to remember.
- Human-oriented names are usually variable-length strings, often with structure; thus they are easy for humans to remember, but expensive to process by machines.

System-Oriented Names

As mentioned, system-oriented names are usually implemented as one or more fixed-sized numerals to facilitate efficient handling. Moreover, they typically need to be unique identifiers and may be sparse to convey access rights, e.g. capabilities. Depending on whether they are globally or locally unique, we also call them structured or unstructured.

The structuring may be over multiple levels. Structured name is always not pure. Global uniqueness without further mechanism requires a centralised generator with the usual drawbacks regarding scalability and reliability. In contrast, distributed generation without excessive communication usually leads to structured names. For example, a globally unique structured name can be constructed by combining the local time with a locally unique identifier. Both values can be generated locally and do not require any communication.

Human-Oriented Names

In many systems, the most important attribute bound to a human-oriented name is the system-oriented name of the object. All further information about the entity is obtained via the system-oriented name. This enables the system to perform the usually costly resolution of the human-oriented name just once and implement all further operations on the basis of the system-oriented name (which is more efficient to handle). Often a whole set of human-oriented names is mapped to a single system-oriented name (symbolic links, relative addressing and so on).

As an example of all this, consider the naming of files in Unix. A pathname is a human-oriented name that, by means of the directory structure of the file system, can be resolved to an inode number, which is a system-oriented name. All attributes of a file are accessible via the inode, i.e. the system-oriented name. By virtue of symbolic and hard links multiple human-oriented names may refer to the same inode, which makes equality testing of files merely by their human-oriented name impossible.

The design space for human-oriented names is considerably wider than that for system-oriented names. As such naming systems for human-oriented names usually require considerably greater implementation effort.

Name Spaces

Names are grouped and organised into name spaces. A structured name space is represented as a labelled directed graph, with two types of nodes. A leaf node represents a named entity and stores information about the entity. This information could include the entity itself, or a reference to the entity, e.g. an address. A directory node (also called a context) is an inner node and does not represent any single entity. Instead it stores a directory table, containing (node 'id, edge' label) pairs, that describes the node's children. A leaf node only has incoming edges, while a directory node has both incoming and outgoing edges. A third kind of node, a root node, is a directory node with only outgoing edges.

A structured name space can be strictly hierarchical or can form a directed acyclic graph (DAG). In a strictly hierarchical name space a node will only have one incoming edge. In a DAG name space any node can have multiple incoming edges. It is also possible to have name spaces with multiple root nodes. Scalable systems usually use hierarchically structured name spaces. A sequence of edge labels leading from one node to another is called a path name. A path name is used to refer to a node in the graph. An absolute path name always starts from a root node. A relative path name is any path name that does not start at the root node. Many name spaces support aliasing, in which case an entity may be reachable by multiple paths from a root node and will, therefore, be named by numerous path names. There are two types of alias. A hard link is when there are two or more paths that directly lead to that entity. A soft link, on the other hand, occurs when a leaf node holds a pathname that refers to another node. In this case the leaf node implicitly refers to the file named by the pathname.

Ideally we would have a global, homogeneous name space that contains names for all entities used. However, we are often faced with the situation where we already have a collection of name spaces that have to be combined into a larger name space. One approach is to simply create a new name that combines names from the other name spaces. An example of the composition of name spaces is mounting a name space onto a mount point in a different (external) name space. This approach is often applied to merge file systems, e.g. mounting a remote file system onto a local mount point. In terms of a name space graph, mounting requires one directory node to contain information about another directory node in the external name space. This is similar to the concept of soft linking, except that in this case the link is to a node outside of the name space. The information contained in the mount point node must, therefore, include information about where to find the external name space.

10.18.8.3 Name Resolution

The process of determining what entity a name refers to is called name resolution. Resolving a name results in a reference to the entity that the name refers to. Resolving a name in a name space often results in a reference to the node that the name refers to. Path name resolution is a process that starts with the resolution of the first element in the path name, and ends with resolution of the last element in the name. There are two approaches to this process, iterative resolution and recursive resolution.

In iterative resolution the resolver contacts each node directly to resolve each individual element of the path name. In recursive resolution the resolver only contacts the first node and asks it to resolve the name. This node looks up the node referred to by first element of the name and then passes the rest of the name onto that node. The process is repeated until the last element is resolved after which the result is returned back through the nodes to the resolver. A problem with name resolution is how to determine which node to start resolution at. Knowing how and where to start name resolution is referred to as the closure mechanism. One approach is to keep an external reference (e.g. in a file) to the root node of the name space. Another approach is to keep a reference to the 'current' directory node for dealing with relative names. Note that the actual closure mechanism is always implicit, that is it is never explicitly defined in a name. The reason for this is that if a closure mechanism was defined in a name there would have to be a way to resolve the name used for that closure mechanism. This would require the use of a closure mechanism to bootstrap the original closure mechanism. Because this could be repeated indefinitely, at a certain point an implicit mechanism will always be required.

10.18.8.4 Naming Service

A naming service is a service that provides access to a name space allowing clients to perform operations on the name space. These operations include adding and removing directory or leaf nodes, modifying the contents of nodes and looking up names. The naming service is implemented by name servers. Name resolution is performed on behalf of clients by resolvers. A resolver can be implemented by the client itself, in the kernel, by the name server, or as a separate service.

(i) Distributed Naming Service

As with most other system services, naming becomes more involved in a distributed environment. A distributed naming service is implemented using multiple name servers over which the name space is partitioned and/or replicated. The goal of a distributed naming service is to distribute both the management and name resolution load over these name servers. Before discussing implementation aspects of distributed naming services it is useful to split a name space up into several layers according to the role the nodes play in the name space. These layers help to determine how and where to partition and replicate that part of the name space. The highest level nodes belong to the global layer. A main characteristic of nodes in this layer is that they are stable, meaning that they do not change much. As such, replicating these nodes is relatively easy because consistency does not cause much of a problem. The next layer is the administrational layer. The nodes in this layer generally represent a part of the name space that is associated to a single organisational entity, e.g. a company or a university. They are relatively stable (but not as stable as the nodes in the global layer). Finally the lowest layer is the managerial layer. This layer sees much change. Nodes may be added or removed as well as have their contents modified. The nodes in the top layers generally see the most traffic and, therefore, require more effort to keep their performance at an acceptable level.

Typically, a client does not directly converse with a name server, but delegates this to a local resolver that may use caching to improve performance. Each of the name servers stores one or more naming contexts, some of which may be replicated. We call the name servers storing attributes of an object this object's authoritative name servers.

Directory nodes are the smallest unit of distribution and replication of a name space. If they are all on one host, we have one central server, which is simple, but does not scale and does not provide fault tolerance. Alternatively, there can be multiple copies of the whole name space, which is called full replication. Again, this is simple and access may be fast. However, the replicas will have to be kept consistent and this may become a bottleneck as the system grows. In the case of a hierarchical name space, partial sub-trees (often called zones) may be maintained by a single server. In the case of the Internet Domain Name Service (DNS), this distribution also matches the physical distribution of the network. Each zone is associated with a name prefix that leads from the root to the zone. Now, each node maintains a prefix table (essentially, a hint cache for name servers corresponding to zones) and, given a name, the server corresponding to the zone with the longest matching prefix is contacted. If it is not the authoritative name server, the next zone's prefix is broadcast to obtain the corresponding name server (and update the prefix table). As an alternative to broadcasting, the contacted name server may be able to provide the address of the authoritative name server for this zone. This scheme can be efficiently implemented, as the prefix table can be relatively small and, on average, only a small number of messages are needed for name resolution. Consistency of the prefix table is checked on use, which removes the need for explicit update messages.

For smaller systems, a simpler structure-free distribution scheme may be used. In this scheme contexts can be freely placed on the available name servers (usually, however, some distribution policy is in place). Name resolution starts at the root and has to traverse the complete resolution chain of contexts. This is easy to reconfigure and, for example, used in the standard naming service of CORBA.

(ii) Implementation of Naming Services

In the following, we consider a number of issues that must be addressed by implementations of name services. First, a starting point for name resolution has to be fixed. This essentially means that the resolver must have a list of name servers that it can contact. This list will usually not include the root name server to avoid overloading it. Instead, physically close servers are normally chosen. For example, in the BIND (Berkeley Internet Name Domain) implementation of DNS, the resolver is implemented as a library linked to the client program. It expects the file /etc./resolv.conf to contain a list of name servers. Moreover, it facilitates relative naming in form of the search option.

10.18.8.5 Name Caches

Name resolution is expensive. For example, studies found that a large proportion of Unix system calls (and network traffic in distributed systems) is due to name-mapping operations. Thus, caching of the results of name resolution on the client is attractive:

- High degree of locality of name lookup; thus, a reasonably sized name cache can give good hit ratio.
- Slow update of name information database; thus, the cost for maintaining consistency is low.
- On-use consistency of cached information is possible; thus, no invalidation on update: stale entries are detected on use.

There are three types of name caches:

- ***Directory cache:*** Directory node data is cached. Directory caches are normally used with iterative name resolution. They require large caches, but are useful for directory listings, etc.
- ***Prefix cache:*** Path name prefix and zone information is cached. Prefix caching is unsuitable with structure-free context distribution.
- ***Full-name cache:*** Full path name information is cached. Full-name caching is mostly used with structure-free context distribution and tends to require larger cache sizes than prefix caches.

A name cache can be implemented as a process-local cache, which lives in the address space of the client process. Such a cache does not need many resources, as it typically will be small in size, but much of the information may be duplicated in other processes. More seriously, it is a short-lived cache and incurs a high rate of start-up misses, unless a scheme such as cache inheritance is used, which propagates cache information from parent to child processes. The alternative is a kernel cache, which avoids duplicate entries and excessive start-up misses, but access to a kernel cache is slower and it takes up valuable kernel memory. Alternatively, a shared cache can be located in a user-space cache process that is utilised by clients directly or by redirection of queries via the kernel (the latter is used in the CODA file system). Some Unixvariants use a tool called 'name server cache daemon' (nscd) as a user-space cache process.

Example: Domain Name System (DNS).

Attribute-Based Naming

Whereas names as described above encode at most one attribute of the named entity (e.g. a domain name encodes the entity's administrative or geographical location) in attribute-based naming an entity's name is composed of multiple attributes. An example of an attribute-based name is given below:

/C = AU/O = UNSW/OU = CSE/CN = WWW Server Hardware = Sparc/OS = Solaris/Server = Apache.

The name not only encodes the location of the entity (/C = AU/O = UNSW/OU = CSE, where C is the attribute country, O is organisation, OU is organisational unit—these are standard attributes in X. 500 and LDAP), it also identifies it as a Web server, and provides information about the hardware that it runs on, the operating system running on it, and the software used. Although an entity's attribute-based name contains information about all attributes, it is common to also define a distinguished name (DN), which consists of a subset of the attributes and is sufficient to uniquely identify the entity.

In attribute-based naming systems the names are stored in directories, and each distinguished name refers to a directory entry. Attribute-based naming services are normally called directory services. Similar to a naming service, a directory service implements a name space that can be flat or hierarchical. With a hierarchical name space its structure mirrors the structure of distinguished names.

The structure of the name space (i.e. the naming graph) is defined by a directory information tree (DIT). The actual contents of the directory (that is the collection of all directory entries) are stored in the directory information base (DIB).

10.18.9 Distributed File Systems

In a distributed file system (DFS), multiple clients share files provided by a shared file system. In the DFS model communication between processes is done using these shared files. The basic model provided by distributed file systems is that of clients accessing files and directories that are provided by one or more file servers. A file server provides a client with a file service interface and a view of the file system. Note that the view provided to different clients by the same server may be different, for example, if clients only see files that they are organized to access. Access to files is achieved by clients performing operations from the file service interface such as create, delete, read, write, etc. on a file server. Depending on the implementation the operations may be executed by the servers on the actual files, or by the client on local copies of the file. The key challenges of distributed systems apply to DFS as follows:

Transparency

- *Location:* A client cannot tell where a file is located.
- *Migration:* A file can transparently move to another server.
- *Replication:* Multiple copies of a file may exist.
- *Concurrency:* Multiple clients access the same file.

Flexibility

In a flexible DFS it must be possible to add or replace file servers. Also, a DFS should support multiple underlying file system types, e.g. various Unix file systems, various Windows file systems, etc.

Reliability

- *Consistency:* Employing replication and allowing concurrent access to files may introduce consistency problems.
- *Security:* Clients must authenticate themselves and servers must determine whether clients are organized to perform requested operation. Furthermore communication between clients and the file server must be secured.
- *Fault tolerance:* Clients should be able to continue working if a file server crashes. Likewise, data must not be lost and a restarted file server must be able to recover to a valid state.

Performance

In order for a DFS to offer good performance it may be necessary to distribute requests across multiple servers. Multiple servers may also be required if the amount of data stored by a file system is very large.

Scalability

A scalable DFS will avoid organized components such as an organized naming service, an organized locking facility and an organized file store. A scalable DFS must be able to handle an increasing number of files and users. It must also be able to handle growth over a geographic area (e.g. clients that are widely spread over the world) as well as clients from different administrative domains.

Client's Perspective: File Services

The File Service Interface represents files as an uninterpreted sequence of bytes that are associated with a set of attributes (owner, size, creation date, permissions, etc.) including information regarding protection, i.e. access control lists or capabilities of clients. Moreover, there is a choice between the upload/download model and the remote access model. In the first model, files are downloaded from the server to the client. Modifications are performed directly at the client after which the file is uploaded back to the server. In the second model all operations are performed at the server itself, with clients simply sending commands to the server.

There are benefits and drawbacks to both models. The first model, for example, can avoid generating traffic every time it performs operations on a file. Also, a client can potentially use a file even if it cannot access the file server. A drawback of performing operations locally and then sending an updated file back to the server is that concurrent modification of a file by different clients can cause problems. The second approach makes it possible for the file server to order all operations and therefore, allow concurrent modifications to the files. A drawback is that the client can only use files if it has contact with the file server. If the file server goes down, or the network connection is broken, then the client loses access to the files.

10.18.9.1 File Access Semantics

Ideally, the client would perceive remote files just like local ones. Unfortunately, the distributed nature of a DFS makes this goal hard to achieve. In the following we present the various file access semantics available, and discuss how appropriate they are to a DFS.

The first type of access semantics that we consider are called Unix semantics and they imply the following:

- A read after a write returns the value just written.
- When two writes follow in quick succession, the second persists.

In the case of a DFS, it is possible to achieve such semantics if there is only a single file server and no client-side caching is used. In practice, such a system is unrealistic because caches are needed for performance and write-through caches (which would make Unix semantics possible to combine with caching) are expensive. Furthermore deploying only a single file server is bad for scalability. Because of this it is impossible to achieve Unix semantics with distributed file systems.

Alternative semantic models that are better suited for a distributed implementation include:

- Session semantics
- Immutable files
- Atomic transactions.

In the case of session semantics, changes to an open file are only locally visible. Only after a file is closed, are changes propagated to the server (and other clients). This raises the issue of what happens if two clients modify the same file simultaneously. It is generally up to the server to resolve conflicts and merge the changes. Another problem with session semantics is that parent and child processes cannot share file pointers if they are running on different machines.

Immutable files cannot be altered after they have been closed. In order to change a file, instead of overwriting the contents of the existing file a new file must be created. This file may then replace the old one as a whole. This approach to modifying files does require that directories (unlike files) be updatable. Problems with this approach include a race condition when two clients try to replace the same file as well as the question of what to do with processes that are reading a file at the same time as it is being replaced by another process.

In Atomic Transaction model, a sequence of file manipulations can be executed indivisibly, which implies that two transactions can never interfere. This is the standard model for databases, but it is expensive to implement.

Server's Perspective: Implementation

Observations about the expected use of a file system can be used to guide the design of a DFS.

For instance a study on Unix reveals the following which guides in designing a DFS.

- Most files are small—less than 10 k.
- Reading is much more common than writing.
- Usually access is sequential; random access is rare.
- Most files have a short lifetime.
- File sharing is unusual.
- Most processes use only a few files.
- Distinct files classes with different properties exist.

These usage patterns (small files, sequential access, high read-write ratio) would suggest that an upload/download model for a DFS would be appropriate. Note, however, that different usage patterns may be observed at different kinds of institutions. In situations where the files are large, and are updated more often it may make more sense to use a DFS that implements a remote access model.

Besides the usage characteristics, implementation tradeoffs may depend on the requirements of a DFS. These include supporting a large file system, supporting many users, the need for high performance, and the need for fault tolerance. Thus, for example, a fault tolerant DFS may sacrifice some performance for better reliability guarantees, while a high performance DFS may sacrifice security and wide-area scalability in order to achieve extra performance.

10.18.9.2 Stateful Vs Stateless Servers

The file servers that implement a distributed file service can be stateless or stateful. Stateless file servers do not store any session state. This means that every client request is treated independently, and not as part of a new or existing session. Stateful servers, on the other hand, do store session state. They may, therefore, keep track of which clients have opened which files, current read and write pointers for files, which files have been locked by which clients, etc. The main advantage of stateless servers is that they can easily recover from failure. Because there is no state that must be restored, a failed server can simply restart after a crash and immediately provide services to clients as though nothing happened. Furthermore, if clients crash the server is not stuck with abandoned opened or locked files. Another benefit is that the server implementation remains simple because it does not have to implement the state accounting associated with opening, closing and locking of files.

The main advantage of stateful servers, on the other hand, is that they can provide better performance for clients. Because clients do not have to provide full file information every time they perform an operation, the size of messages to and from the server can be significantly decreased. Likewise the server can make use of knowledge of access patterns to perform read-ahead and do other optimisations. Stateful servers can also offer clients extra services such as file locking, and remember read and write positions.

10.18.9.3 Replication

The main approach to improving the performance and fault tolerance of a DFS is to replicate its content. A replicating DFS maintains multiple copies of files on different servers. This can prevent data loss, protect a system against down time of a single server, and distribute the overall workload.

There are three approaches to replication in a DFS:

Explicit replication: The client explicitly writes files to multiple servers. This approach requires explicit support from the client and does not provide transparency.

Lazy file replication: The server automatically copies files to other servers after the files are written. Remote files are only brought up to date when the files are sent to the server. The frequency of occurrence is up to the implementation and affects the consistency of the file state.

Group file replication: Write requests are simultaneously sent to a group of servers. This keeps all the replicas up to date, and allows clients to read consistent file state from any replica.

10.18.9.4 Caching

Besides replication, caching is often used to improve the performance of a DFS. In a DFS caching involves storing either a whole file, or the results of file service operations. Caching can be performed at two locations: at the server and at the client. Server-side caching makes use of file caching provided by the host operating system. This is transparent to the server and helps to improve the server's performance by reducing costly disk accesses. Client-side caching comes in two flavours:

1. On-disk caching
2. In-memory caching.

On-disk caching involves the creation of (temporary) files on the client's disk. These can either be complete files (as in the upload/download model) or they can contain partial file state, attributes, etc. In-memory caching stores the results of requests in the client-machine's memory. This can be process-local (in the client process), in the kernel, or in a separate dedicated caching process.

The issue of cache consistency in DFS has obvious parallels to the consistency issue in shared-memory systems, but there are other tradeoffs (for example, disk access delays come into play, the granularity of sharing is different, sizes are different, etc.). Furthermore, because write-through caches are too expensive to be useful, the consistency of caches will be weakened. This makes implementing Unix semantics impossible. Approaches used in DFS caches include, delayed writes where writes are not propagated to the server immediately, but in the background later on, and write-on-close where the server receives updates only after the file is closed. Adding a delay to write-on-close has the benefit of avoiding superfluous writes if a file is deleted shortly after it has been closed.

10.18.9.5 Case Study

Example: Network File System (NFS).

NFS is a remote access DFS that was introduced by Sun in 1985. The currently used version is version 3, however, a new version (4) has also been defined. NFS integrates well into Unix's model of mount points, but does not implement Unix semantics. NFS servers are stateless, i.e. NFS does not provide open and close operations. It supports caching, but no replication. NFS has been ported to many platforms and, because the NFS protocol is independent of the underlying file system, supports many different underlying file systems. On Unix, an NFS server runs as a daemon and reads the file /etc./export to determine what directories are exported to whom under which policy (for example, who is allowed to mount them, who is allowed to access them, etc.). Server-side caching makes use of file caching as provided by the underlying operating system and is, therefore, transparent. On the client side, exported file systems can be explicitly mounted or mounted on demand (called automounting). NFS can be used on diskless workstations so does not require local disk space for caching files. It does, however, support client-side caching, and allows both file contents as well as file attributes to be cached. Although NFS allows caching, it leaves the specifics up to the implementation. As such, file caching details are implementation specific. Cache entries are generally discarded after a fixed period of time and a form of delayed write-through is employed.

Traditionally, NFS trusts clients and servers and thus has only minimal security mechanisms in place. Typically, the clients simply pass Unix user ID and group ID of the process performing a request to the server. This implies that NFS users must not have root access on the clients, otherwise they could simply switch their identity to that of another user and then access that user's files. New security mechanisms have been put in place, but they also have their drawbacks: Secure NFS using Diffie-Hellman public key cryptography is more complex to implement and to manage the keys, and the key lengths used are too short to provide security in practice. Using Kerberos would turn NFS more secure, but it has high entry costs.

Example: Andrew File System (AFS).

The Andrew File System (AFS) is a DFS that came out of the Andrew research project at Carnegie Mellon University (CMU). Its goal was to develop a DFS that would scale to all computers on the university's campus. It was further developed into a commercial product and an open-source branch was later released under the name 'OpenAFS'. AFS offers the same API as Unix, implements Unix semantics for processes on the same machine, but implements write-on-close semantics globally. All data in AFS is mounted in the /afs directory and organised in cells, e.g. /afs/cs.cmu.edu. Cells are administrative units that manage users and servers.

Files and directories are stored on a collection of trusted servers called Vice. Client processes accessing AFS are redirected by the file system layer to a local user-level process called Venice (the AFS daemon), which then connects to the servers. The servers serve whole files, which are cached as a whole on the clients' local disks. For cached files a callback is installed on the corresponding server. After a process finishes modifying a file by closing it, the changes are written back to the server. The server then uses the callbacks to invalidate the file in other clients' caches. As a result, clients do not have to validate cached files on access (except after a reboot) and hence, there is only very little cache validation traffic. Data is stored on flexible volumes, which can be resized and moved between the servers of a cell. Volumes can be marked as read only, e.g. for software installations.

AFS does not trust Unix user IDs and instead uses its own IDs which are managed at a cell level. Users have to authenticate with Kerberos by using the klog command. On successful authentication, a token will be installed in the client's cache managers. When a process tries to access a file, the cache manager checks if there is a valid token and enforces the access rights. Tokens have a timp stamp and expire, so users have to renew their token from time to time. Authorisation is implemented by directory-based ACLs, which allow finer grained access rights than Unix.

Example: Coda.

Coda is an experimental DFS which is the successor of the Andrew File System (AFS) but supports disconnected, mobile operation of clients. Its design is much more ambitious than that of NFS. Coda has quite a number of similarities with AFS. On the client side, there is only a single mount point /coda. This means that the name space appears the same to all clients (and files, therefore, have the same name at all clients). File names are location transparent (servers cannot be distinguished). Coda provides client-side caching of whole files. The caching is implemented in a user-level cache process called

Venus. Coda provides Unix semantics for files shared by processes on one machine, but applies write-on-close (session) semantics globally. Because high availability is one of Coda's goals access to a cached copy of a file is only denied if it is known to be inconsistent.

In contrast to AFS, Coda supports disconnected operation, which works as follows. While disconnected (a client is disconnected with regards to a file if it cannot contact any servers that serve copies of that file) all updates are logged in a client modification log (CML). Upon reconnection, the operations registered in the CML are replayed on the server. In order to allow clients to work in disconnected mode, Coda tries to make sure that a client always has up-to-date cached copies of files that they might require. This process is called file hoarding. The system builds a user hoard database which it uses to update frequently used files using a process called a hoard walk. Conflicts upon reconnection are resolved automatically where possible, otherwise, manual intervention becomes necessary.

Files in Coda are organised in organisational units called volumes. A volume is a small logical unit of files, e.g. the home directory of a user or the source tree of a program. Volumes can be mounted anywhere below the /coda mount point (in particular, within other volumes). Coda allows files to be replicated on read/write servers. Replication is organised on a per volume basis, that is, the unit of replication is the volume. Updates are sent to all replicas simultaneously using multicast RPCs (Coda defines its own RPC protocol that includes a multicast RPC protocol). Read operations can be performed at any replica.

Example: Google File System.

The Google File System (GFS) is a distributed file system developed to support a system with very different requirements than traditionally assumed when developing file systems. GFS was designed and built to support operations (both production and research) at Google that typically involve large amounts of data, run distributed over very large clusters, and include much concurrent access to files. GFS assumes that most data operations are large sequential reads and large concurrent appends. One of the key assumptions driving the design is that, because very large clusters (built from commodity parts) are used, failure (of hardware or software resulting in crashes or corrupt data) is a regular occurrence rather than an anomaly.

Example: Sprite System.

In contrast to NFS, Sprite uses state on the file server in order to increase performance, but it must recover this state during a file server reboot. For example, some of the state on the file servers is used to keep track of which workstations are caching which files. If a client workstation asks to read a file that is cached for writing on another client, the file server knows to find the most up-to-date copy of the file on the client writing the file. It also knows to turn off client caching if a file is being write-shared between workstations. If a server crashes and reboots, it must recover its knowledge of which clients have which files cached, so that it can enforce cache consistency on future open requests. The solution in Sprite is to use the file system state replicated on the client workstations. Clients are aware of the set of files they have cached. When a client detects a reboot of a server, it recovers with the server by transferring its pertinent file system state to the server. After all interested clients have done this, the server once again has a consistent view of client caching. If a server suffers a hardware failure and cannot reboot quickly, distributed state and disk arrays provide recovery possibilities. If the file server's disk is undamaged and can be accessed from another machine, the clients can push the appropriate file system state to the new machine, recovering with it instead. Sprite is also a part of the XPRS which is a reliable array of inexpensive disks to address recovery from disk failures.

The problem in distributed state recovery is to make sure its performance scales as well as the size of the system scales, and we are currently testing several improvements to reduce the client recovery time. As the number of Sprite client workstations has increased, we've found that the first bottle neck in recovery is the number of RPC requests that the file sever can handle concurrently. In response, we have added negative acknowledgements to our RPC system so that when a server cannot allocate an RPC server process to a client request, it can inform the client that it is not down, but merely busy. This way, the client knows that it has not lost communication with the server and can back off and try again later. This reduced our client state recovery time with 40 clients from an intolerable 15 minutes (or more) to 100 seconds. With these and several other techniques we believe we can easily reduce client state recovery to about ½ second per client, or about 25 seconds with 50 clients.

11

Protection and Security

11.1 INTRODUCTION

In general protection is a mechanism for controlling the access to programs, processes or users to the resources defined by the computer system. The protection mechanism ensures the enforcement of a certain policy. This policy is established in several ways. Some of them are system design, system management and others may be user defined.

The purpose of a protection system is to prevent accidental or intentional misuse of a system.

- *Accidents:* Problems of this kind are easy to solve (can do things to make the likelihood small).
- *Malicious abuse:* Problems of this kind are very hard to completely eliminate (cannot leave any loopholes, cannot play on probabilities).

There are three aspects to a protection mechanism:

- ***User identification (authentication):*** This is to make sure we know who is doing what.
- ***Authorization determination:*** Must figure out what the user is and is not allowed to do. Need a simple database for this.
- ***Access enforcement:*** Must make sure there are no loopholes in the system.

Even the slightest flaw in any of these areas may ruin the whole protection mechanism.

Authentication

User identification is most often done with *passwords*. This is a relatively weak form of protection.

- A password is a secret piece of information used to establish the identity of a user.
- Passwords should not be stored in a readable form.
- One-way transformations should be used.
- Passwords should be relatively long and obscure.
- Another form of identification: badge or key.
- Does not have to be kept secret.
- Should not be able to be forged or copied.
- Can be stolen, but the owner should know if it is.

Key paradox: Key must be cheap to make, hard to duplicate. This means there must be some trick (i.e. secret) that has to be protected. Once identification is complete, the system must be sure to protect the identity since other parts of the system will rely on it.

Authorization Determination

Must indicate who is allowed to do what with what. Draw the general form as in access matrix (Fig. 11.1) with one row per user, one column per file. Each entry indicates the privileges of that user on that object. There are two general ways of storing this information: *access lists* and *capabilities*.

Access lists: With each file, indications on which users are allowed to perform which operations are made.

- In the most general form, each file has a list of pairs.
- It would be tedious to have a separate listing for every user, so they are usually grouped into classes. For example, in

Unix there are three classes: self, group, anybody else (nine bits per file).

- Access lists are simple, and are used in almost all file systems.

Capabilities: With each user, make indications on which files may be accessed, and in what ways.

- Store a list of pairs with each user. This is called a *capability list*.
- Typically, capability systems use a different naming arrangement, where the capabilities are the only names of objects. Naming objects that are not referred to in the capability list is impossible.
- In access-list systems, the default is usually for everyone to be able to access a file. In capability-based systems, the default is for no-one to be able to access a file unless they have been given a capability. There is no way of even naming an object without a capability.
- Capabilities are usually used in systems that need to be very secure. However, capabilities can make it difficult to share information: nobody can get access to the capability unless explicitly given to them.

Matrix of Protection

Objects

Actors	1	2	3	A	B	C	
A	Execute	Read write		Control			
B	Execute		Read write		Control	Control	*Capability*
C	Execute		Read			Control	
			Access list				

Fig. 11.1: Matrix of protection

11.2 CRYPTOGRAPHY

Cryptography might be summed up as the study of techniques and applications that depend on the existence of difficult problems. *Cryptanalysis* is the study of how to defeat the cryptographic mechanisms, and *cryptology* meaning 'hidden word' is the discipline of cryptography and cryptanalysis combined. In general cryptography is concerned with keeping communications private. Indeed, the protection of sensitive communications has been the emphasis of cryptography throughout the history. However, this is only one part of today's cryptography.

Encryption is the transformation of data into a form that is as close to impossible as possible to read without the appropriate knowledge. Its purpose is to ensure privacy by keeping information hidden from anyone for whom it is not intended, even those who have access to the encrypted data. *Decryption* is the reverse of encryption; it is the transformation of encrypted data back into an understandable form.

Encryption and decryption generally require the use of some secret information, referred to as a *key*. For some encryption mechanisms, the same key is used for both encryption and decryption; for other mechanisms, the keys used for encryption and decryption are different.

Authentication is as fundamentally a part of our lives as privacy. It is very much essential at an instance where our decisions and agreements are communicated electronically, we need to have electronic techniques for providing authentication.

Cryptography provides mechanisms for such procedures. A *digital signature* binds a document to the possessor of a particular key, while a *digital timestamp* binds a document to its creation at a particular time. These cryptographic mechanisms can be used to control access to a shared disk drive, a high security installation, or a pay-per-view TV channel.

The field of cryptography encompasses other uses as well. With just a few basic cryptographic tools, it is possible to build elaborate schemes and protocols that allow us to pay using electronic money, to prove we know certain information without revealing the information itself, and to share a secret quantity in such a way that a subset of the shares can reconstruct the secret.

While modern cryptography is growing increasingly diverse, cryptography is fundamentally based on problems that are difficult to solve. A problem may be difficult because its solution requires some secret knowledge, such as decrypting an encrypted message or signing some digital document. The problem may also be hard because it is intrinsically difficult to complete, such as finding a message that produces a given hash value.

11.2.1 Popular Techniques in Cryptography

There are two types of cryptosystems: *secret-key* and *public-key cryptography*. In secret-key cryptography, also referred to as symmetric cryptography, the same key is used for both encryption and decryption. The most popular secret-key cryptosystem in use today is the *Data Encryption Standard*.

In public-key cryptography, each user has a *public key* and a *private key*. The public key is made public while the private key remains secret. Encryption is performed with the public key while decryption is done with the private key. The *RSA public-key cryptosystem* is the most popular form of public-key cryptography. RSA stands for Rivest, Shamir, and Adleman, the inventors of the RSA cryptosystem.

The *Digital Signature Algorithm* is also a popular public-key technique, though it can only be used only for signatures, not encryption. *Elliptic curve cryptosystems* are cryptosystems based on mathematical objects known as elliptic curves. Elliptic curve cryptography has been gaining in popularity recently. Finally the *Diffie-Hellman key agreement protocol* is a popular public-key technique for establishing secret keys over an insecure channel.

11.2.2 Cryptography—Applications

Cryptography is extremely useful; there is a multitude of applications, many of which are currently in use. A typical application of cryptography is a system built out of the basic techniques. Such systems can be of various levels of complexity. Some of the more simple applications are secure communication, identification, authentication, and secret sharing. More complicated applications include systems for electronic commerce, certification, secure electronic mail, key recovery and secure computer access.

In general, the less complex the application, the more quickly it becomes a reality. Identification and authentication schemes exist widely, while electronic commerce systems are just beginning to be established. However, there are exceptions to this rule; namely, the adoption rate may depend on the level of demand. For example, SSL-encapsulated HTTP gained a lot more usage much more quickly than simpler link-layer encryption has ever achieved. The adoption rate may depend on the level of demand.

(i) Secure Communication

Secure communication is the most straightforward use of cryptography. Two people may communicate securely by encrypting the messages sent between them. This can be done in such a way that a third party eavesdropping may never be able to decipher the messages. While secure communication has existed for centuries, the key management problem has prevented it from becoming commonplace. Thanks to the development of public-key cryptography, the tools exist to create a large-scale network of people who can communicate securely with one another even if they had never communicated before.

(ii) Identification and Authentication

Identification and authentication are two widely used applications of cryptography. Identification is the process of verifying someone's or something's identity. For example, when withdrawing money from a bank, a teller asks to see identification (for example, a driver's licence) to verify the identity of the owner of the account. This same process can be done electronically using cryptography. Every automatic teller machine (ATM) card is associated with a 'secret' personal identification number (PIN), which binds the owner to the card and thus to the account. When the card is inserted into the ATM, the machine prompts the cardholder for the PIN. If the correct PIN is entered, the machine identifies that person as the rightful owner and grants access. Another important application of cryptography is authentication. Authentication is similar to identification, in that both allow an entity access to resources (such as an Internet account), but authentication is broader because it does not necessarily involve identifying a person or entity. Authentication merely determines whether that person or entity is authorized for whatever is in question.

(iii) Secret Sharing

Another application of cryptography, called secret sharing, allows the trust of a secret to be distributed among a group of people. For example, in a (k, n)-threshold scheme, information about a secret is distributed in such a way that any k out of the n people (k ? n) have enough information to determine the secret, but any set of $k - 1$ people do not. In any secret sharing scheme, there are designated sets of people whose cumulative information suffices to determine the secret. In some implementations of secret sharing schemes, each participant receives the secret after it has been generated. In other implementations, the actual secret is never made visible to the participants, although the purpose for which they sought the secret is allowed.

(iv) Electronic Commerce

Over the past few years there has been a growing amount of business conducted over the Internet. This form of business is called electronic commerce or *e*-commerce. *E*-commerce is comprised of online banking, online brokerage accounts, and Internet shopping, to name a few of the many applications. One can book plane tickets, make hotel reservations, rent a car, transfer money from one account to another, buy compact disks (CDs), clothes, books and so on all while sitting in front of a computer. However, simply entering a credit card number on the Internet leaves one open to fraud.

One cryptographic solution to this problem is to encrypt the credit card number when it is entered online, another is to secure the entire session. When a computer encrypts this information and sends it out on the Internet, it is incomprehensible to a third party viewer. The web server (Internet shopping center) receives the encrypted information, decrypts it, and proceeds with the sale without fear that the credit card number (or other personal information) slipped into the wrong hands. As more and more business is conducted over the Internet, the need for protection against fraud, theft and corruption of vital information increases.

(v) Certification

Another application of cryptography is certification; certification is a scheme by which trusted agents such as certifying authorities vouch for unknown agents, such as users. The trusted agents issue vouchers called certificates with each having some inherent meaning. Certification technology was developed to make identification and authentication possible on a large scale.

(vi) Key Recovery

Key recovery is a technology that allows a key to be revealed under certain circumstances without the owner of the key revealing it. This is useful for two main reasons: first of all, if a user loses or accidentally deletes his or her key, key recovery could prevent a disaster. Secondly, if a law enforcement agency wishes to eavesdrop on a suspected criminal without the suspect's knowledge, the agency must be able to recover the key. Key recovery techniques are in use in some instances; however, the use of key recovery as a law enforcement technique is somewhat controversial.

(vii) Remote Access

Secure remote access is another important application of cryptography. The basic system of passwords certainly gives a level of security for secure access, but it may not be enough in some cases. For instance, passwords can be eavesdropped, forgotten, stolen or guessed. Many products supply cryptographic methods for remote access with a higher degree of security.

(viii) Other Applications

Cryptography is not confined to the world of computers. Cryptography is also used in cellular (mobile) phones as a means of authentication; that is, it can be used to verify that a particular phone has the right to bill to a particular phone number. This prevents people from stealing (cloning) cellular phone numbers and access codes. Another application is to protect phone calls from eavesdropping using voice encryption.

11.2.3 Importance of Cryptography

Cryptography allows people to carry over the confidence found in the physical world to the electronic world, thus allowing people to do business electronically without worries of deceit and deception. Every day hundreds of thousands of people interact electronically, whether it is through *e*-mail, *e*-commerce (business conducted over the Internet), ATM machines or cellular phones. The perpetual increase of information transmitted electronically has led to an increased reliance on cryptography.

Cryptography on the Internet

The Internet, comprised of millions of interconnected computers, allows nearly instantaneous communication and transfer of information, around the world. People use *e*-mail to correspond with one another. The World Wide Web is used for online business, data distribution, marketing, research, learning and a myriad of other activities.

Cryptography makes secure websites and electronic safe transmissions possible. For a website to be secure all of the data transmitted between the computers where the data is kept and where it is received must be encrypted. This allows people to do online banking, online trading, and make online purchases with their credit cards, without worrying that any of their account information is being compromised. Cryptography is very important to the continued growth of the Internet and electronic commerce.

E-commerce is increasing at a very rapid rate. By the turn of the century, commercial transactions on the Internet are expected to total hundreds of billions of dollars a year. This level of activity could not be supported without cryptographic security. It has been said that one is safer using a credit card over the Internet than within a store or restaurant. It requires much more work to seize credit card numbers over computer networks than it does to simply walk by a table in a restaurant and lay hold of a credit card receipt. These levels of security, though not yet widely used, give the means to strengthen the foundation with which *e*-commerce can grow.

People use *e*-mail to conduct personal and business matters on a daily basis. *E*-mail has no physical form and may exist electronically in more than one place at a time. This poses a potential problem as it increases the opportunity for an eavesdropper to get a hold of the transmission. Encryption protects *e*-mail by rendering it very difficult to read by any unintended party. Digital signatures can also be used to authenticate the origin and the content of an *e*-mail message.

In some cases cryptography allows you to have more confidence in your electronic transactions than you do in real life transactions. For example, signing documents in real life still leaves one vulnerable to the following scenario. After signing your will, agreeing to what is put forth in the document, someone can change that document and your signature is still attached. In the electronic world this type of falsification is much more difficult because digital signatures are built using the contents of the document being signed.

Access Control

Cryptography is also used to regulate access to satellite and cable TV. Cable TV is set up so people can watch only the channels they pay for. Since there is a direct line from the cable company to each individual subscriber's home, the cable company will only send those channels that are paid for. Many companies offer pay-per-view channels to their subscribers. Pay-per-view cable allows cable subscribers to 'rent' a movie directly through the cable box. What the cable box does is decode the incoming movie, but not until the movie has been 'rented'. If a person wants to watch a pay-per-view movie, he/she calls the cable company and requests it. In return, the cable company sends out a signal to the subscriber's cable box, which unscrambles (decrypts) the requested movie.

Satellite TV works slightly differently since the satellite TV companies do not have a direct connection to each individual subscriber's home. This means that anyone with a satellite dish can pick up the signals. To alleviate the problem of people getting free TV, they use cryptography. The trick is to allow only those who have paid for their service to unscramble the transmission; this is done with receivers. Each subscriber is given a receiver; the satellite transmits signals that can only be unscrambled by such a receiver (ideally). Pay-per-view works in essentially the same way as it does for regular cable TV.

As seen, cryptography is widely used. Not only is it used over the Internet, but also it is used in phones, televisions and a variety of other common household items. Without cryptography, hackers could get into our *e*-mail, listen in on our phone conversations, tap into our cable companies and acquire free cable service, or break into our bank/brokerage accounts.

11.3 AUTHENTICATION

Authentication is any process by which one can verify that someone is who they claim they are. This usually involves a username and a password, but can include any other method of demonstrating identity, such as a smart card, retina scan, voice recognition or fingerprints. Authentication is equivalent to showing your drivers licence at the ticket counter at the airport.

Basic authentication is the simplest method of authentication, and for a long time was the most common authentication method used.

(i) How Basic Authentication Works

When a particular resource has been protected using basic authentication, server sends an 'authentication required header' with the response to the request, in order to notify the client that user credentials must be supplied in order for the resource to be returned as requested.

Upon receiving a 401 response header, the client's browser, if it supports basic authentication, will ask the user to supply a username and password to be sent to the server. If you are using a graphical browser, such as Netscape or Internet Explorer, what you will see is a box which pops up and gives you a place to type in your username and password, to be sent back to the server. If the username is in the approved list, and if the password supplied is correct, the resource will be returned to the client.

Because the HTTP protocol is stateless, each request will be treated in the same way, even though they are from the same client. That is, every resource which is requested from the server will have to supply authentication credentials over again in order to receive the resource. Fortunately, the browser takes care of the details here, so that you only have to type in your username and password one time per browser session, that is, you might have to type it in again the next time you open up your browser and visit the same website.

Along with the response, certain other information will be passed back to the client. In particular, it sends a name which is associated with the protected area of the website. This is called the *realm*, or just the authentication name. The client browser caches the username and password that you supplied, and stores it along with the authentication realm, so that if other resources are requested from the same realm, the same username and password can be returned to authenticate that request without requiring the user to type them in again. This caching is usually just for the current browser session, but some browsers allow you to store them permanently, so that you never have to type in your password again. The authentication name, or realm, will appear in the pop-up box, in order to identify what the username and password are being requested for.

Configuration: Protecting content with basic authentication.

There are two configuration steps which you must complete in order to protect a resource using basic authentication. Or three, depending on what you are trying to do.

1. Create a password file
2. Set the configuration to use this password file
3. Optionally, create a group file

(ii) Biometrics and Smart Card

For centuries, security was competing with secrecy. Even in this age of electronics and supercomputers, passwords and PINs are shared between the user and the computer or ATM machine to which access is needed. But secret passwords require a great deal of trust between parties sharing the secret. This traditional paradigm of shared-secret computer security could soon be a thing of the past with smart card-based cryptographic credentials and biometric authentication for access control.

Some individuals and companies are replacing shared secret security with the Public Key Infrastructure (PKI) approach. PKI uses a standardized set of transactions using asymmetric public key cryptography, a more secure and potentially much more functional mechanism for access to digital resources. The same system could also be used for securing physical access to controlled environments, such as your home or office.

In a PKI world, everyone would be issued at least one cryptographic key pair. Each key pair would consist of a secret (private) cryptographic key and a public cryptographic key. These keys are typically a 1024-bit or 2048-bit string of binary digits with a unique property: when one is used with an encoding algorithm to encrypt data, the other can be used with the same algorithm to decrypt the data. The encoding key cannot be used for decoding. Public keys are certified by a responsible party such as a notary public, passport office, government agency or trusted third party. The public key is widely distributed, often through a directory or database that can be searched by the public. But the private key remains a tightly guarded secret by the owner. Between sender and receiver, secure messaging (or other secure transaction) would work as described below (Figs 11.2 and 11.3).

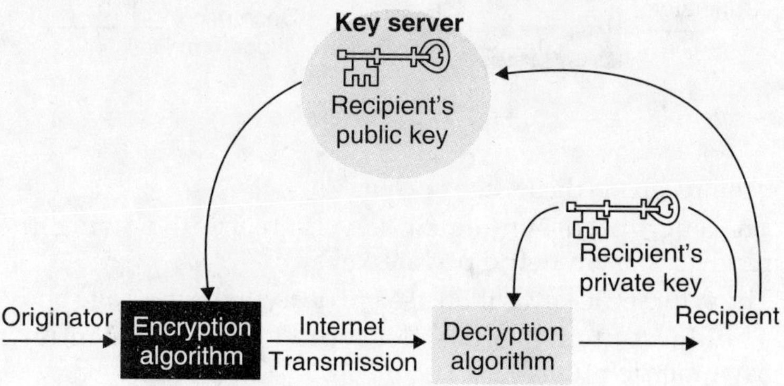

Fig. 11.2: Sender

For the sender, the following steps occur:

1. Message data is hashed; that is, a variable-length input string is converted to a fixed-length output string. Hash functions are mainly used with public key algorithms to create digital signatures.
2. A symmetric key is created and used to encrypt the entire message. DES and IDEA are examples of symmetric key cryptography.
3. The symmetric key is encrypted with the receiver's asymmetric public key.
4. The message hash is encrypted with the sender's asymmetric private key, creating a digital signature independent of the encrypted message.
5. The encrypted message, encrypted symmetric key and signed message hash are sent to the receiver.

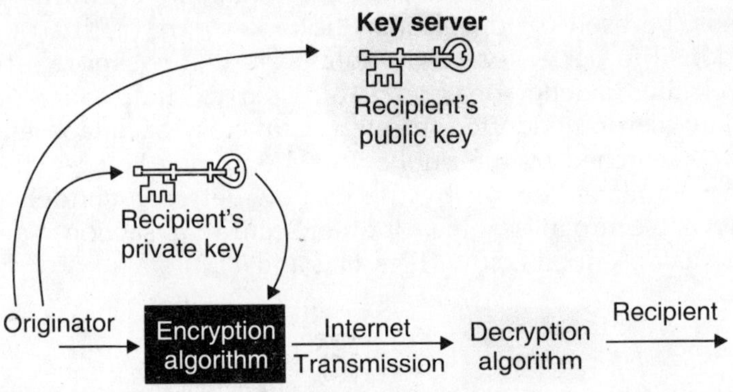

Fig. 11.3: Receiver

For the receiver, these steps occur:

1. The encrypted symmetric key is decrypted using the receiver's asymmetric private key.
2. The symmetric key is then used to decrypt the message body.
3. The encrypted hash is decrypted with the sender's asymmetric public key.
4. The decrypted message is then rehashed with the original hashing algorithm.

5. The two hashes are compared to verify the sender's identity and serves as proof that the message was not altered in transit.

Several technical issues must be solved before this scenario can be realized:

- Secure key storage.
- Secure authentication to the key store.
- Directory services (central public key database).
- Key escrow or other emergency recovery method for encrypted data.
- Cross-platform standards.
- International export and usage regulations for strong cryptography.

If these issues seem daunting, remember how impossible a common network strategy once seemed. Today, the Internet is everywhere and connected to almost every type of computer. Let's consider the PKI issues one by one.

1. Secure Key Storage

A few possibilities exist for key storage. Remember that these keys are long bit strings and memorizing them is out of the question. There are three storage possibilities: hard disk, floppy disk and smart card.

Hard disk storage provides a low-cost solution. The user's key pair is stored directly on the user's machine. The user authenticates with a shared-secret password to unlock their private key for signing. This solution does not allow for easy mobility in a desktop environment, and it puts constraints on terminal applications. A user cannot easily use another machine without off-loading the information to the machine they are trying to use. Problems also arise if a user tries to log into another machine and the network is unavailable. Hard disk storage also lends itself to physical attacks, such as theft of the terminal or hard drive, both of which can be used for leisurely password cracking.

Floppy disk storage addresses the mobility problem. Now the user has a quite inexpensive and portable way of using mobile digital credentials. Someone could use another machine simply by inserting the floppy and using a traditional shared secret password for authentication. However, floppy disks are not well known for long-term, robust data retention, particularly when carried around. Floppy disks are susceptible to magnetic fields (airport security stations, for example) and do not fit conveniently into your pocket or wallet.

Smart card storage presents the best scenario. Smart cards have been used for many years in Europe for a variety of applications. These credit-card-sized computers have a rugged and familiar form that fits nicely into a wallet or pocket and can take lots of physical stress. Some modern processor-based smart cards even have on-board cryptographic co-processors that allow signing and key generation to be done entirely on the card, so the private key might never need to be revealed or off-loaded. The microprocessor gives the smart card a big advantage over magnetic or optical media storage. A smart-card-based PKI might be very secure indeed, eliminating any possibility of the key pair being spoofed out during creation and transmission. The initial expense is higher, since smart cards require a reader. But this additional cost is offset by much higher security for the private key and by convenient porting.

2. Secure Authentication with Biometrics

All three storage methods—hard disk, floppy or smart card—could use shared-secret password or PIN to secure the private key. This accommodates single sign-on, since once a user authenticates to the key store, cryptographic protocols can be used for subsequent authentication to different applications. This would be good from an administrative point of view, but makes the security situation much worse. Now, if a cracker gains access to the shared secret password or PIN that secures the cryptographic keys, he also gains access to every cryptographically protected application or data element available to the authorized user. What we need is an authentication method to which only the authorized party has access to enter biometrics.

The word biometrics comes from the Greek words bio and metric, meaning 'life measurement'. By measuring something unique about an individual and using that to identify them, we can achieve a dramatic improvement in security of the key store. Newer biometric measurements include DNA from tissue samples, voice pattern, face pattern or even the arrangement of blood vessels in the retina or pattern of coloration in the cornea of the eye. The oldest and most widely accepted biometric is the fingerprint. The tip of every finger has a characteristic called 'friction ridges'. While generally similar, no two friction ridges are exactly the same. By imaging the ridges of the fingertips, we get the fingerprint.

Most implementations of fingerprint biometrics create a template from the original image, which is a fraction of the size of the original fingerprint image. This template can be used only to compare the fingerprint against other templates, and it cannot be used to recreate the original image. Template implementations of biometrics fit well with smart cards for two reasons. First, they usually range from 100 to 600 bytes in size and can easily fit on a smart card. Second, there is no need to worry about an attacker reproducing your fingerprints from your templates and using them to impersonate you. Biometrics can aid authentication. Here is a rough outline of the procedure for authenticating oneself to a computer application:

1. Insert the smart card into a reader. The smart card contains the cryptographic keys and biometric fingerprint data.
2. Enter the shared-secret PIN (or password), in order to unlock the digital representation of the fingerprint. In the trade, this is known as the minutia data.
3. Place the finger on the scanner. The scanned fingerprint is compared to the fingerprint data on the smart card.
4. If the data matches, the smart-card fingerprint data is converted into a number and combined with the smart-card secret PIN (retrieved in Step 2) and used as a symmetric cryptographic key to decrypt the private key.
5. A nonce (random number) is passed from the computer application to the smart card.
6. The private key on the smart card is used to encrypt the nonce and pass it back to the application.
7. The application verifies that a certified public key obtained from the network-based directory service or from the card does, in fact, decrypt the encrypted message from the card

and reveal the same nonce that was originally passed to the card.

This process undoubtedly authenticates the person presenting the card as the same person to whom the cryptographic keys belong and provides the necessary tight binding between the cryptographic key storage and the authorized user of the cryptographic keys.

Two terms describe the functionality of biometrics. The false acceptance rate (FAR) is the probability that an intruder is accepted with a measurement that does not belong to the enrolled user. The false rejection rate (FRR) is the probability that an enrolled user is not recognized. Good biometrics have low FAR and low FRR, but unfortunately few standardized tests are available to determine these results, as each biometric read takes measurements in a slightly different way. Thus, third-party verification is very important when evaluating any biometric.

As a rule, there is usually a trade-off between security and convenience. Biometrics are no exception. In general, the better their security (the lower the FAR), the more inconvenience there is to the user, because more false rejections occur. Similarly, the more convenient the system is to use, the poorer the security is. Good biometric systems allow the user to choose from a wide range of possible FAR/FRR levels, so that convenience can be maximized for the desired level of security.

Exposure to a few detective movies can cause the average person to ask the macabre but pertinent question, 'How can these devices ensure that the finger is alive?' Attempts have been made to solve this problem. Some vendors measure the heat of the finger to ensure that it is at body temperature, which makes the system difficult to use in cold climates or with people who are predisposed to cold hands. Other vendors measure the conductivity of the finger to prevent forged fingerprints (for example, silicone castings). This does not address the dead finger issue, but it is worth noting that conductivity measurements can be fooled with a bit of saline solution on the silicone casting. The best solutions spectroscopically measure the amount of oxygenated hemoglobin in the blood, as this measurement is the most difficult to fool and is radically different for live and dead fingers, but again there is a trade-off between price and necessity.

3. The Central Public Key Database

Directory services play an essential role in any PKI system. Applications must be able to verify the certificate authority of the public key contained on the smart card. The certificate authority is the organization that initially issued the encryption keys and smart card. The certificate authority verifies that the person is who they claim to be. If privacy concerns can be overcome, public keys (for the certificate authority and for the individual) should be available to all applications that need cross verification.

PKI at the office: A person has a smart card containing cryptographic keys secured with biometrics and signed (validated) by a government agency. Now the person applies for a job in the private sector. If the company verifies that the government signature is valid, the person's public key can be used for employment verification. The smart card is essentially reusable as identification.

Personal banking: This application makes a binding between the application, the public cryptographic key and personal data stored in an employee directory. Again, the original single identity token is reused. Directory services and biometrically secured cryptographic key storage would truly enable electronic commerce. Such a scheme, if widely adopted, would allow an individual to carry a single convenient token to authenticate themselves to applications anywhere.

Card management tracks communication speeds and the currently selected file. Consider the following example: Applicant B wants to off-load data from elementary file 2000. Applicant A is in wait state but currently has selected file 1000. The card manager must keep track of this file so that when Applicant B takes control, selects 2000 and performs data transfer, Applicant A can regain control upon completion and reselect elementary file 1000. Without such resource management, a user must assume another transaction has occurred and do a cold reset before any file or verification-related transaction.

Cards contain specific functions that make them unique. The most common is the cryptographic-capable smart card. In this card, it is necessary to have yet another common API which communicates with the card manager. This API is known as the *cryptographic service provider*. The cryptographic API performs functions such as key generation, secure signing, hashing, encryption and key verification.

Integrating smart cards, biometrics and public key cryptography provides a solid foundation for developing secure applications and communications. The highest level of security uses three-factor authentication:

- Something you know (password or PIN).
- Something you have (smart card, magnetic stripe card or a physical key).
- Something you are (your fingerprint, retinal/iris scan or voice pattern).

An individual gains three-factor authentication by combining a smart card, biometric and PIN. If the user loses the smart card, the card is inoperable without the biometric. Forged fingerprints are weeded out with use of the PIN.

In a smart-card-secure world, no one is locked into one form of authentication, such as the ever-vulnerable password. One can control the identity because it is contained on the card one carries. Even if attackers run Crack 5.0 on the Internet provider's password file, they cannot gain access without possession of the smart card tucked safely in the owner's front pocket.

11.4 SECURITY ATTACKS

(i) Cryptanalysis

Cryptanalysis refers to the study of ciphers, ciphertext, or cryptosystems (that is, to secret code systems) with a view to finding weaknesses in them that will permit retrieval of the plaintext from the ciphertext, without necessarily knowing the key or the algorithm. This is known as *breaking* the cipher, ciphertext or cryptosystem.

Breaking is sometimes used interchangeably with *weakening*. This refers to finding a property (fault) in the design or implementation of the cipher that reduces the number of keys required in a brute force attack (that is, simply trying every possible key until the correct one is found). For example, assume that a symmetric cipher implementation uses a key length of 2^128 bits (2 to the power of 128): this means that a brute force attack would need to try up to all 2^128 possible combinations (rounds) to be certain of finding the correct key (or, on average, 2^127 possible combinations) to convert the ciphertext into plaintext, which is not possible given present and near future computing abilities. However, a cryptanalysis of the cipher reveals a technique that would allow the plaintext to be found in 2^40 rounds. While not completely broken, the cipher is now much weaker and the plaintext can be found with moderate computing resources.

There are numerous techniques for performing cryptanalysis, depending on what access the cryptanalyst has to the plaintext, ciphertext or other aspects of the cryptosystem. Below are some of the most common types of attacks:

1. ***Known-plaintext analysis:*** With this procedure, the cryptanalyst has knowledge of a portion of the plaintext from the ciphertext. Using this information, the cryptanalyst attempts to deduce the key used to produce the ciphertext.
2. ***Chosen-plaintext analysis (also known as differential cryptanalysis):*** The cryptanalyst is able to have any plaintext encrypted with a key and obtain the resulting ciphertext, but the key itself cannot be analyzed. The cryptanalyst attempts to deduce the key by comparing the entire ciphertext with the original plaintext. The Rivest-Shamir-Adleman encryption technique has been shown to be somewhat vulnerable to this type of analysis.
3. ***Ciphertext-only analysis:*** The cryptanalyst has no knowledge of the plaintext and must work only from the ciphertext. This requires accurate guesswork as to how a message could be worded. It helps to have some knowledge of the literary style of the ciphertext writer and/or the general subject matter.
4. ***Man-in-the-middle attack:*** This differs from the above in that it involves tricking individuals into surrendering their keys. The cryptanalyst/attacker places him or herself in the

communication channel between two parties who wish to exchange their keys for secure communication (via asymmetric or public key infrastructure cryptography). The cryptanalyst/attacker then performs a key exchange with each party, with the original parties believing they are exchanging keys with each other. The two parties then end up using keys that are known to the cryptanalyst/attacker. This type of attack can be defeated by the use of a hash function.

5. ***Timing/differential power analysis:*** This is a new technique made public in June 1998, particularly useful against the smart card, that measures differences in electrical consumption over a period of time when a microchip performs a function to secure information. This technique can be used to gain information about key computations used in the encryption algorithm and other functions pertaining to security. The technique can be rendered less effective by introducing random noise into the computations, or altering the sequence of the executables to make it harder to monitor the power fluctuations. This type of analysis was first developed by Paul Kocher of Cryptography Research, though Bull Systems claims it knew about this type of attack over four years before.

In addition to the above, other techniques are available, such as convincing individuals to reveal passwords/keys, developing Trojan horse programs that steal a victim's secret key from their computer and send it back to the cryptanalyst, or tricking a victim into using a weakened cryptosystem. All of these are valid techniques in cryptanalysis, even though they may be considered unorthodox.

Successful cryptanalysis is a combination of mathematics, inquisitiveness, intuition, persistence, powerful computing resources—and more often than many would like to admit—luck. However, successful cryptanalysis has made the enormous resources often devoted to it more than worthwhile: the breaking of the German Enigma code during WWII, for example, was one of the key factors in an early Allied victory.

Today, cryptanalysis is practised by a broad range of organizations: governments try to break other governments' diplomatic and military transmissions; companies developing security products send them to cryptanalysts to test their security features and to a hacker or cracker to try to break the security of websites by finding weaknesses in the securing protocols. It is this constant battle between cryptographers trying to secure information and cryptanalysts trying to break cryptosystems that moves the entire body of cryptology knowledge forward.

(ii) Denial of Service Attack

A denial of service (DoS) attack is an incident in which a user or organization is deprived of the services of a resource they would normally expect to have. In a distributed denial of service, a large number of compromised systems (sometimes called a botnet) attack a single target.

Although a DoS attack does not usually result in the theft of information or other security loss, it can cost the target person or company a great deal of time and money. Typically, the loss of service is the inability of a particular network service, such as e-mail, to be available or the temporary loss of all network connectivity and services. A denial of service attack can also destroy programming and files in affected computer systems. In some cases, DoS attacks have forced websites accessed by millions of people to temporarily cease operation. Denial of service attacks can be difficult to distinguish from common network activity, but there are some indications that an attack is in progress.

In a denial of service (DoS) attack, an attacker attempts to prevent legitimate users from accessing information or services. By targeting your computer and its network connection, or the computers and network of the sites you are trying to use, an attacker may be able to prevent you from accessing e-mail, websites, online accounts (banking, etc.) or other services that rely on the affected computer.

The most common and obvious type of DoS attack occurs when an attacker 'floods' a network with information. When you type a URL for a particular website into your browser, you are sending a request to that site's computer server to view the page. The server can only process a certain number of requests at once, so if an attacker overloads the server with requests, it can't process your request. This is a 'denial of service' because you can't access that site.

An attacker can use spam e-mail messages to launch a similar attack on your e-mail account. Whether you have an e-mail account supplied by your employer or one available through a free service such as Yahoo or Hotmail, you are assigned a specific quota, which limits the amount of data you can have in your account at any given time. By sending many, or large, e-mail messages to the account, an attacker can consume your quota, preventing you from receiving legitimate messages.

Unfortunately, there are no effective ways to prevent being the victim of a DoS or DDoS attack, but there are steps you can take to reduce the likelihood that an attacker will use your computer to attack other computers:

- Install and maintain anti-virus software.
- Install a firewall, and configure it to restrict traffic coming into and leaving your computer.

Follow good security practices for distributing your e-mail address. Applying e-mail filters may help you manage unwanted traffic.

Not all disruptions to service are the result of a denial of service attack. There may be technical problems with a particular network, or system administrators may be performing maintenance. However, the following symptoms *could* indicate a DoS or DDoS attack:

- Unusually slow network performance (opening files or accessing websites).
- Unavailability of a particular website.
- Inability to access any website.
- Dramatic increase in the amount of spam you receive in your account.

There are two types of DoS attacks, both of which are described in the next major section:

1. ***Operating system attacks:*** Which target bugs in specific operating systems and can be fixed with patches.
2. ***Networking attacks:*** Which exploit inherent limitations of networking and may require firewall protection.

Operating System Attacks

These attacks exploit bugs in a specific operating system (OS), which is the basic software that the computer runs, such as Windows XP. In general, when these problems are identified, they are promptly fixed by the company such as Microsoft, so this vulnerability can be reduced by frequently applying the latest security patches. All Windows users should regularly visit Microsoft's Windows Update Site which automatically checks to see if they need any updates. If possible, set the PC to check for updates automatically and at least weekly.

Networking Attacks

These attacks exploit inherent limitations of networking to disconnect the user from the IRC server or from ISP, but do not usually cause crash to computer. Generally, it does not matter what kind of operating system is used, and there is essentially nothing can be done personally to defend against the attacks. Even large companies like Yahoo, Amazon and Microsoft have been crippled by such large scale attacks. Network attacks include outright floods of data to overwhelm the finite capacity of the connection, spoofed unreach/redirect aka 'click' which tricks the computer into thinking there is a network failure and voluntarily breaking the connection, and a whole new generation of distributed denial of service attacks (although these are seldom used against individuals unless you've really upset somebody).

Just because one gets disconnected with some unusual error message such as the ubiquitous 'Connection reset by peer' (external link) for Windows users doesn't mean he is attacked. Almost all disconnects are due to natural network failures. On the other hand, if disconnected repeatedly, especially if it happens only when certain IRC channels or talk to certain people is made, it is suspicious.

Common forms of denial of service attacks are:

Buffer Overflow Attacks

The most common kind of DoS attack is simply to send more traffic to a network address than the programmers who planned its data buffers anticipated someone might send. The attacker may be aware that the target system has a weakness that can be exploited or the attacker may simply try the attack in case it might work. A few of the better-known attacks based on the buffer characteristics of a program or system include:

- Sending e-mail messages that have attachments with 256-character file names to Netscape and Microsoft mail programs.
- Sending oversized Internet Control Message Protocol (ICMP) packets (this is also known as the Packet Internet or Inter-Network Groper (ping) of death).
- Sending to a user of the Pine e-mail progam a message with a 'From' address larger than 256 characters.

SYN Attack

When a session is initiated between the Transport Control Program (TCP) client and server in a network, a very small buffer space exists to handle the usually rapid 'hand-shaking' exchange of messages that sets up the session. The session-establishing packets include a SYN field that identifies the sequence in the message exchange. An attacker can send a number of connection requests very rapidly and then fail to respond to the reply. This leaves the first packet in the buffer so that other, legitimate connection requests can't be accommodated. Although the packet in the buffer is dropped after a certain period of time without a reply, the effect of many of these bogus connection requests is to make it difficult for legitimate requests for a session to get established. In general, this problem depends on the operating system providing correct settings or allowing the network administrator to tune the size of the buffer and the timeout period.

Teardrop Attack

This type of denial of service attack exploits the way that the Internet Protocol (IP) requires a packet that is too large for the next router to handle be divided into fragments. The fragment packet identifies an offset to the beginning of the first packet that enables the entire packet to be reassembled by the receiving system. In the teardrop attack, the attacker's IP puts a confusing offset value in the second or later fragment. If the receiving operating system does not have a plan for this situation, it can cause the system to crash.

Smurf Attack

In this attack, the perpetrator sends an IP ping (or 'echo my message back to me') request to a receiving site. The ping packet specifies that it be broadcast to a number of hosts within the receiving site's local network. The packet also indicates that the request is from another site, the target site that is to receive the denial of service. (Sending a packet with someone else's return address in it is called spoofing the return address.) The result will be lots of ping replies flooding back to the innocent, spoofed host. If the flood is great enough, the spoofed host will no longer be able to receive or distinguish real traffic.

Viruses

Computer viruses, which replicate across a network in various ways, can be viewed as denial of service attacks where the victim is not usually specifically targetted but simply a host unlucky enough to get the virus. Depending on the particular virus, the denial of service can be hardly noticeable ranging all the way through to be disastrous.

Physical Infrastructure Attacks

Here, someone may simply snip a fiber optic cable. This kind of attack is usually mitigated by the fact that traffic can sometimes quickly be rerouted.

11.5 ATTACK PREVENTION AND SECURITY SOLUTIONS

Firewalls

A firewall is hardware, software, or a combination of both that is used to prevent unauthorized programs or Internet users from accessing a private network and/or a single computer. Firewalls make it possible to filter incoming and outgoing traffic that flows through your system. A firewall can use one or more sets of 'rules' to inspect the network packets as they come in or go out of your network connections and either allows the traffic through or blocks it. These rules can inspect one or more characteristics of the packets including the source or destination host address, and the source or destination port.

It can do the following:

- Protect a trusted network from an untrusted network.
- Evaluate each incoming or outgoing packet.
- Hide the internal network.

Hardware Vs Software Firewalls

Hardware firewalls protects an entire network and is implemented on the router level. It is usually more expensive and harder to configure whereas the software firewalls protects a single computer and is usually less expensive and easier to configure.

In the following discussion we move on with the working of a firewall. It inspects each individual packet that arrives at both sides of the firewall and determines whether it should be allowed to pass through it or not. Windows Firewall monitors all network traffic on the connections for which it is enabled. The firewall keeps track of all communications that have originated from your computer, and it prevents unsolicited traffic from reaching your computer. If necessary, the firewall dynamically opens ports and allows your computer to receive traffic that you have specifically requested, such as a Web page for which you have clicked the address. A "port" is a networking term that identifies the point at which a type of network traffic reaches your computer. The exact ports that you open depend on the type of traffic you want to send and receive. If you have not requested the incoming traffic, Windows Firewall helps to block it before it can reach your computer. For special uses, such as networking, hosting online games, or hosting your own Web server, you can select ports that you want to leave open. This allows others to make connections to your computer, but it can also reduce security.

Firewall Types

We have mainly the following types of firewalls:

- Application-level proxy.
- Transparent proxy.

- Packet filter.
- Stateful packet filtering.
- SOCKS.
- Network address translation.

1. Application-Level Proxy Firewall

Application-level firewalls first determine if a requested connection between a computer on the internal network and one on the outside is permitted. If the connection is authorized, the firewall mimics the requesting software and sets up the necessary communication links between the two computers. As an intermediary, the firewall can monitor the communication between the two networks and suppress any unauthorized activity.

2. Transparent Proxy Firewall

A network administrator configures the firewall to intercept requests for streaming media.

3. Packet Filtering

Rather than impersonating an application, network-level firewalls examine the packets of information sent at the transport level to determine whether a particular packet should be blocked. Each packet is either forwarded or blocked based on a set of rules defined by the firewall administrator. A common configuration for network-level-filtering firewalls is to allow all connections initiated by machines inside the firewall, and to restrict or prohibit all connections made by machines outside the firewall. For most programs, this works well since they usually only establish a single outbound TCP connection.

4. Stateful Packet Filtering Firewall

A stateful packet filtering firewall monitors the communication between the client and the Internet to ensure that inbound packets are being sent at the request of a client inside the firewall. Similar to packet filters, it may include additional options that allow more sophisticated actions to be taken with individual packets:

5. Network Address Translation Firewall

A network address translation firewall converts the client's internal address to an external address before it forwards the client's requests to Helix Universal Server. Once it receives a request, Helix Universal Server will send its UDP packets directly to the firewall, rather than to the client, and the firewall may not know which client requested the packets. Network address translation is often implemented as part of packet filtering firewalls or stateful packet filtering firewalls.

6. SOCKS Firewall

Only software with built-in SOCKS support, that must additionally be configured by the user, can send data through a SOCKS firewall; In some cases, a user can install a Winsock.dll that supports SOCKS, and configure it to point to the SOCKS firewall.

	Whether client configuration required or not?	**Which IP address being seen by the client?**	**Which IP address being seen by the server?**	**Valid inside addresses required?**
Application level proxy	Yes	Firewall's address	Firewall's address	No
Transparent proxy	No	Server	Firewall	No
Packet filter	No	Server	Client	Yes
Stateful packet filtering	No	Server	Client	Yes
SOCKS	Yes	Firewall	Firewall	No

Intrusion Detection Systems

In recent years, the network technology has evolved a lot. Now Internet is changing the computing theory. The possibilities and opportunities are growing and also the risks and chances of malicious intrusions. The security mechanisms of a system are to be designed so as to *prevent* unauthorized access to system resources and data. In today's situation; however, completely preventing breaches of security is impossible. But these intrusion attempts can be detected and the damage can be repaired later. This field of security is called **Intrusion Detection**.

Anderson introduced the concept of intrusion detection in 1980, where he defined an **intrusion attempt** or a **threat** to be the potential possibility of a deliberate unauthorized attempt to

- Access information,
- Manipulate information, or
- Render a system unreliable or unusable.

Intrusion Detection Systems—Importance

A computer system should provide *confidentiality, integrity* and *assurance* against denial of service. However, due to increased number of connections in network (especially on the Internet) more and more systems are subject to attack by intruders. These resulted in the attacks on operating system as well as in application programs.

One way to prevent intrusion is building a completely secure system. It may, for instance, *require* all users to identify and authenticate themselves; we could protect data by various cryptographic methods and very tight access control mechanisms. However, this is not really feasible because:

1. In practice, it is not possible to build a completely secure system. Miller's report on bugs seems to indicate that bug free software is still a dream and no one seems to want to make the effort to try to develop such software. Designing and implementing a totally secure system is thus an extremely difficult task.
2. The vast installed base of systems worldwide guarantees th`at any transition to a secure system (if it is ever developed) will be long in coming.
3. Cryptographic methods have their own problems. Passwords can be cracked, users can lose their passwords, and entire crypto-systems can be broken.
4. Even a truly secure system is vulnerable to abuse by insiders who abuse their privileges.

5. It has been seen that the relationship between the level of access control and user efficiency is an inverse one, which means that the stricter the mechanisms, the lower the efficiency becomes.

If there are attacks on a system, it is preferable to detect them as soon as possible in real-time and take necessary immediate action. This is called as **Intrusion Detection System (IDS)**. An IDS does not usually take preventive measures when an attack is detected; it is a reactive rather than pro-active agent.

The most popular way to detect intrusions has been by using the *audit data* generated by the operating system. An *audit trail* is a record of activities on a system that are logged to a file in chronologically sorted order. Since almost all activities are logged on a system, it is possible that a manual inspection of these logs would allow intrusions to be detected. But, auditing large sizes of audit data (in the order of 100 Megabytes per day) by manual analysis is impossible. Intrusion Detection System automates the auditing. Audit trails are particularly useful because they can be used to establish the work of attackers, and are often the only way to detect unauthorized user activity.

Many times, even after an attack has occurred, it is important to analyze the audit data so that the extent of damage can be determined, the tracking down of the attackers is facilitated, and steps may be taken to prevent such attacks in future. An IDS can also be used to analyze audit data. Thus, IDS is a valuable real-time post-mortem analysis tools.

Some definitions in intrusion detection:

- *Risk:* Accidental or unpredictable exposure of information, or violation of operations integrity due to the malfunction of hardware or incomplete or incorrect software design.
- *Vulnerability:* A known or suspected flaw in the hardware or software or operation of a system that exposes the system to penetration or its information to accidental disclosure.
- *Attack:* A specific formulation or execution of a plan to carry out a threat.
- *Penetration:* A successful attack—the ability to obtain unauthorized (undetected) access to files and programs or the control state of a computer system.

Anderson also classified intruders into two types:

- The *external* intruders who are unauthorized users of the machines they attack, and
- *Internal* intruders, who have permission to access the system, but limited to certain portions.

Classification of Intrusion Detection Systems

Intrusions can be divided into 6 main types:

1. Attempted break-ins, which are detected by atypical behavior profiles or violations of security constraints.
2. Masquerade attacks, which are detected by atypical behavior profiles or violations of security constraints.
3. Penetration of the security control system, which are detected by monitoring for specific patterns of activity.
4. Leakage, which is detected by atypical use of system resources.
5. Denial of service, which is detected by atypical use of system resources.
6. Malicious use, which is detected by atypical behavior profiles, violations of security constraints, or use of special privileges.

However, we can divide the techniques of intrusion detection into two main types as anomaly detection and misuse detection.

Type 1: Anomaly detection: Anomaly detection techniques assume that all intrusive activities are necessarily anomalous. This means that if we could establish a 'normal activity profile' for a system, we could, in theory, flag all system states varying from the established profile by statistically significant amounts as intrusion attempts. However, if we consider that the set of intrusive activities only intersects the set of anomalous activities instead of being exactly the same, we find a couple of interesting possibilities: (1) Anomalous activities that are not intrusive are flagged as intrusive. (2) Intrusive activities that are not anomalous result in false negatives (events are not flagged intrusive, though they actually are). This is a dangerous problem, and is far more serious than the problem of false positives.

The main issues in anomaly detection systems thus become the selection of threshold levels so that neither of the above 2 problems is unreasonably magnified. Anomaly detection systems are also computationally expensive because of the overhead of keeping track of, and possibly updating several system profile metrics.

Anomaly detection compares observed activity against expected normal usage profiles which may be developed for users, groups of users, applications, or system resource usage. Audit event records which fall outside the definition of normal behavior are considered anomalies.

Anomaly Detection Systems

There have been a few major approaches to anomaly intrusion detection systems, some of which are described below.

Statistical approaches: In this method, initially, behavior profiles for subjects are generated. As the system continues running, the anomaly detector constantly generates the variance of the present profile from the original one. There may be several measures that affect the behavior profile, like activity measures, CPU time used, number of network connections in a time period, etc. In some systems, the current profile and the previous profile are merged at intervals, but in some other systems profile generation is a one time activity. The main advantage to statistical systems is that they adaptively learn the behavior of users; they are thus potentially more sensitivte than human experts. However, there are a few problems with statistical approaches: they can gradually be trained by intruders so that eventually, intrusive events are considered normal.

Static methods of determining these measures are sometimes misleading because of the unique features of a particular system. Thus, it seems that a combination of static and dynamic determination of the set of measures should be done. Some problems associated with this technique have been remedied by other methods, including the method involving *Predictive Pattern Generation*, which takes past events into account when analyzing the data.

Predictive pattern generation: This method of intrusion detection tries to predict future events based on the events that have already occurred. Therefore, we could have a rule:

$$E1 - E2 \rightarrow (E3 = 80\%, E4 = 15\%, E5 = 5\%)$$

This would mean that given that events $E1$ and $E2$ have occurred, with $E2$ occurring after $E1$, there is an 80% probability that event $E3$ will follow, a 15% chance that event $E4$ will follow and a 5% probability that event $E5$ will follow. The problem with this is that some intrusion scenarios that are not described by the rules will not be flagged intrusive. Thus, if an event sequence $A - B - C$ exists that is intrusive, but not listed in the rulebase, it will be classified as unrecognized. This problem can be partially solved by flagging any unknown events as intrusions (increasing the probability of false positives), or by flagging them as non-intrusive (thus increasing the probability of false negatives). In the normal case, however, an event is flagged intrusive if the left hand side of a rule is matched, but the right hand side is statistically very deviant from the prediction.

There are several advantages to this approach. First, rule based sequential patterns can detect anomalous activities that were difficult with traditional methods. Second, systems built using this model are highly adaptive to changes. This is because low quality patterns are continuously eliminated, finally leaving the higher quality patterns behind. Third, it is easier to detect users who try to train the system during its learning period. And fourth, anomalous activities can be detected and reported within seconds of receiving audit events.

Another approach taken in intrusion detection systems is the use of **neural networks**. The idea here is to train the neural network to predict a user's next action or command, given the window of n previous actions or commands. The network is trained on a set of representative user commands. After the training period, the network tries to match actual commands with the actual user profile already present in the net. Any incorrectly predicted events (events and commands are used interchangeably in this discussion) actually measure the deviation of the user from the established profile. Some advantages of using neural networks are: they cope well with noisy data, their success does not depend on any statistical assumption about the nature of the underlying data, and they are easier to modify for new user communities. However, they have some problems. First, a small window will result in false positives while a large window will result in irrelevant data as well as increase the chance of false negatives. Second, the net topology is only determined after considerable trial and error. And third, the intruder can train the net during its learning phase.

Type 2: Misuse detection: The concept behind misuse detection schemes is that there are ways to represent attacks in the form of a pattern or a signature so that even variations of the same attack can be detected. This means that these systems are not unlike virus detection systems—they can detect many or all *known* attack patterns, but they are of little use for as yet unknown attack methods. An interesting point to note is that anomaly detection systems try to detect the complement of 'bad' behavior. Misuse detection systems try to recognize known 'bad' behavior. The main issues in misuse detection systems are how to write a signature that encom-passes *all* possible variations of the pertinent attack, and how to write signatures that do not also match non-intrusive activity.

Keystroke monitoring is a very simple technique that monitors keystrokes for attack patterns. Unfortunately the system has several defects—features of shells like *bash*, *ksh*, and *tcsh* in which user definable aliases are present defeat the technique unless alias expansion and semantic analysis of the commands is taken up. The method also does not analyze the running of a program, only the keystrokes. This means that a malicious program cannot be flagged for intrusive activities. Operating systems do not offer much support for keystroke capturing, so the keystroke monitor should have a hook that analyses keystrokes before sending them onto their intended receiver. An improvement to this would be to monitor system calls by application programs as well, so that an analysis of the program's execution is possible.

Model-based intrusion detection states that certain scenarios are inferred by certain other observable activities. If these activities are monitored, it is possible to find intrusion attempts by looking at activities that infer a certain intrusion scenario. The model-based scheme consists of three important modules. The *anticipator* uses the active models and the scenario models to try to predict the next step in the scenario that is expected to occur. A scenario model is a knowledge base with specifications of intrusion scenarios. The *planner* then translates this hypothesis into a format that shows the behavior as it would occur in the audit trail. It uses the predicted information to plan what to search for next. The *interpreter* then searches for this data in the audit trail. The system proceeds this way, accumulating more and more evidence for an intrusion attempt until a threshold is crossed; at this point, it signals an intrusion attempt.

This is a very clean approach. Because the planner and the interpreter know what they are searching for at each step, the large amounts of noise present in audit data can be filtered, leading to excellent performance improvements. In addition, the system can predict the attacker's next move based on the intrusion model. These predictions can be used to verify an intrusion hypothesis, to take preventive measures, or to determine what data to look for next. However, there are some critical issues related to this system. First, patterns for intrusion scenarios must be easily recognized. Second, patterns must always occur in the behavior being looked for. And finally, patterns must be *distinguishing*; they must *not* be associated with any other normal behavior.

In the **State Transition Analysis** technique, the monitored system is represented as a state transition diagram. As data is analyzed, the system makes transitions from one state to another. A transition takes place on some Boolean condition being true (for example, the user opening a file). The approach followed in USTAT is to have state transitions from safe to unsafe states based on known attack patterns.

This is where the attack occurs. Whenever a link to a file is created, a new inode with the target's original permissions is created.

However, there are also a few problems with state transition systems. First, attack patterns can specify only a sequence of events, rather than more complex forms. Second, there are no general purpose methods to prune the search except through the assertion primitives described above. And finally, they cannot detect denial of service attacks, failed logins, variations from normal usage, and passive listening—this is because these items are either not recorded by the audit trail mechanism, or they cannot be represented by state transition diagrams.

A new misuse detection system based on **Pattern Matching** is also proposed. This model encodes known intrusion signatures as patterns that are then matched against the audit data. Like the state transition analysis model, this model attempts to match incoming events to the patterns representing intrusion scenarios. The difference between this and the state transition model is that the state transition model associates the security tips with states, rather than transitions. The important advantages of this model are:

1. ***Declarative specification:*** It only needs to be specified what patterns need to be matched, not how to match them.
2. Multiple event streams can be used together to match against patterns for each stream without the need to combine streams. This means that streams can be processed independently, and their results can be analyzed together to give evidence of intrusive activity.
3. ***Portability:*** Since intrusion signatures are written in a system independent script, they need not be rewritten for different audit trails. The patterns' declarative specifications enable them to be exchanged across different Operating Systems and different audit trails.
4. It has excellent real-time capabilities. Kumar reports a CPU overhead of 5–6% when scanning for 100 different patterns, which is excellent.
5. It can detect some attack signatures like the failed logins signature that the state transition model cannot do.

One problem with this model is it can only detect attacks based on known vulnerabilities. This is a problem with misuse detection systems in general. In addition, pattern matching is not very useful for representing ill-defined patterns and it is not an easy task to translate known attack scenarios into patterns that can be used by the model. Also, it cannot detect passive wire-tapping intrusions, nor it detects spoofing attacks where a machine pretends to be another machine by using its IP address.

Anti-intrusion Approaches

Over the past fifteen years a great deal of emphasis has been placed on detection as the most fruitful area for research and development to fight against intrusion. As work environments become more interconnected and exposed, service providers should rely on a wide range of anti-intrusion techniques, not just IDS's.

The six anti-intrusion approaches are discussed here.

- **Prevention** precludes or severely handicaps the likelihood of a particular intrusion's success.
  - *Hire hulking bodyguards and avoid bad neighborhoods.* A definitive approach when it works, but expensive and troublesome and unlikely to be operationally 100% foolproof. Still leaves opportunity for successful attack if bodyguards can be distracted or bribed.
- **Preemption** strikes offensively against likely threat agents prior to an intrusion attempt to lessen the likelihood of a particular intrusion occurring later.
  - *Support vigilante patrols.* Non-specific and may affect innocents.
- **Deterrence** deters the initiation or continuation of an intrusion attempt by increasing the necessary effort for an attack to succeed, increasing the risk associated with the attack, and/or devaluing the perceived gain that would come with success.
  - *Dress down and walk with excitable Chihuahua dog.* Many attackers will move on to richer-looking easier prey, but if it has been a lean night, a little annoying yapping dog is not going to stop a determined mugger.
- **Deflection** leads an intruder to believe that he has succeeded in an intrusion attempt, whereas instead he has been attracted or shunted off to where harm is minimized.
  - *Carry two wallets so that when attacked,* a decoy wallet with canceled credit cards can be handed over. Can learn more about how attackers operate, but probably only works for newbie muggers and it is inconvenient having to carry two wallets.
- **Detection** discriminates intrusion attempts and intrusion preparation from normal activity and alerts the authorities.

  - *Carry a whistle and blow to attract attention from beat cop if attacked*. Limited usefulness if attack is too far from a donut shop for whistle to be heard, or if car-alarm-syndrome causes authorities to ignore as a false alarm. Also you may not detect in time that your wallet was stolen if it is surreptitiously pickpocketed.
- **Counter measures** actively and autonomously counter an intrusion as it is being attempted.
  - *Carry a can of mace, attach mouse trap to wallet, and know karate to counter attack*. Run the risk of being sued by accidentally breaking the arm of Hari Krishna solicitor offering flowers. With a booby trapped wallet, a pickpocket can be autonomously countered with necessary speed without conscious detection. However you, as an authorized user, might mistakenly get your fingers snapped if you forget about the mousetrap.

Intrusion Prevention

Intrusion Prevention techniques (enforced internally or externally to the system) seek to preclude or at least severely handicap the likelihood of success of a particular intrusion. These techniques help ensure that a system is so well conceived, designed, implemented, configured, and operated that the opportunity for intrusions is minimal. Because built-in prevention seeks to make it impossible for an intrusion to occur on the target system, it may be considered the strongest anti-intrusion technique. Ideally, this approach would prevent all intrusions, negating the need for detection and consequent reaction techniques. Add-on prevention measures of an existing system include vulnerability scanning tools and network firewalls.

- **Correct design/implementation** techniques represent classic INFOSEC mechanisms (e.g. identification and authentication, mandatory and discretionary access control, physical security) and are appropriate to be developed into the target system itself. These techniques are well explored, but may be cumbersome and expensive, and care must be taken that they are not poorly configured.
- **Vulnerability scanning tools** examine system and network configurations for oversights and vulnerabilities. Static

configuration scanners are programs and scripts periodically run manually by the System Security Officer (SSO) to detect system vulnerabilities. Dynamic configuration scanning tools perform much the same function but run constantly as a low priority task in the background. Configuration scanning tools can monitor for a wide range of system irregularities including: unauthorized software, unauthorized accounts, unprotected logins, inappropriate resource ownership, inappropriate access permissions, weak passwords, and ghost nodes on a network. Other vulnerability scanning tools can check for evidence of previous intruder activity, susceptibility to known attacks, and dormant viruses. Representative UNIX configuration scanning tools include: Security Profile Inspector (SPI), Internet Security Scanner (ISS), Security Analysis Tool for Auditing Networks (SATAN), COPS, and Tripwire (FIS94).

11.6 KEY AGREEMENT PROTOCOLS

Introduction to Key Agreement Protocol

A *key agreement protocol*, also called a *key exchange protocol*, is a series of steps used when two or more parties need to agree upon a key to use for a secret-key cryptosystem. These protocols allow people to share keys freely and securely over any insecure medium, without the need for a previously established shared secret.

Suppose Alice and Bob want to use a secret-key cryptosystem to communicate securely. They first must decide on a shared key. Instead of Bob calling Alice on the phone and discussing what the key will be, which would leave them vulnerable to an eavesdropper; they decide to use a key agreement protocol. By using a key agreement protocol, Alice and Bob may securely exchange a key in an insecure environment. One example of such a protocol is called the Diffie-Hellman key agreement. In many cases, public-key cryptography is used in a key agreement protocol. Another example is the use of digital envelopes for key agreement.

The key agreement problem is stated as follows: the entities wish to agree on keying information in secret over a distributed network. By Diffie-Hellman key exchange suppose if entity i wishes to agree on secret keying information with entity j. Each party desires an assurance that no party other than j and i can possibly compute the keying information agreed. This is the authenticated key agreement (AK) problem. In Key agreement problem i does not care who is agreeing on a key with.

Always the problem of proving security comes in five stages:

1. Specification of model.
2. Definition of goals within the model.
3. Statement of assumptions.
4. Description of protocol.
5. Proof that the protocol meets its goals within the model.

Properties of Key Agreement Protocols

Before analysing any protocol it is necessary to identify what attacks a protocol should withstand and what are the desired attributes of a protocol.

First we identify the two types of attacks:

1. ***Passive attacks:*** An adversary attempts to prevent a protocol from achieving its goal by merely observing honest entities carrying out the protocol.
2. ***Active attacks:*** An adversary additionally subverts the communications themselves in any way possible. It may be by injecting messages, intercepting messages, replaying messages, altering messages and some like.

It is essential for any secure protocol to withstand both passive and active attacks, since an adversary can reasonably be assumed to have these capabilities in a distributed network.

A number of desirable attributes of key agreement protocols have been identified as:

1. ***Known session keys:*** A protocol still achieves its goal in the face of an adversary who has learned some previous session keys.
2. ***Forward secrecy:*** If long-term secrets of one or more entities are compromised, the secrecy of previous session key is not affected.
3. ***Unknown key-share:*** Entity i cannot be coerced into sharing a key with entity j without i's knowledge.

4. ***Key-compromise impersonation:*** Suppose i's secret value is disclosed. Clearly an adversary that knows this value can now impersonate i, since it is precisely this value that identifies i. However, it may be desirable that this loss does not enable an adversary to impersonate other entities to i .
5. ***Loss of information:*** Compromise of other information that would not ordinarily be available to an adversary does not affect the security of the protocol.
6. ***Message independence:*** Individual flows of a protocol run between two honest entities are unrelated.

Key Management

Key management deals with the secure generation, distribution, and storage of keys. Secure methods of key management are extremely important. Once a key is randomly generated, it must remain secret to avoid unfortunate mishaps (such as impersonation). In practice, most attacks on public-key systems will probably be aimed at the key management level, rather than at the cryptographic algorithm itself.

Users must be able to securely obtain a key pair suited to their efficiency and security needs. There must be a way to look up other people's public keys and to publicize one's own public key. Users must be able to legitimately obtain others' public keys; otherwise, an intruder can either change public keys listed in a directory, or impersonate another user. Certificates are used for this purpose. Certificates must be unforgeable. The issuance of certificates must proceed in a secure way, impervious to attack. In particular, the issuer must authenticate the identity and the public key of an individual before issuing a certificate to that individual.

If someone's private key is lost or compromised, others must be made aware of this, so they will no longer encrypt messages under the invalid public key nor accept messages signed with the invalid private key. Users must be able to store their private keys securely, so no intruder can obtain them, yet the keys must be readily accessible for legitimate use. Keys need to be valid only until a specified expiration date but the expiration date must be chosen properly and publicized in an authenticated channel.

Digital signatures are electronic stamps that can be used to identify the sender or the signer of a digital document. Think of digital signatures as the digital equivalent of the signature placed on a contract or a check. Digital signatures use public and private key pairs to ensure the authenticity of an electronic document. The creator of the document will have the private portion of a digital signature scheme which is encoded onto the document when it is signed. Then the recipient of the document would receive the public key of the digital signature scheme. This would allow the recipient of the document to know that the document was authentic and really did come from the sender.

Keeping with a paper document analogy, the purpose of a signature is to verify that the signer is the originator of the document. Sometimes documents require signatures in person to have a witness to the signature. The public key/private key pair allows electronic documents to be verified in much the same way.

A digital signature scheme generates a key pair, and the public key will only match the corresponding private key and vice versa. This ensures that the document which contains the private key is authentic and has not been changed since signing.

One thing to note is that a digital signature is altogether different from a digital certificate, which verifies content on a website with a third party. A digital signature is also very different from an e-mail signature. While an e-mail signature is a digital representation of the senders name and contact information, it does nothing to guarantee the origin of the message or document.

E-mail messages can be signed with digital signatures to verify their origin just like other electronic documents. Using digital signatures will allow recipients of these documents to feel comfortable in trusting that the document really came from the listed sender. This process can also help guarantee that the document has not been modified since being sent.

In today's commercial environment, establishing a framework for the authentication of computer-based information requires a familiarity with concepts and professional skills from both the legal and computer security fields.

Combining these two disciplines is not an easy task. Concepts from the information security field often correspond only loosely to concepts from the legal field, even in situations where the terminology is similar. For example, from the information security point of view, 'digital signature' means the result of applying to specific information certain specific technical processes described below. The historical legal concept of 'signature' is broader. It recognizes any mark made with the intention of authenticating the marked document. In a digital setting, today's broad legal concept of 'signature' may well include markings as diverse as digitized images of paper signatures, typed notations such as '/s/ John Smith,' or even addressing notations, such as electronic mail origination headers.

Signatures and the Law

A signature is not part of the substance of a transaction, but rather of its representation or form. Signing writings serve the following general purposes.

- *Evidence:* A signature authenticates a writing by identifying the signer with the signed document. When the signer makes a mark in a distinctive manner, the writing becomes attributable to the signer.
- *Ceremony:* The act of signing a document calls to the signer's attention the legal significance of the signer's act, and thereby helps prevent 'inconsiderate engagements'.
- *Approval:* In certain contexts defined by law or custom, a signature expresses the signer's approval or authorization of the writing, or the signer's intention that it has legal effect.
- *Efficiency and logistics:* A signature on a written document often imparts a sense of clarity and finality to the transaction and may lessen the subsequent need to inquire beyond the face of a document. Negotiable instruments, for example, rely upon formal requirements, including a signature, for their ability to change hands with ease, rapidity, and minimal interruption.

The formal requirements for legal transactions, including the need for signatures, vary in different legal systems, and also vary with the passage of time. There is also variance in the legal consequences of failure to cast the transaction in a required form. The statute of frauds of the common law tradition, for example, does not render a transaction invalid for lack of a 'writing signed by the party to be charged,' but rather makes it unenforceable in court, a distinction which has caused the practical application of the statute to be greatly limited in case law.

During this century, most legal systems have reduced formal requirements, or at least have minimized the consequences of failure to satisfy formal requirements. Nevertheless, sound practice still calls for transactions to be formalized in a manner which assures the parties of their validity and enforceability. In current practice, formalization usually involves documenting the transaction on paper and signing or authenticating the paper. Traditional methods, however, are undergoing fundamental change. Documents continue to be written on paper, but sometimes merely to satisfy the need for a legally recognized form. In many instances, the information exchanged to effect a transaction never takes paper form. Computer-based information can also be utilized differently than its paper counterpart. For example, computers can 'read' digital information and transform the information or take programmable actions based on the information. Information stored as bits rather than as atoms of ink and paper can travel near the speed of light, may be duplicated without limit and with insignificant cost.

Although the basic nature of transactions has not changed, the law has only begun to adapt to advances in technology. The legal and business communities must develop rules and practices which use new technology to achieve and surpass the effects historically expected from paper forms.

To achieve the basic purposes of signatures outlined above, a signature must have the following attributes:

- ***Signer authentication:*** A signature should indicate who signed a document, message or record, and should be difficult for another person to produce without authorization.
- ***Document authentication:*** A signature should identify what is signed, making it impracticable to falsify or alter either the signed matter or the signature without detection.

Signer authentication and document authentication are tools used to exclude impersonators and forgers and are essential ingredients of what is often called a "nonrepudiation service" in the terminology of the information security profession. A nonrepudiation service provides assurance of the origin or delivery of data in order to protect the sender against false denial by the recipient that the data has been received, or to protect the recipient against false denial by the sender that the data has been sent. Thus, a nonrepudiation service provides evidence to prevent a person from unilaterally modifying or terminating legal obligations arising out of a transaction effected by computer-based means.

- *Affirmative act:* The affixing of the signature should be an affirmative act which serves the ceremonial and approval functions of a signature and establishes the sense of having legally consummated a transaction.
- *Efficiency:* Optimally, a signature and its creation and verification processes should provide the greatest possible assurance of both signer authenticity and document authenticy, with the least possible expenditure of resources.

Digital signature technology generally surpasses paper technology in all these attributes. To understand why, one must first understand how digital signature technology works.

How Digital Signature Technology Works

Digital signatures are created and verified by cryptography, the branch of applied mathematics that concerns itself with transforming messages into seemingly unintelligible forms and back again. Digital signatures use what is known as 'public key cryptography,' which employs an algorithm using two different but mathematically related 'keys;' one for creating a digital signature or transforming data into a seemingly unintelligible form, and another key for verifying a digital signature or returning the message to its original form. Computer equipment and software utilizing two such keys are often collectively termed an 'asymmetric cryptosystem.'

The complementary keys of an asymmetric cryptosystem for digital signatures are arbitrarily termed the private key, which is known only to the signer and used to create the digital signature, and the public key, which is ordinarily more widely known and is used by a relying party to verify the digital signature. If many people need to verify the signer's digital signatures, the public key must be available or distributed to all of them, perhaps by publication in an on-line repository or directory where it is easily accessible. Although the keys of the pair are mathematically related, if the asymmetric cryptosystem has been designed and implemented securely it is 'computationally infeasible to derive the private key from knowledge of the public key. Thus, although many people may know the public key of a given signer and use it to verify that signer's signatures, they cannot discover that signer's private key and use it to forge digital signatures. This is sometimes referred to as the principle of 'irreversibility.'

Another fundamental process, termed a 'hash function,' is used in both creating and verifying a digital signature. A hash function is an algorithm which creates a digital representation or 'fingerprint' in the form of a 'hash value' or 'hash result' of a standard length which is usually much smaller than the message but nevertheless substantially unique to it. Any change to the message invariably produces a different hash result when the same hash function is used. In the case of a secure hash function, sometimes termed a 'one-way hash function,' it is computationally infeasible to derive the original message from knowledge of its hash value. Hash functions, therefore, enable the software for creating digital signatures to operate on smaller and predictable amounts of data, while still providing robust evidentiary correlation to the original message content, thereby efficiently providing assurance that there has been no modification of the message since it was digitally signed.

Thus, use of digital signatures usually involves two processes, one performed by the signer and the other by the receiver of the digital signature:

- **Digital signature creation** uses a hash result derived from and unique to both the signed message and a given private key. For the hash result to be secure, there must be only a negligible possibility that the same digital signature could be created by the combination of any other message or private key.

- **Digital signature verification** is the process of checking the digital signature by reference to the original message and a given public key, thereby determining whether the digital signature was created for that same message using the private key that corresponds to the referenced public key.

To sign a document or any other item of information, the signer first delimits precisely the borders of what is to be signed. The delimited information to be signed is termed the "message" in these guidelines. Then a hash function in the signer's software computes a hash result unique (for all practical purposes) to the message. The signer's software then transforms the hash result into a digital signature using the signer's private key. The resulting digital signature is thus unique to both the message and the private key used to create it.

Typically, a digital signature (a digitally signed hash result of the message) is attached to its message and stored or transmitted with its message. However, it may also be sent or stored as a separate data element, so long as it maintains a reliable association with its message. Since a digital signature is unique to its message, it is useless if wholly dissociated from its message.

Verification of a digital signature is accomplished by computing a new hash result of the original message by means of the same hash function used to create the digital signature. Then, using the public key and the new hash result, the verifier checks: (1) whether the digital signature was created using the corresponding private key; and (2) whether the newly computed hash result matches the original hash result which was transformed into the digital signature during the signing process. The verification software will confirm the digital signature as "verified" if: (1) the signer's private key was used to digitally sign the message, which is known to be the case if the signer's public key was used to verify the signature because the signer's public key will verify only a digital signature created with the signer's private key; and (2) the message was unaltered, which is known to be the case if the hash result computed by the verifier is identical to the hash result extracted from the digital signature during the verification process.

Various asymmetric cryptosystems create and verify digital signatures using different algorithms and procedures, but share this overall operational pattern.

The processes of creating a digital signature and verifying it accomplish the essential effects desired of a signature for many legal purposes:

- *Signer authentication:* If a public and private key pair is associated with an identified signer, the digital signature attributes the message to the signer. The digital signature cannot be forged, unless the signer loses control of the private key (a 'compromise' of the private key) such as by divulging it or losing the media or device in which it is contained.
- *Message authentication:* The digital signature also identifies the signed message, typically with far greater certainty and precision than paper signatures. Verification reveals any tampering, since the comparison of the hash results (one made at signing and the other made at verifying) shows whether the message is the same as when signed.
- *Affirmative act:* Creating a digital signature requires the signer to use the signer's private key. This act can perform the 'ceremonial' function of alerting the signer to the fact that the signer is consummating a transaction with legal consequences.
- *Efficiency:* The processes of creating and verifying a digital signature provide a high level of assurance that the digital signature is genuinely the signer's. As with the case of modern electronic data interchange ('EDI') the creation and verification processes are capable of complete automation (sometimes referred to as 'machinable'), with human interaction required on an exception basis only. Compared to paper methods such as checking specimen signature cards—methods so tedious and labor-intensive that they are rarely actually used in practice—digital signatures yield a high degree of assurance without adding greatly to the resources required for processing.

The processes used for digital signatures have undergone thorough technological peer review for over a decade. Digital signatures have been accepted in several national and international standards developed in cooperation with and accepted by many corporations, banks, and government agencies. The likelihood of malfunction or a security problem in a digital signature cryptosystem designed and implemented as prescribed in the industry standards is extremely remote, and is far less than the risk of undetected forgery or alteration on paper or of using other less secure electronic signature techniques.

Public Key Certificates

To verify a digital signature, the verifier must have access to the signer's public key and have assurance that it corresponds to the signer's private key. However, a public and private key pair has no intrinsic association with any person; it is simply a pair of numbers. Some convincing strategy is necessary to reliably associate a particular person or entity to the key pair.

In a transaction involving only two parties, each party can simply communicate (by a relatively secure 'out-of-band' channel such as a courier or a secure voice telephone) the public key of the key pair each party will use. Such an identification strategy is no small task, especially when the parties are geographically distant from each other, normally conduct communication over a convenient but insecure channel such as the Internet, are not natural persons but rather corporations or similar artificial entities, and act through agents whose authority must be ascertained. As electronic commerce increasingly moves from a bilateral setting to the many-on-many architecture of the World Wide Web on the Internet, where significant transactions will occur among strangers who have no prior contractual relationship and will never deal with each other again, the problem of authentication/non-repudiation becomes not merely one of efficiency, but also of reliability. An open system of communication such as the Internet needs a system of identity authentication to handle this scenario.

To that end, a prospective signer might issue a public statement, such as: 'Signatures verifiable by the following public key are mine.' However, others doing business with the signer may for good reason be unwilling to accept the statement, especially where there is no prior contract establishing the legal effect of that published statement with certainty. A party relying upon such an unsupported published statement in an open system would run a great risk of trusting a phantom or an imposter, or of attempting to disprove a false denial of a digital signature (nonrepudiation) if a transaction should turn out to prove disadvantageous for the purported signer.

The solution to these problems is the use of one or more trusted third parties to associate an identified signer with a specific public key. That trusted third party is referred to as a "certification authority" in most technical standards and in these guidelines.

To associate a key pair with a prospective signer, a certification authority issues a certificate, an electronic record which lists a public key as the 'subject' of the certificate, and confirms that the prospective signer identified in the certificate holds the corresponding private key. The prospective signer is termed the 'subscriber. A certificate's principal function is to bind a key pair with a particular subscriber. A 'recipient' of the certificate desiring to rely upon a digital signature created by the subscriber named in the certificate (whereupon the recipient becomes a 'relying party') can use the public key listed in the certificate to verify that the digital signature was created with the corresponding private key. If such verification is successful, this chain of reasoning provides assurance that the corresponding private key is held by the subscriber named in the certificate, and that the digital signature was created by that particular subscriber.

To assure both message and identity authenticity of the certificate, the certification authority digitally signs it. The issuing certification authority's digital signature on the certificate can be verified by using the public key of the certification authority listed in another certificate by another certificate authority (which may but need not be on a higher level in a hierarchy), and that other certificate can in turn be authenticated by the public key listed in yet another certificate, and so on, until the person relying on the digital signature is adequately assured of its genuineness. In each case, the issuing certification authority must digitally sign its own certificate during the operational period of the other certificate used to verify the certification authority's digital signature.

A digital signature, whether created by a subscriber to authenticate a message or by a certification authority to authenticate its certificate (in effect a specialized message) should be reliably time-stamped to allow the verifier to determine reliably whether the digital signature was created during the 'operational period' stated in the certificate, which is a condition upon verifiability of a digital signature under these guidelines.

To make a public key and its identification with a specific subscriber readily available for use in verification, the certificate may be published in a repository or made available by other means. Repositories are on-line databases of certificates and other information available for retrieval and use in verifying digital signatures. Retrieval can be accomplished automatically by having the verification program directly inquired of the repository to obtain certificates as needed.

Once issued, a certificate may prove to be unreliable, such as in situations where the subscriber misrepresents his identity to the certification authority. In other situations, a certificate may be reliable enough when issued but come to be unreliable sometime thereafter. If the subscriber loses control of the private key ("compromise" of the private key), the certificate has become unreliable, and the certification authority (either with or without the subscriber's request depending on the circumstances) may suspend (temporarily invalidate) or revoke (permanently invalidate) the certificate. Immediately upon suspending or revoking a certificate, the certification authority must publish notice of the revocation or suspension or notify persons who inquire or who are known to have received a digital signature verifiable by reference to the unreliable certificate.

Components of Digital Signature

1. *Your public key:* This is the part that any one can get a copy of and is part of the verification system.
2. *Your name and e-mail address:* This is necessary for contact information purposes and to enable the viewer to identify the details.

3. ***Expiration date of the public key:*** This part of the signature is used to set a shelf life and to ensure that in the event of prolonged abuse of a signature eventually the signature is reset.
4. ***Name of the company:*** This section identifies the company that the signature belongs too.
5. ***Serial number of the digital ID:*** This part is a unique number that is bundled to the signature for tracking and extra identification reasons.
6. ***Digital signature of the CA (certification authority):*** This is a signature that is issued by the authority that issues the certificates.

11.7 SECURE COMMUNICATION PROTOCOLS

(i) Secure Socket Layer

Security of data in transit over the Internet becomes increasingly necessary because of steadily growing data volume and importance. Nowadays, every user of a public network sends various types of data, from e-mail to credit card details daily, and he would, therefore, like them to be protected when in transit over a public network. To this end, a practical SSL protocol has been adopted for protection of data in transit that encompasses all network services that use TCP/IP to support typical application tasks of communication between servers and clients.

Netscape, to ensure security of data transported and routed through HTTP, LDAP or POP3 application layers, originally developed the SSL protocol. SSL is designed to make use of TCP as a communication layer to provide a reliable end-to-end secure and authenticated connection between two points over a network (for example, between the service client and the server). Notwithstanding this SSL can be used for protection of data in transit in situations related to any network service, it is used mostly in HTTP server and client applications. Today, almost each available HTTP server can support an SSL session, whilst IE or Netscape Navigator browsers are provided with SSL-enabled client software (Fig. 11.4).

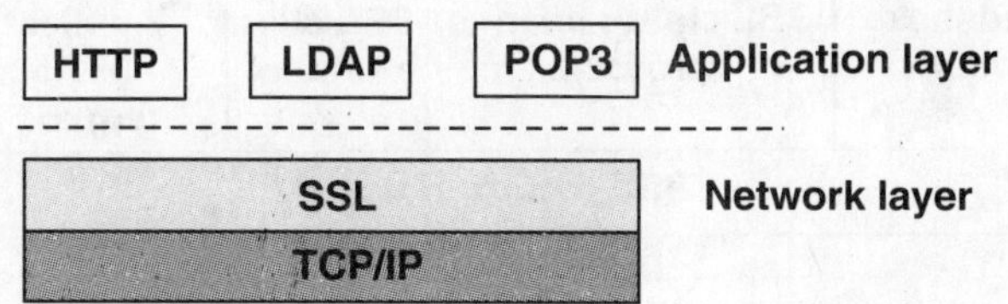

Fig. 11.4: SSL between application protocols and TCP/IP

SSL Objectives and Architecture

The main objectives for SSL are:

1. Authenticating the client and server to each other: The SSL protocol supports the use of standard key cryptographic techniques (public key encryption) to authenticate the communicating parties to each other. Though the most frequent application consists in authenticating the service client on the basis of a certificate, SSL may also use the same methods to authenticate the client.
2. Ensuring data integrity: During a session, data cannot be either intentionally or unintentionally tampered with.
3. Securing data privacy: Data in transport between the client and the server must be protected from interception and be readable only by the intended recipient. This prerequisite is necessary for both the data associated with the protocol itself (securing traffic during negotiations) and the application data that is sent during the session itself. SSL is in fact not a single protocol but rather a set of protocols that can additionally be further divided in two layers:
   - The protocol to ensure data security and integrity: This layer is composed of the SSL Record Protocol,
   - The protocols that are designed to establish an SSL connection: Three protocols are used in this layer: the SSL Handshake Protocol, the SSL Change Cipher Spec-Protocol and the SSL Alert Protocol.

The SSL protocol stack is illustrated in Fig. 11.5.

SSL uses these protocols to address the tasks as described above. The SSL record protocol is responsible for data encryption and integrity. It is also used to encapsulate data sent by other SSL protocols, and therefore, it is also involved

SSL handshake protocol	SSL cipher change protocol	SSL alert protocol	Application protocol (e.g. HTTP)
SSL record protocol			
TCP			
IP			

Fig. 11.5: The SSL protocol stack

in the tasks associated with the SSL check data. The other three protocols cover the areas of session management, cryptographic parameter management and transfer of SSL messages between the client and the server. Prior to going into a more detailed discussion of the role of individual protocols and their functions let us describe two fundamental concepts related to the use of SSL.

SSL Session and Connection

The concepts as mentioned above are fundamental for a connection between the client and the server, and they also encompass a series of attributes. Let's try to give some more details:

- *Connection:* This is a logical client/server link, associated with the provision of a suitable type of service. In SSL terms, it must be a peer-to-peer connection with two network nodes.
- *Session:* This is an association between a client and a server that defines a set of parameters such as algorithms used, session number, etc. An SSL session is created by the Handshake Protocol that allows parameters to be shared among the connections made between the server and the client, and sessions are used to avoid negotiation of new parameters for each connection. This means that a single session is shared among multiple SSL connections between the client and the server. In theory, it may also be possible that multiple sessions are shared by a single connection, but this feature is not used in practice. The concepts of an SSL session and connection involve several parameters that are used for SSL-enabled communication between the client and

the server. During the negotiations of the handshake protocol, the encryption methods are established and a series of parameters of the session state are subsequently used within the session. A session state is defined by the following parameters:

- ***Session identifier:*** This is an identifier generated by the server to identify a session with a chosen client,
- ***Peer certificate:*** X.509 certificate of the peer,
- ***Compression method:*** A method used to compress data prior to encryption,
- ***Algorithm specification termed CipherSpec:*** Specifies the bulk data encryption algorithm (for example, DES) and the hash algorithm (for example, MD5) used during the session,
- ***Master secret:*** 48-byte data being a secret shared between the client and server,
- ***'Is resumable':*** This is a flag indicating whether the session can be used to initiate new connections. According to the specification, the SSL connection state is defined by the following parameters:
  - ***Server and client random:*** Random data generated by both the client and server for each connection,
  - ***Server write MAC secret:*** The secret key used for data written by the server,
  - ***Client write MAC secret:*** The secret used for data written by the client,
  - ***Server write key:*** The bulk cipher key for data encrypted by the server and decrypted by the client,
  - ***Client write key:*** The bulk cipher key for data encrypted by the client and decrypted by the server,
  - ***Sequence number:*** Sequence numbers maintained separately by the server for messages transmitted and received during the data session.

The abbreviation MAC used in the above definitions means Message Authentication Code that is used for transmission of data during the SSL session. The role of MAC will be explained further when discussing the record protocols. A brief description of the terms was necessary to be able to explain the next issues connected with the functioning of the SSL protocol, namely the SSL record protocol.

The SSL Record Protocol

The SSL record protocol involves using SSL in a secure manner and with message integrity ensured. To this end it is used by upper layer SSL protocols. The purpose of the SSL record protocol is to take an application message to be transmitted, fragment the data which needs to be sent, encapsulate it with appropriate headers and create an object just called a record, which is encrypted and can be forwarded for sending under the TCP protocol. The first step in the preparation of transmission of the application data consists in its fragmentation, i.e. breaking up the data stream to be transmitted into 16Kb (or smaller) data fragments followed by the process of their conversion in a record. These data fragments may be further compressed, although the SSL 3.0 protocol specification includes no compression protocol, thus at present, no data compression is used. At this moment, creation of the record is started for each data portion by adding a header to it, possible information to complete the required data size and the MAC. The record header that is added to each data portion contains two elementary pieces of information, namely the length of the record and the length of the data block added to the original data. In the next step, the record data constructed consists of the following elements:

- Primary data,
- Some padding to complete the data gram as required,
- MAC value.

MAC is responsible for the verification of integrity of the message included in the transmitted record. It is the result of a hash function that follows a specific hash algorithm, for example, MD5 or SHA-1. MAC is determined as a result of a hash function that receives the following data: MAC = Hash function (secret key, primary data, padding, sequence number). A secret key in creation of MAC is either a client write MAC secret or a server write MAC secret respectively, it depends on which party prepares the packet. After receiving the packet, the receiving party computes its own value of the MAC and compares it with that received. If the two values match, this means that data has not been modified during the transmission over the network. The length of the MAC obtained in this way depends on the method uses for its computing. Next, the data plus the MAC are encrypted using a preset symmetric encryption algorithm, for example, DES or triple DES. Both data and MAC are encrypted. This prepared data is attached with the following header fields:

- ***Content type:*** Identifies what payload is delivered by the packet to determine which higher protocols are to be used for processing of data included in the packet. The possible values are change_cipher_spec, alert, handshake, and application_data that refer to the appropriate protocols.
- ***Major version:*** Establishes the main portion of the protocol version to be used. For SSL 3.0, the value is 3.
- ***Minor version:*** Establishes the additional portion of the used version of the protocol. For SSL 3.0 the value is 0.

With the addition of fields, the process of record preparation is completed. Afterwards, the record is sent to the targeted point. The entire process of preparation of the packet to be sent is illustrated in Fig. 11.6.

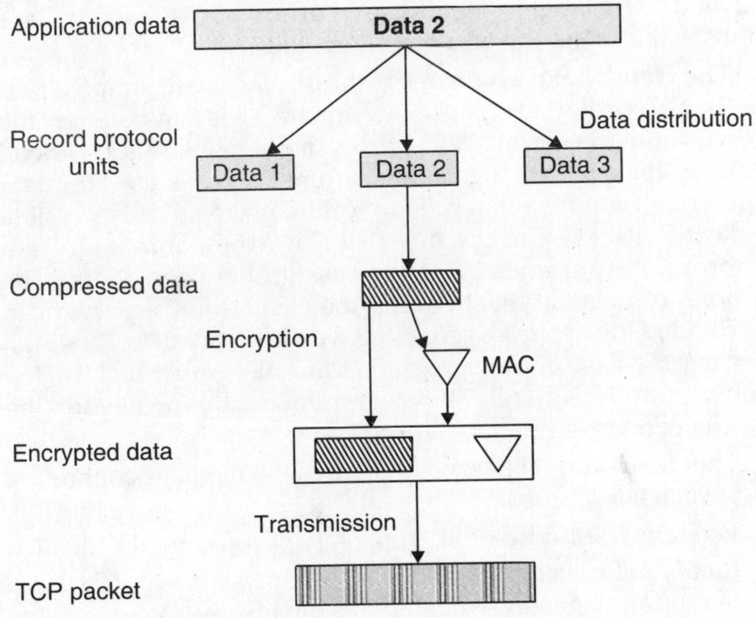

Fig. 11.6: Creating a packet under SSL record protocol

The SSL Record protocol is used to transfer any data within a session, both messages and other SSL protocols (for example, the handshake protocol), as well as for any application data.

The Alert protocol is used by parties to convey session messages associated with data exchange and functioning of the protocol. Each message in the alert protocol consists of two bytes. The first byte always takes a value, 'warning' (1) or 'fatal' (2), that determines the severity of the message sent. Sending a message having a 'fatal' status by either party will result in an immediate termination of the SSL session. The next byte of the message contains one of the defined error codes, which may occur during an SSL communication session.

The Change Cipher Spec protocol is the simplest SSL protocol. It consists of a single message that carries the value of 1. The sole purpose of this message is to cause the pending session state to be established as a fixed state, which results, for example, in defining the used set of protocols. This type of message must be sent by the client to the server and vice versa. After exchange of messages, the session state is considered agreed. This message and any other SSL messages are transferred using the SSL record protocol.

The Handshake protocol constitutes the most complex part of the SSL protocol. It is used to initiate a session between the server and the client. Within the message of this protocol, various components such as algorithms and keys used for data encryption are negotiated. Due to this protocol, it is possible to authenticate the parties to each other and negotiate appropriate parameters of the session between them. The process of negotiations between the client and the server can be divided into 4 phases separated with horizontal broken lines. During the first phase, a logical connection must be initiated between the client and the server followed by the negotiation on the connection parameters.

The client sends the server a client_hello message containing data such as:

- ***Version:*** The highest SSL version supported by the client,
- ***Random:*** Data consisting of a 32-bit timestamp and 28 bytes of randomly generated data. This data is used to protect the key exchange session between the parties of the connection.

- ***Session ID:*** A number that defines the session identifier. A nonzero value of this field indicates that the client wishes to update the parameters of an existing connection or establish a new connection on this session. A zero value in this field indicates that the client wishes to establish a new connection.
- ***CipherSuite:*** A list of encryption algorithms and key exchange method supported by the client. The server, in response to the client_hello message sends a server_hello message, containing the same set of fields as the client message, placing the following data:

– ***Version:*** The lowest version number of the SSL protocol supported by the server,

– ***Random data:*** The same fashion as used by the client, but the data generated is completely independent,

– ***Session ID:*** If the client field was nonzero, the same value is sent back; otherwise the server's session ID field contains the value for a new session,

– ***CipherSuite:*** The server uses this field to send a single set of protocols selected by the server from those proposed by the client. The first element of this field is a chosen method of exchange of cryptographic keys between the client and the server. The next element is the specification of encryption algorithms and hash functions, which will be used within the session being initiated, along with all specific parameters.

The set of encryption algorithms and key exchange method sent in the CipherSuite field establishes three components:

1. The method of key exchange between the server and client,
2. The encryption algorithm for data encryption purposes,
3. A function used for obtaining the mac value.

The server begins the next phase of negotiations by sending its certificate to the client for authentication. The message sent to the client contains one or a chain of X509 certificates. These are necessary for authentication of both the server and the certification path towards a trusted certification official of the certificating body for the server. This step is not obligatory and may be omitted, if the negotiated method of key exchange does not require sending the certificate (in the case of anonymous Diffie-Hellman method). Depending on the negotiated method of key exchange, the server may send an additional server_key_exchange message, which is, however, not required in the case when the fixed Diffie-Hellman method or RSA key exchange technique has been negotiated. Moreover, the server can request a certificate from the client. The final step of Phase 2 is the server_done message, which has no parameters and is sent by the server merely to indicate the end of the server messages. After sending this message, the server waits for a client response. Upon receipt of the message, the client should verify the server's certificate, the certificate validation data and path, as well as any other parameters sent by the server in the server_hello message. The client's verification consists of:

- Validation date check of the certificate and comparison with the current date, to verify whether the certificate is still valid.
- Checking whether the certifying body is included in the list of trusted Certifying Authorities in possession of the client. If the CA, which has issued the server's certificate is not included in the CA's list, the client attempts to verify the CA signature. If no information about the CA can be obtained, the client terminates the identification procedure by either returning the error signal or signalling the problem for the user to solve it.
- Identifying the authenticity of the public key of the CA which has issued the certificate: if the Certifying Authority is included in the client's list of trusted CAs, the client checks the CA's public key stated in the server's certificate with the public key available from the list. This procedure verifies the authenticity of the certifying body.
- Checking whether the domain name used in the certificate matches the server name shown in the server's certificate.

Upon successful completion of all steps the server is considered authenticated. If all parameters are matched and the server's certificate correctly verified, the client sends the server one or multiple messages. Next is the client__key_exchange message, which must be sent to deliver the keys. The content of this message depends on the negotiated method of key exchange. Moreover, at the server's request, the client's certificate is sent along with the message enabling verification of the certificate. This procedure ends Phase 3 of negotiations. Phase 4 is to confirm the messages so far received and to verify whether the pending data is correct. The client sends a change_cipher_spec message (in accordance with the pending SSL Change Cipher Spec), and then sets up the pending set of algorithm parameters and keys into the current set of the same. Then the client sends the finished message, which is first protected with just negotiated algorithms, keys and secrets. This is to confirm that the negotiated parameters and data are correct. The server in response to the client sends the same message sequence. If the finished message is correctly read by either party this confirms that the transmitted data, negotiated algorithms and the session key are correct. This indicates that the session has been terminated and that it is possible to send the application data between the server and the client, via SSL. At this point the TCP session between the client and the server is closed, however, a session state is maintained, allowing it to resume communications within the session using the retained parameters. It is worth noticing that both Phases 2 and 3 are used by both parties to verify the authenticity of the server's certificate and possibly the client's certificate during the handshake step. If the server cannot be successfully authen-ticated by the client on the basis of the delivered certificate, the handshake terminates and the client will generate an error message. The same will occur at the server if the client's certificate authenticity cannot be confirmed, establishing the SSL session between the client and the server (red coloured—messages that are non-mandatory).

At first glance this process seems to be somewhat complicated, however, this takes place at each connection with the server of an SSL-enabled service, for example, while requesting the address of a site beginning with HTTPS://.

(ii) Virtual Private Network

A virtual private network (VPN) is the extension of a private network that encompasses links across shared or public networks like the Internet. A VPN enables you to send data between two computers across a shared or public internetwork in a manner that emulates the properties of a point-to-point private link. The act of configuring and creating a virtual private network is known as virtual private networking.

To emulate a point-to-point link, data is encapsulated, or wrapped, with a header that provides routing information allowing it to traverse the shared or public transit internetwork to reach its endpoint. To emulate a private link, the data being sent is encrypted for confidentiality. Packets that are intercepted on the shared or public network are indecipherable without the encryption keys. The portion of the connection in which the private data is encapsulated is known as the tunnel. The portion of the connection in which the private data is encrypted is known as the virtual private network (VPN) connection.

VPN connections allow users working at home or on the road to connect in a secure fashion to a remote corporate server using the routing infrastructure provided by a public internetwork (such as the Internet). From the user's perspective, the VPN connection is a point-to-point connection between the user's computer and a corporate server. The nature of the intermediate internetwork is irrelevant to the user because it appears as if the data is being sent over a dedicated private link.

VPN technology also allows a corporation to connect to branch offices or to other companies over a public internetwork (such as the Internet), while maintaining secure communications. The VPN connection across the Internet logically operates as a wide area network (WAN) link between the sites.

In both of these cases, the secure connection across the internetwork appears to the user as a private network communication—despite the fact that this communication occurs over a public internetwork—hence the name virtual private network.

VPN technology is designed to address issues surrounding the current business trend toward increased telecommunicating and widely distributed global operations, where workers must be able to connect to central resources and must be able to communicate with each other.

Basic VPN Requirements

Typically, when deploying a remote networking solution, an enterprise needs to facilitate controlled access to corporate resources and information. The solution must allow roaming or remote clients to connect to LAN resources, and the solution must allow remote offices to connect to each other to share resources and information (router-to-router connections). In addition, the solution must ensure the privacy and integrity of data as it traverses the Internet. The same concerns apply in the case of sensitive data traversing a corporate internetwork. Therefore, a VPN solution should provide at least all of the following:

- ***User authentication:*** The solution must verify the VPN client's identity and restrict VPN access to authorized users only. It must also provide audit and accounting records to show who accessed what information and when.
- ***Address management:*** The solution must assign a VPN client's address on the intranet and ensure that private addresses are kept private.
- ***Data encryption:*** Data carried on the public network must be rendered unreadable to unauthorized clients on the network.
- ***Key management:*** The solution must generate and refresh encryption keys for the client and the server.
- ***Multiprotocol support:*** The solution must handle common protocols used in the public network. These include IP, Internetwork Packet Exchange (IPX), and so on.

An Internet VPN solution based on the Point-to-Point Tunneling Protocol (PPTP) or Layer Two Tunneling Protocol (L2TP) meets all of these basic requirements and takes advantage of the broad availability of the Internet. Other solutions, including Internet Protocol Security (IPSec), meet only some of these requirements, but remain useful for specific situations.

Index

Reader's Notes

Reader's Notes

Reader's Notes

Reader's Notes